The Third **Oldie** Annual

Edited by

Richard Ingrams

Oldie Publications Ltd
London

This compilation first published by Oldie Publications Ltd

Copyright© 1997 Oldie Publications Ltd
Text copyright © 1997 Oldie Publications Ltd
Illustrations copyright © Oldie Publications Ltd

The moral right of the authors and illustrators has been asserted.

Oldie Publications Ltd, 45/46 Poland Street, London W1V 4AU.

The publishers would like to thank the respective copyright owners for permission to include material in this volume
A CIP catalogue record for this book is available from The British Library.

Distributed by World Leisure Marketing, 9 Downing Road, West Meadows Ind. Estate, Derby DE21 6HA.

ISBN 1 901170 03 9

Cover illustration by Derek W Rains

ACKNOWLEDGEMENTS
Thanks to all the authors, writers and cartoonists whose work appears in this book and all of whom have waived their copyright for this book.
Thanks also to Caroline Law, Caroline Fitton, James Pembroke, Ben Tisdall and Rory Campbell

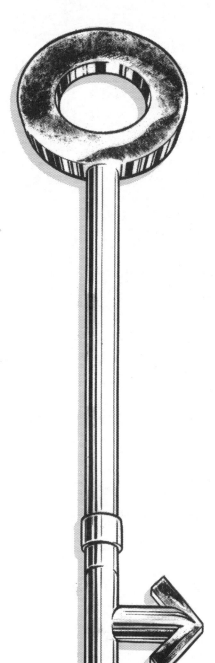

Editor's Introduction

The Oldie was launched in February 1992 with the general aim of redressing the balance of a world apparently dominated by 'yoof'. Like any new magazine founded with a limited amount of capital it has had a rocky ride and even one near-death experience. In the summer of 1994 we faced closure and were only saved at the eleventh hour when we transformed *The Oldie* into a monthly from a fortnightly.

This transformation explains the rather large gap between this, the third *Oldie* 'annual' and its predecessor – there being half the amount of material available on previous occasions. Nevertheless I hope there has been no falling off in the quality and variety of the contributions.

Readers will notice a number of well-known names – John Mortimer, Jane Gardam,

Hugh Cudlipp – as well as some of our faithful regulars like Miles Kington, Edward Enfield and John Michell. But for me the greatest pleasure of editing *The Oldie* has been the amount of unsolicited material I have received. Writing is something that anyone can do, yet the majority of my fellow editors persist in believing that it is a highly specialised art which can only be practised by trained professionals who have preferably gained a diploma in media studies. *The Oldie*, on the contrary, has always given a warm welcome to 'the punter', anyone with a story to tell. Our 'I Once Met' feature (the brainwave of our one-time literary editor James Michie) has attracted a wonderful variety of pieces and if I had to select my favourite from the current anthology I think it would be Gill McLaren Rowe's long and fascinating account of her association with the late Dame Rebecca West – which also arrived on my desk out of the blue.

Finally I would like to salute the cartoonists who have supported *The Oldie* in droves since the very beginning. Even in my long sojourn at *Private Eye* I don't remember such a variety of ages and styles. Nor should the illustrators be forgotten – John Cramer, Paul Hogarth, Robert Geary and John O'Connor – to name but four.

To them and all the contributors my heartfelt thanks,

Richard Ingrams

Contents

*'Harry! there's a spider
in the bath'*

Christopher is learning to say 'Thank you'.

There is nothing out of the ordinary about Christopher. However, this little boy will grow up understanding sign language. You see, Mum is profoundly deaf. She will never hear him, and this is how they will talk to each other.

Helping families like Christopher's is just part of RAD's work among hundreds of people who are deaf, or people who have other disabilities, with deafness: deafblind people, for example, or those with learning difficulties.

We help meet their spiritual and social needs. We help with a multitude of practical problems. We provide centres and help set up social clubs. We hold sign-language church services; we give pastoral care. We provide interpreters when needed: at the doctors, for example, or the solicitors. Our work is wide-ranging and, quite literally, 'hands on'.

But we need a hand, too. Inevitably, we need money most of all. Please help deaf people with your donation and legacy. And if you would like to know more, do get in touch.

The Royal Association in aid of
Deaf people

Patron **Her Majesty The Queen**

RAD helps Deaf people make the most of life by offering:
**Advocacy ● Chaplaincy ● Counselling ● Information ● Interpreting
Leisure Facilities ● Support Groups**

27 Old Oak Road, London W3 7HN. Tel: 0181-743 6187

Founded 1841 Registered Charity: 207358

Too Old To Fight -

Nepal, home of Mt. Everest the highest peak in the world, is also home of the Gurkhas, the legendary soldiers. Renowned for their loyalty, the Gurkhas have won 13 Victoria Crosses for conspicuous bravery. The Gurkhas have served the British Crown since 1815. Gurkhas served in both World Wars, and their sons and grandsons continue to serve the British Army.

Always serving abroad, they return home to one of the poorest countries in the world, which has no state welfare system, and where natural disasters are common-place. For these Gurkhas, retirement and old age means a continued struggle to exist. Many ex-Gurkhas do not even have a Service pension. We help over 11,000 each month and need to help more. Please help them face the hardships and challenges of home.

Too Proud To Ask

THE GURKHA WELFARE TRUST

3rd Floor, 88 Baker Street, London. W1M 2AX

Tel: 0171-707 1925
Fax: 0171-707 1929

Registered Charity Number 1034080

Iain Topliss

writes – and draws – the astonishing truth about…

The Speed of the Deer Bot Fly

The most cherished piece of information I possessed as a child was that the Deer Bot Fly flew at 818 miles an hour. I came across this fact in the following way. In the summer of 1953 the Headmistress of the school I attended summoned my parents and told them that I was on the road to becoming a juvenile delinquent. She added that I was also unlikely to pass the 11-plus, already looming like a great dark cloud on my personal horizon. My anxious parents arranged for me to attend the Castle House Preparatory School for Boys – a genteel name, I now realise, for what was a private cramming institution. I received a special Christmas present that year, *The Schoolboy's Pocket Book*, edited by Carlton Wallace and published by Evans Brothers at five shillings a copy. The gift was designed to equip me for the strenuous intellectual regime of the Castle House. (As it turned out, the regime was not so strenuous after all. I remember that on the day everyone in the class spelt 'excite' properly we were given a half-holiday.)

The Schoolboy's Pocket Book exuded the innocent self-confidence of the brave, post-war world of the 'New Elizabethans'. It tackled everything. It listed the constellations, explained how Parliament worked, printed common mathematical formulae, showed you (with diagrams) how to signal 'I am slowing down or stopping' on a bicycle. From a section entitled 'Common Abbreviations' I gathered that FIDO meant 'Fog Investigation and Dispersal Operation'. I discovered that a day on the planet Mercury lasted 88 earth days (not unlike the Castle House). But in some areas *The Schoolboy's Pocket Book* had to be treated with caution. The parsec was supposedly the new unit of astronomical distance, 'a little

more than 19,000,000,000,000 miles', fast replacing the light year in scientific discourse. (I loved the drollery of 'a little more'.) I gave interstellar distances in parsecs whenever I had the chance, but no one else had ever heard of the term. Then there was the Deer Bot Fly. My favourite page in *The Schoolboy's Pocket Book* was the one headed 'Comparative Animal Speeds'. It showed a chart that began with salmon moving upstream at seven miles an hour. Then came animals like the African Racing Cheetah, 70 miles an hour, and the Golden Eagle, 150 miles an hour. At the top of the table stood this wondrous item: 'Deer Bot Fly, 818 mph'.

The scene is a quiet classroom in a small market town in the English Midlands. Outside, in the afternoon sunlight, the leaves of the old chestnut and plane trees that reach over the school grounds fall softly to the asphalt. Inside, the science-master – an ignorant but well-meaning fellow, the kind of person who talks about light-years and thinks that FIDO is the name of a dog – innocently poses a question: 'What is the fastest animal known to man?' My friends, unfamiliar with the work of Carlton Wallace, make the usual suggestions – seven-mile-an-hour salmon; 70-mile-an-hour cheetahs; 150-mile-an-hour golden eagles. My hand goes up. 'Please, sir! The Deer Bot Fly, sir!' 'The what?' 'The Deer Bot Fly, sir! 818 miles an hour!' 'Rubbish, boy.' 'Please, sir! It says so in my book!' 'Don't waste our time, boy. It's the Golden Eagle. Everyone knows that. And what was that stupid and dangerous hand-waving you were doing on your bicycle this morning?'

Years later, holidaying in a house on the Norfolk coast, I was spending the afternoon lazing on a sofa leafing through some old magazines dating from the 40s and 50s. There, on the page before me, was a brief reference to the Deer Bot Fly. I realised, as I never had before, that my fact was a real fact; my fly a real fly. The Deer Bot Fly actually existed. Someone had measured its speed (how would you do this?). Someone had reported their findings to the world (where?). A week later in Cambridge, I went to the university library and immersed myself in newspaper indexes. In a few hours I had the outline of the Deer Bot Fly's rise and fall. Filling in the details took longer, but at the end of two weeks I believed I had the story.

The Deer Bot Fly (*Cephenomuyia pratti*) is a rare North American insect about the size of a bumble-bee, parasitic on deer and similar ruminants. Its range has not been finally determined. In one account its habitat is placed within a southerly arc extending from the south-west Pacific coast to the south Atlantic coast of the United States (including the Gulf coast regions and the Sierra Madre range in Mexico); in another account it is confined to the triangle formed between the lowlands of California, Durango in Mexico, and west Texas. The Deer Bot Fly lays its eggs in the nasal cavity of its host… etc, etc.

Every word of this is true but it is the wrong sort of beginning. It seems better to begin with a strange sight, one to arouse the curiosity of any traveller passing through the Sierra Madre range of western Chihauhau in Mexico in the summer of 1899. A man in his forties is blasting away with a .22 shotgun at nothing more than the thin empty mountain air. He strides around after firing a few times and stoops down picking up small scattered objects and putting them into a bag. The man is an entomologist called Charles Henry Tyler Townsend (not Charles Henry Townsend, also an entomologist, but no relation). The shotgun is loaded with sand, and Townsend is shooting Deer Bot Fly.

There are many ways to catch insects but shooting is not normally one of them. The reason that Townsend is shooting Deer Bot Fly is that they travel at very great speed – although at this stage no one was saying how great. 'The flies are seldom met with and usually difficult to capture… About the only impression left by them on the eye was a blur or streak of orange or reddish black, the red dominant.' The description comes from an article that Townsend published in the *Journal of the New York Entomological Society* in June 1917. It is a scholarly assessment of the known data on a rare insect. It makes no amazing claims about the speed of the insect. At the time he wrote it, Townsend was an entomologist in the Bureau of Entomology at the United States Department of Agriculture. But the dry academic protocols of this article conceal a wayward streak in its author.

Around 1920, Townsend gave up his post at the Department of Agriculture and removed himself and his family to Itaquaquecetuba in Sao Paulo, Brazil. It wasn't long before he went into print over the Deer Bot Fly once more. This time

Townsend turned to what had clearly fascinated him about the insect all along – its speed. In an article published in 1926 he tackled the matter head-on: 'Can the speed attained by *Cephenomyia* be calculated with any degree of accuracy? … In extended flight their passing is of such an incredible swiftness that one is utterly unable to initiate any movement whatever toward capture before they vanished [*sic*] from sight. Form is not sensed by the eye as they pass, but merely a blur or streak of color and only a fleeting glimpse at that. It may be safely estimated, in the opinion of the writer, who has given much thought to the subject, that *these flies attain a speed upward of 400 yards per second.*' Townsend supplied the italics but such an astonishing claim, advanced for the first time in print, hardly required emphasis. Four hundred yards a second is equivalent to 818 miles an hour.

Any other entomologist coming across insects flying at 818 miles an hour would publish as quickly as possible. It is the kind of coup that makes a career. What does Charles Townsend do? He sits on his discovery for a quarter of a century. When he finally publishes, the speed of the Deer Bot Fly is anything but central to the article in question. The article in which the Deer Bot Fly is claimed to be the fastest creature on earth is not about the Deer Bot Fly at all. It is entirely devoted to speculations about whether aeroplanes will ever attain speeds fast enough to circumnavigate the globe keeping pace with the sun.

'Around the World in a Daylight Day: a Problem in Flight' appeared in the popular *Scientific Monthly* in April 1926. Townsend asks whether the possibility suggested in his title will ever be realised. The development of flight has owed much to man's observation of birds. Is it not a reasonable inference that by a further investigation of the flight of lower animals, man might attain 'whatever speed is an accomplished fact among them'? As a model there is the Deer Bot Fly, zooming around the Sierra Madre ranges at 818 miles an hour. Townsend works out the implications of being able to travel at the speed of the Deer Bot Fly. 'Setting out from New York at 4am, we could take *coffee* over Omaha, *breakfast* over Reno, *tiffin* over Peking, *tea* over Constantinople and *dinner* over Madrid, while arrival in New York would complete the schedule.' He then appends a schedule of this imaginary journey, giving a full list of distances, meals and times between the various cities.

A surreal correspondence sprang up around this article. People wrote to complain that Townsend had miscalculated the length of the 40th parallel, the route of his flight. People wrote to point out that a plane travelling at 800 miles an hour would overtake the sun, and that a speed of 466 miles an hour would be quite fast enough. No one wrote to ask Townsend how come the Deer Bot Fly flies at 818 miles an hour and no one has even heard about it before? Townsend replied in equally surreal articles which argued that the problem of high-speed flight was an energy problem. He pointed out that the vibrating wing of an insect is far more rapid in its motions than the flapping wing of a bird – and hence far more efficient. This was true. But Townsend also appeared to think there was a 'trend' in aviation research towards the development of wing-flapping machines ('ornithopters'), whereas attention would be better directed at inventing vibrating wing aeroplanes ('myiopters'). If Townsend was aware that no successful man-carrying, wing-flapping aeroplane had ever been built, and that research into wing-flapping aeroplanes did not represent the cutting edge of aeronautical science, he was not letting on. (Nor did the vibrating wing aeroplane come to much.)

Meanwhile, the fantastic speed of the Deer Bot Fly began to be reported in the popular press and was featured as a novelty item in local newspapers in places like Omaha and Baton Rouge. It began its journey as a factoid, a fragment of semi-factual information, without origin, without provenance, but all the more tenacious in the public mind for those very reasons. It was perhaps natural that it should attract the attention of Roy Chapman Andrews, Director of the American Museum of Natural History. In a varied career Andrews had been a zoologist, an explorer and an archaeologist. In the Gobi desert in 1928 he came across a nest of two dozen fossilised dinosaur eggs, the first ever to be found. The discovery made him a famous man. Andrews published an article on animal speeds in *Natural History* in October 1937. 'Wings Win' featured a photograph of the Deer Bot Fly – looking absolutely unlike anything that could fly at 800 miles an hour – and a fold-out chart showing the comparative speeds of air, land and sea creatures with the golden eagle and African racing cheetah in their usual role of supporting cast.

1937 is the Deer Bot Fly's climacteric. It has an article and a photograph in one of the leading natural history magazines in the world; the title of 'speed champion of the world'; something very close to universal acceptance and scientific respectability. But waiting in the wings is a shadowy nemesis. The story in *Natural History* was picked up by the *Illustrated London News* in the New Year's Day issue for 1938. Fatefully, a copy of the magazine landed on the desk of Irving Langmuir.

Now, Townsend and Andrews are jolly, insouciant, eccentric figures. You can just see them, taking tiffin over Peking in a vibrating wing aeroplane flying at 800 miles an hour… But Langmuir (the very name has a damp Scots-Presbyterian dourness clinging to it) is a gloomy killjoy and truth-teller; the exploder of myths; the swatter of the Deer Bot Fly. You can tell from his name that *he* would never live in a place called Itaquaquecetuba, but some dull town like Schenectady, NY (which is just where he did live). (Omitted from this description are certain uninteresting details like Langmuir's reputation as a brilliant researcher, his Nobel Prize in Chemistry and his personal feats like walking over 50 miles in one day and climbing the Matterhorn, past 40, without any preparation…)

Langmuir devised a simple experiment to test Townsend's claims. Townsend had written of Deer Bot Fly that 'their passing is of such incredible swiftness that… form is not sensed by the eye as they pass, but merely a blur or streak of colour, and only a fleeting glimpse at that.' Langmuir stuck a blob of solder the size of the fly on a length of string. He whirled it round his head. He came to the following conclusions: at 26mph the 'fly' is barely visible; at 43mph it appears only as a faint line or streak; at 64mph it is completely invisible.

There were other, more sophisticated experiments as well, and Langmuir published the results in a terse article in *Science* in March 1939. He showed that the build up of wind-pressure against the fly's blunt head would be nearly eight pounds per square inch at 800 miles an hour – enough to squash the fly to a pulp. The energy needed to get to such a speed was one-half horsepower – as Langmuir laconically noted, 'a good deal for a fly'. Moreover the insect would need to be eating one and a half times its own weight *per second* to generate that amount of energy in the first place.

Townsend attempted to reply to these charges but his arguments seem a trifle desperate. Under pressure from Langmuir he was forced to admit that 'the fly is of course totally invisible at top speed and leaves a visible blur in the air only when it suddenly decelerates to veer off and thus avoid collision with the observer'. (Langmuir had fun imagining the injury caused to any 'observer' unfortunate enough to come into collision with a fly that hadn't managed to veer away at the last moment.) All this was tantamount to agreeing that he could never have been in a position to estimate the insect's speed in the first place. The house of cards collapsed around him.

Many years later Brian Hocking, a Professor in the Department of Entomology at the University of Alberta, published a lengthy report on his investigations into the speed and flight range of insects, paying fulsome tribute to Langmuir's pioneering work. Its conclusions can be briefly stated: the maximum continuous speed attained by any living insect is about 27 mph, and the maximum in short bursts no more than 36 mph. Popular publications since then have been far more cautious about insect speeds. Later editions of *The Schoolboy's Pocket Book* go quiet on the whole matter. The *Guinness Book of Speed Facts* follows Hocking and adds that his figures disprove 'the fanciful claim of an American entomologist who claimed in 1926 to have observed a deer-bot fly travelling at 1316 km/h (818 miles an hour)'. 'The fanciful claim of an American entomologist'! How terrible to see Charles Townsend ridiculed and condemned to anonymity in such a way. Triumph for Langmuir was complete indeed.

In his time, of course, Townsend had genuflected often enough before the altar of science. He had discovered the vector of the disfiguring skin disease verruga. He published over 1,000 scientific papers. His magnum opus, *A Manual of Myiology*, ran to 12 volumes and nearly 4,000 pages of text. But I could not help noticing that his brief obituary in the *Annals of the Entomological Society of America* included the cryptic phrase 'aspects of his work have aroused considerable controversy'. The Deer Bot Fly, of course – but what other 'aspects'? Like many scientists, Townsend prepared a personal profile for use in the standard professional biographical guides. After covering his work as an entomologist it outlines his other career achievements: 'explained gravity; recorded exact atomic weights; determined exact velocity of light; defined cosmic units of length, time and mass; explained moon's origin and earth's axial inclination…' It is a mystifying list. What, for instance, can 'explained gravity' actually mean? For a while a new compulsion took over and I became obsessed by Townsend. The man grew more shadowy and more elusive the more I pieced together the few bits of information about him I could discover. The speed of the Deer Bot Fly had turned out to be a factoid rather than a fact – perhaps Townsend was a kind of factoid, too.

I remember the day I finished reading Langmuir's article, which I had tracked down with much difficulty to an obscure London library. Somewhat dispirited, I came out into the hot, dusty, summer streets. When I got to Liverpool Street I did not feel like catching the train back home, so I set off along Bishopsgate, through the City, to London Bridge and the river. I had lived in London for six months when I was 12 and on certain Saturdays I had been permitted to take the bus to London Bridge station where I would spend pleasant hours wandering around the streets on both sides of the Thames. I came to know the area well – the narrow ways around Billingsgate and the Monument, the soot-blackened façade of St Magnus Martyr, the warehouses of Bermondsey, streets deep in afternoon shadow… A memory of those times came back to me. A friend and I had once made paper boats which we tossed off London Bridge. We could see them bobbing on the ebb tide. We ran frantically down Tooley Street on the south bank to see if we could beat them to Tower Bridge. But either the tide was too swift or the boats sank, because we never saw them again.

East
of Islington

Sam Taylor *continues her Stoke Newington adventures with Gay Opera Singer and Co*

'GET YOUR FILTHY hands off me, you deranged loony!' Annual visit of the poshest woman in the world is heralded by an all-out attack on our new neighbours, the Yemeni refugees. Spying her souped-up shag-mobile approaching, Mr Yemen lunges forth and attempts to beg for currency, sterling preferably, through the mugger-friendly sun-roof. He could be offering his services as a sperm donor; there is a small language barrier.

'Call the police immediately!' Poshest Woman in the World lives in a smaller version of the V&A in Canterbury – a place where the police respond and the Yemen is somewhere bad breath comes from. The Turkish Trotskys from the garage come to the rescue, drag off frothing, blind, desperate, Yemeni refugee and free Poshest Woman in the World. Pausing to admire her souped up shag mobile, Turkish Trotskys explain that Mr Yemen has been tortured and had his eyes burnt out. This accounts for his lack of social graces. Poshest Woman in the World splutters that only fools send their children to Gordonstoun and that he probably deserved it. Poshest Woman in the World is having serious assimilation problems.

Since her last visit, an industrial sized launderette has been built in the basement of the house next door. This is kept constantly whirring with the hundreds of faux 16th century Polish costumes worn by the Hasidic adolescents at the trainee rabbi school two doors along. The Yemeni refugees are squeezed in around the laundry.

In the three minutes afforded for planning opposition in the chambers of the local council, Weirdie Woman upstairs, for some reason only known to herself, insisted that as a manager of a building society she should do the talking for all three flats in our house. Consequently the Hasidim now happily trolley their laundry baskets along a four foot high concrete ramp through two gardens into the back of the house next door, with full legal blessing. They wash for Israel. Except on Saturdays when they pray for Israel and I pray for my money back.

The Yemeni refugees pray for cash advances and leave trays of soggy food offerings in the front garden.

Attempt to drag Poshest Woman in the World into flat. Hindered by Mr Yemen's blind flailing. Turkish Trotskys no longer restraining him due to confusion over Poshest Woman's education comment. She sprays perfume at her assailant.

Gay Opera Singer descends wearing dinner jacket.

'*Darleeeng…*'

Mr Yemen lunges, the fully adorned shape of the capitalist West being too much for him to resist. Make mental note to attempt, in nice liberal way, to have blind begging Yemeni refugees removed from doorstep. Gay Opera Singer tries to convince Mr Yemen that he has a future in opera ; that with a small amount of stage direction he could tackle the lead in *Nabucco*.

Despite the evident chaos, I have higher things on my mind. Poopy, the West Highland terrier, is currently under a drier at Pampered Pets hair salon where I left her this morning – a trip undertaken with guidance from my extremely sensible sister, who will be returning here shortly with the newly-shaven one.

Clarice at Pampered Pets had explained the drill. 'Do you want the Westie or do you want the summer crop?'

'What's the Westie?' I enquired.

'No hair on back, with fringes round the side.'

'Fringes?'

'Yeah, fringes.'

'What kind of fringes?' I mean fringes could be anything – Elton John, Michael Portillo… I didn't want just any old fringe.

'Just fringes. No frills, just fringes.'

'We'll have the summer crop.' Extremely Sensible Sister had decided to take control.

'But I don't know, what will it look like? Hair is important.'

Poopy, it seems, doesn't mind at all; she is firmly ensconced in a pampered pet booth alongside a dashing black Westie called Hamish. I can tell that Clarice is getting bored. Hair is hair to Clarice. Preferably bleached and blow dried or else on the cutting room floor. 'I'll show you,' she says.

She grabs Hamish, sticks him in the middle of the pampering bench and proceeds to mow a straight, two inch wide gap down the middle of his back.

'Like that,' she points dismissively, 'but all over.' I am confused as to the use of the word 'Pampering' here; so is Hamish.

'We'll have it.' Sensible Sister has decided. In order to facilitate the complete removal of all Poopy's hair I have to sign a waiver that states if, on seeing my pampered pet, I go into deep shock, I forgo my rights to sue. It happens a lot, apparently. It seems to be happening now and the dog isn't even back yet.

The rest of the Yemeni refugee cast emerge from the laundry next door carrying sticks of furniture that can surely have only come from Brian Keenan's cell. They proceed to put these in their front garden alongside the offerings of soggy food.

'Please can you not put that stuff there… if you don't mind.'

The refugees ignore my plaintive plea for gentrification. They live in a laundry and don't speak any English. I attempt mime. Midway through this non-dialogue, Sensible Sister draws up and all hell breaks loose again.

'What's going on?' Sensible Sister is keen to get a measure of the situation. So am I. Poopy is bald. She will need thousands of pounds worth of counselling.

'Stop that immediately.' Mr Yemen has lunged at Extremely Sensible Sister and earned a smack round the ear. Poshest Woman in the World applauds, Gay Opera Singer is upstaged.

'Why do you let them leave this rubbish in the front garden?'

I feebly mumble something back to Sensible Sister about the right of neighbours to culturally express themselves but she is having none of it and orders them to get rid of their junk.

Within seconds the scene is cleared and Sensible Sister is back in her car. It's a miracle.

'Wait!' I suddenly remember my bald dog. 'What about Poopy's hair?' Hoping for a second miracle…

After a moment's pause she looks up. 'Get a wig.'

'*Who's up for pizza?*'

Modern Life

What is...
Slide?

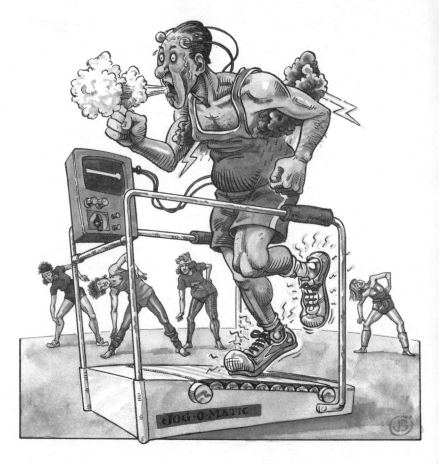

AS MOST *Oldie* readers will understand, entering one's forties is a tricky business, filled with insecurity, doubt and self-re-evaluation. Top of the list of worries, to one as dedicated to venery as I, is the fear that one is reaching a stage of life when lust becomes mere lechery, when women laugh at one's advances, and when one irritates one's tailor with technical questions about waistbands.

So I joined a gym. 'Gym', at school, was what you were forced to do three times a week. Now it is where you go of your own accord. People are nice to you, and when you get into the stomach-muscle machine upside down and fall on to the floor, they show you how to do it properly instead of mining a rich seam of naval oaths while hitting you with a plimsoll. They don't even have plimsolls any more, but pimp-soles: complicated 'cross-trainers' which force you to walk with a cocky, in-your-face roll, pre-eminent among which are 'Air Jordans'. Not knowing what a Jordan is, let alone an Air one, I scoured London for plimsolls, with eventual success.

In this, I was wrong. The gym I went to was an easy-going one, relatively speaking, but there are gyms – at Chelsea Harbour, for example, or the one in the businessmen's hotel in Piccadilly – where

you would be a hissing and a byword for wearing plimsolls. Why, there is even a gym, run by one of those people who isn't as posh as he thinks he is (otherwise why would he be running a gym?) where you have to do your sweating and grunting in a special uniform.

At first I thought I had an excuse. I was off to Australia to do a travel book about flying around the Outback (which is where I am writing this) and decided I had to be Fit. But that was nonsense. The light aeroplane is the ultimate Gentleman's Touring Machine. You don't even have to keep your eyes on the road. Fit? Unnecessary. Kenneth Clarke would be in perfectly acceptable shape for this job.

So I had to confront the truth: that it was a potent mixture of fear and vanity which took me to the gym. And in its turn, the gym, like all sects trading upon those emotions, demanded that I learn new liturgies and orthodoxies, while itself being riven with dissenters, schismatics

and periodic convulsions of dogma. Certain types of weight-lifting were suddenly Bad for you. Other types of weight-lifting, hitherto anathematized, overnight became part of the Magisterium. Debates ranged about bananas, hydrogenated poly-unsaturated fats, anabolic regimes, and the US Rapid Deployment Force's three-day anti-stress diet. 'Trouble in Korea? No problem! I'll just put the boys on the three-day anti-stress diet, and we'll see you on Friday.'

And aerobics; merciful Lord, aerobics. As far as I understand it, there's one sort of exercise which makes you ache and bulge, and another sort which makes you sweat and your heart pound. Aerobics is the second sort, and is supposed to be Very Good for you, instead of just making you Big and Strong.

Personally, I hate it. Sweating seems so undignified in the 1990s. But it's all the go. And never mind that you can work up a lather running on the spot; aerobics is a complex science, and if you do it wrong (that is, for free at home) you could end up dead.

The trouble is that it's eerily dull. The people at the gym, pounding away on the stair-climbing machine (I suppose they live in bungalows themselves) or jogging endlessly on the treadmill (they have ones with realistic screens of rolling country-side now, and I hear the next generation will have virtual muggers to hit you on the head and nick your watch) clearly don't mind the dullness. They run or plod for hours, mouths open, steaming feet and monsoon armpits, brain-scan flat as a sitcom. The ethical committee of the BMA would have no difficulty in deciding to turn them off at the wall.

But for the rest of us, it's intolerable. So new forms of aerobics keep being invented. There was Step Aerobics, where you jumped on and off little boxes, in a group, to music. There was Ski Aerobics, where you pulled all the muscles in your upper body as well as your legs. The current thing is Slide, where you behave like a beginner learning to skate, sliding around ineptly on a little Teflon pad.

All these things are quite attractive when done by a group of young women in tight leotards. But men really shouldn't do it, particularly since the only men who do it are either weasel-faced sports fanatics with spotty backs and razor haircuts, or podgy, weak, grey-skinned men with bulging red eyes who have been sent there by their doctors or their wives. It is a horrible thing to see. And it doesn't help, either with living longer (which is mostly a question of bloodlines, says my doctor) nor with venery, (which is mostly a matter of wit, charm and attentiveness, say my women).

So why do people do it? Stupidity, I suppose, and the religious vacuum left when the churchmen all went mad in the 70s and started claiming to be personal friends of Jesus. But it won't do. Slide Aerobics, indeed! Here in the Outback men are men. They work a 12-hour day beneath a blazing sun; they all smoke like fish, drink like heavy drinkers, eat too much of all the wrong stuff; they are fat, slovenly and completely out of shape – just as Nature intended. **MICHAEL BYWATER**

Busily doing nothing

Whatever happened to the lost art of the boulevardier, asks **Anthony Sampson** *– and where would you go should you want to become one?*

'WHAT ARE YOU doing now?' I asked a distinguished architect, recently retired, expecting the usual protestations about 'never-been-busier-in-my-life' or 'can't-think-how-I-ever-had-time-for-a-job'. Instead he beamed and replied: 'I've become a boulevardier.'

I was overcome with curiosity and envy. The word conjured up a lost image of leisure, with much more romance than the English translation, 'man about town'. It conveyed a picture of Paris at the turn of the century, with dandies with silver-topped canes parading up and down the *grands boulevards* to attract the ladies, before they took a seat to join their friends in their café society.

How much more adventurous an occupation for a retiree than the British equivalent, the clubman! The club turns its ponderous back on the street, cultivates its exclusiveness with blackballs and rituals, and thrives on competitiveness and name-dropping. But the boulevard is the street, and the café is part of it, always waiting for newcomers and diversions.

How can boulevardism be revived, I asked some cosmopolitan friends. What training and qualifications are required?

Happening to be in Paris soon afterwards I conducted some arduous field research in cafés on boulevards, investigating the current habitat, plumage and mating habits of the species.

There were no signs of silver-topped canes, bowing or kissing of hands. Even the pavements were not what they were. The once-fashionable northern boulevards – of the Italiens, St Denis and Haussmann – have been taken over (I was told) by immigrants who, having no jobs, are the real practitioners of leisure.

Most of the French, in fact, are even more obsessed than the British with appearing as busy as possible, with the help of every new kind of gadgetry – mobile phones, calculators and laptops.

In this futuristic world the nearest equivalent to the organised flirting of the old boulevards is the Internet which allows ambitious young Frenchmen to pick up promising young American women a few thousand miles away, and to start a provocative dialogue over their computer screens, re-inforced by colour photographs to show off their charms.

But they are too busy comparing notes about computer programmes to get down to more intimate discourse; their competitiveness depends on speed, which allows little time for subtle seduction.

The true boulevardier flaunted his leisure. A century ago the rich displayed their wealth through their lack of work and their trappings and clothes which – as the great sociologist Thorstein Veblen analysed at the time – were the results of other people's work.

But today the fear of unemployment has reversed all that. The more spare time there is, the more it is dreaded: while over the last 20 years the rich have become obsessed with working and busy-ness – travelling, phoning, faxing, moving between offices – adopting the activities of people who have to work for a living.

Even the luxury yacht, the old symbol of conspicuous consumption, now has its communication centre, helicopter and satellite dish to keep constantly in touch with the mainland.

So what are the prospects for the would-be boulevardier? What happens to the oldie who has overworked for years to earn enough pension for luxurious leisure?

There is no doubt that he is entering the most difficult and exacting profession of all, which offers rewards like no other – freedom from competitiveness, pressures and speed. But he will have to work at it.

Christie's, SW1

Drawings by **Nick Baker**, *words by* **Huon Mallalieu**

'I SEE YOU WERE at Oxford,' said the Managing Director.

'Yes,' I replied, no doubt smugly.

'Did you actually get a degree?'

'Yes!'

'Well, you'll have to forget all that arty-farty nonsense here.'

Some time later, on Monday, 5th May, 1969, I presented myself at the front counter of Christie's as the auction house's newest recruit.

Every recruit, however eminent, was supposed to do time on the counter where the goods are received, and indeed, even the late Michael Tree, owner and restorer of Mereworth Castle, sat there with a benign smile for a day or two at the beginning of his employment. Most 20-year-olds could expect several months of running errands and learning diplomacy, before being assigned to a department – which, as in the Foreign Office, seldom turned out to be the one you wanted.

In charge of us was Ridley Dranmer Leadbeater, elegant of buttonhole and dapper of waistcoat, whose shining morning face shone still more benignly after lunch. Ridley combined immense kindness with shock tactics when he felt that our manners were less than perfect. A favourite corrective was a jab in the backside with a Biro. He tried that only once on an American girl whom he caught gossiping – she whirled round and almost flattened him.

I too was on the receiving end of the Biro only once. I was leaning over the counter in a casual fashion while dealing with the enquiries of a tall middle-aged gentleman, when I was jabbed upright by Ridley who muttered from the side of his mouth, 'Stand up straight, boy, when you talk to the King of Norway'.

The first job of the day was removing the stamps from all the envelopes of the previous day's post. They were sent to charity, but we found that it was remarkable how many got through the system unfranked. It was some years before I needed to buy a stamp.

The major part of the job was unwrapping people's treasures in the row of waiting rooms, summoning the relevant specialists, or taking the goods to them, and making out receipts. Paintings had to be chalked with stock numbers. Everything else had its sticker or label, and the piles of receipts were taken upstairs to be entered in the daybook by hand. Those vellum-bound ledgers were the spine of the firm, running back to its foundation in 1766. No computer record can have the atmosphere of the shelves of daybooks in the old muniments room.

The point of our existence was to learn by listening, and a very good general education it was. Almost anything might emerge. On one occasion I was dealing with two sharp-suited Americans. They had a trunk of silver and other things that had belonged to Napoleon on St Helena. 'That's his cup; that's some of his hair – and that's his schlong,' said one. I had not heard the word before, and so was able

to act with entire aplomb. I wish I could remember what I put on the receipt.

Once I was working with a friend in the warehouses behind. A colleague from the wine department passed pushing a trolley on which something was leaking. 'It's a bottle of port with a little hole in the shoulder – have it if you want.' We had only a short time, but I have never enjoyed a glass of port as much as that 1912 strained through a handkerchief into a tea cup.

Everything became more of a hustle and bustle as '11 o'clock precisely,' the hour of the morning sales, approached. Some weeks after I joined I was surprised by an unusual hush. 'Ah, there's a doll sale this morning,' said someone more experienced. 'So what?' 'You'll see.' At about 10.45 coachloads of blue rinses from St Louis and Cincinnati erupted through the door.

At night, security consisted of an ancient man and his equally old dog. He moved around at a remarkable pace, but one morning he was not to be seen when we arrived. He was found in one of the waiting rooms with his feet on a chair, having died in his sleep. I often wondered what happened to the dog.

At Christmas everyone was given a turkey – Ridley had an interest in a turkey farm – a bottle of wine, and perhaps a bonus. The picture storage area was transformed into a scene from Brueghel, as porters plucked among the Old Masters. On Christmas Eve, the front counter was quite as unbuttoned, since half the art world seemed to appear bearing bottles.

Ridley Leadbeater died at the beginning of 1995, having retired in 1974, some time after which the firm stopped using trainees on the counter. I do not know how they educate them nowadays but it is a schooling I am glad not to have missed.

Jorge Luis Borges

IT WAS an especially cold January, I think in 1963. I was working as a guide for the British Council in London. My assignment for this particular day was to take an eminent Argentinian writer to three houses in Sussex and Kent with literary vibrations. We were to have a car with a driver.

He was travelling with his mother, Leonora Acevedo de Borges, a small woman in a velvet hat and enormous fur coat, her clear, direct eyes missing nothing. He was not very tall and wore thick glasses, through which I think he could only see shadows. There was a calm smile on his face and he had a soft handshake. He, too, wore an enormous overcoat.

The snow was thick on the pavements before we left London. By the time we got to the lane that led to Bateman's, the home of Rudyard Kipling, it was clear that it was completely impassable. We then made for Rye, to see Lamb House, where Henry

James had lived for so long, only to find that it was never open on that day of the week and certainly not in winter. Someone at headquarters had blundered.

We had an excellent lunch at the Mermaid Hotel.

He called his mother Mama, with the accent on the first syllable, and she called him Jorge. Having heard radio announcers tying their glottises in knots in order to say 'Horche Lueeth Borcheth', I asked her how to pronounce his name correctly. 'Jorge Luis Borges,' she replied, exactly as it is written, the g's and j's very soft, the s's sibilant.

Our third appointment was at the house of H G Wells in Sandgate, near Folkestone, and here we were expected. It was a house in the style of C F A Voysey, probably even by him. Our hostess, in a dirndl skirt and sandals with no stockings, welcomed us into a stone-flagged hall

even colder than outside. She gave us tea in that hall, glancing disapprovingly at Mama's neat suede boots and huge fur coat – which she did not remove – explaining that her sandals were made of plastic and that she was entirely vegetarian. She gave us scones made of stone-ground flour, the proportion of stone to flour approximately equal.

He said very little over tea, a Buddhist smile on his face, enjoying the brittle conversation of the woman. Only in England, he said to me later, did people like that flourish unhindered. HG Wells still haunted the house, we were told. No woman could have a bath in the housemaids' bathroom on the top floor, because H G came in and stared at them, sitting on the lavatory seat with the lid down.

As we prepared to leave he said to me:

'Are we near Canterbury?'

'Yes,' I said.

'Have we time to go?'

He had had a disappointing day. They were not usually very pleased at headquarters when programmes were altered or interfered with, but he obviously wanted to go very much. Fortunately, our driver was one of the more amenable of a very recalcitrant lot.

It was dark when we arrived and evensong was being sung. The nave was only partially lit and I heard Mama catch her breath as we entered. 'Unbelievable,' she said. We sat in the ambulatory behind the choir as the service continued, the treble and base voices seemed to reflect the light and shadow on the ceiling arches. He touched me on the sleeve.

'I want to go back to the nave,' he said.

Together we went down that wide flight of perfectly plain steps until we stood at the bottom.

'Am I in the middle?' We moved.

'Am I facing the altar?'

I manoeuvred him slightly and he said: 'Now you must face me.'

I did so, my back to the choir.

'And now,' he said, 'I fulfil a lifelong ambition. I am here in Canterbury Cathedral and I am going to recite to you the Lord's Prayer in Anglo-Saxon.'

A beatific smile spread slowly over his face and seemed to envelop his entire person.

Only then did he do so.

LAURENCE FLEMING

She gave us scones made of stone-ground flour, the proportion of stone to flour approximately equal

Miles Kington

The Yellow Water Hotel

Sometimes hotels like to boast that they have a homely atmosphere or that they are homes from home, and I never used to question this claim until I stayed a night the other week in a large hotel in a big city centre in the North of England, and while I was endeavouring to manoeuvre my hotel hanger back on to its socket suddenly realised that in almost every respect hotels are as unlike home as they could be.

For a start, you don't have a mini-bar in your bedroom at home, and nor do we all have a TV in our bedroom, and even if we do, we probably don't have an in-house soft porn channel on it.

In a hotel bedroom you have keys which are not keys at all but temporary credit cards. This is to prevent you walking off with them, I suppose.

For some reason (kleptomania among guests) hotels no longer have real clothes hangers either, but those ones with knobs on top which slot into a sliding device on the clothes rail. If I had the energy and the ingenuity I would long since have installed a wardrobe at home which would take hotel hangers so that I could safely go on nicking hangers, but I have never got round to it…

In real life you don't have a kettle in your bedroom accompanied by a posh butter dish full of tea bags, and a short electrical connection and no plug in the wall to stick it into. I actually did feel like a cup of tea when I arrived. I filled the kettle and looked round for the wall plug. Couldn't find it anywhere.

My eye fell on the mock-leather folder which hotels now give you to brief you on your mission. Nothing about wall plugs in there, but there was a message from the manager asking me to get in touch any time I had a problem. Seriously considered ringing him up. 'Room 510 here… Fine, thanks… just want to know where I plug the kettle in… ' Found it just in time, behind the electric trouser press, which I don't have at home either.

In real life you don't have the end of the lavatory paper roll tucked into a V shape by an invisible maid. I have never quite understood the point of

this. Is it to enable you to locate the end of the paper? Is it some personal artistry on the part of the chambermaid, like arranging napkins?

In real life, when someone flushes the loo while you are in the shower, the shower suddenly goes scalding hot as the cold water is called elsewhere to help fill cisterns. This does not happen in hotels, where there is enough water to go round. The shower in a hotel remains absolutely the same temperature. It is never quite the right temperature, but that is what it remains.

In hotels, the radio can only be heard on the television set. This is different from most homes. In hotels you can get tiny bottles of 'Natural Moisturising Shampoo'. This is a fluid unknown to nature, so I do not know why it is called 'Natural Moisturising Shampoo'. Everything in hotel bedrooms comes in unnaturally small portions, of course, but this is only because they know that, being hotel guests and therefore kleptomaniacs, we will abscond with whatever we are given, and they are therefore trying to minimise the danger.

Incidentally, do people really walk away with that curious object known as the courtesy shower cap? If they haven't got any at home, I suppose it might be tempting, and I certainly have never seen any round my place. And there was something in my

'Don't you dare turn your back on me!'

hotel bathroom this time which I had never seen before in any hotel or home. It was a printed card from the hotel people say, 'WATER SUPPLY – Dear Guest, You may notice a slight discolouration of the water supply. This is common in the Leeds area as we are informed by Yorkshire Water that water is filtered through peat in this area. However, I would like to assure you that the water is perfectly safe. Yrs The General Manager.'

Good, eh? Of course, it works better when you are reading it out, and can tell people that water is filtered through peat in this area, and then say: 'That Pete has sure got a tough job, eh?' Hmmm. Anyway, up to that moment I had not been tempted to nick anything from the hotel, but then I succumbed and now our bathroom sports a notice apologising for the slight discolouration of the water.

ACCORDING TO Christianity, the spirits of the dead go to a better, or worse, place than this earth. But a lot of people see ghosts, so there appears to be strong evidence for their visits here — the reason why I made several TV documentaries about them. Ghosts are at their noblest on battlements or in ancient houses, though some turn up in council houses. Ghostly Roman soldiers were once seen walking through underground walls by a sewer worker. I met a man who had been preparing the foundations for an old folk's home, who had been surprised to see the top half of a

Quaker watching him. Because it was a Jewish old folk's home a row broke out concerning the true identity of the apparition; it was asserted that it must have been the top half of a rabbi. But the phantom's cuffs solve d that problem – they had been white, making it a Quaker.

An old lady told me she had observed a ghost on a lavatory during the night. She had retreated when she saw ghostly pyjama knees sticking out beyond the open door. A man was fortunate enough to have a female ghost in his bedroom, although he had made no attempt to approach her,

possibly because he was married. A lady in Scotland told me she was a reincarnation of James IV and saw glimpses of soldiers from the Battle of Flodden. She remembered the flying English Standard and men with swords driving at her.

In Wimbledon, Rosemary Brown was in contact with dead composers. She explained on film how Liszt was standing behind me, that Chopin was to my right dressed in a tartan shirt because of his Scottish connections and that the room was crowded, some on floor level, others above it. Bertrand Russell was standing

A spectre calls

Liszt on a plane, Handel's 'new' Oratorio? **Hugh Burnett** *investigates ghostly goings on*

beside her, dressed in a suit, a silky open-necked shirt, black shoes and without spectacles. 'He wouldn't need spectacles there.' After Russell had died and discovered he was still alive he had been very cross and changed a lot of his ideas, commenting that scientists do that all the time. He felt more alive than when on earth, which surprised him – his physical brain during his life had apparently blurred his perception. 'I felt very honoured when he first came and spoke to me,' said Mrs Brown. 'I wondered why somebody of such an immense intellect should bother himself with a humble person like myself.'

She also described how Liszt went shopping with her to Safeways, assisting in the selection of cheaper bunches of bananas than those she could see. Liszt wore a long robe and was usually smiling, even when he had appeared to her on an aeroplane. 'He seemed quite fascinated by the idea of flying. Somehow or other they seem to get into the plane... They aren't limited by geography as we are,' she said. Once she had been visiting a friend and Wordsworth suddenly appeared – to dictate a new poem. Painters had communicated new works. Van Gogh had come through in charcoal, because she had no oil paints at the time. He had complained about that and she bought some oils, since they painted on the Other Side with brushes and paints. There were buildings Over There she had been told, libraries, musical instruments, landscapes, trees, rivers, beautiful flowers, birds and animals. I raised the problem that animals did not have souls and could therefore not survive. Mrs Brown said this was more likely to happen to animals that had close human contact. A tiger in a zoo, apparently, has a better chance of passing into the afterlife than one in the jungle.

John Lill, the distinguished concert pianist, attended one of Mrs Brown's public meetings. He said she was genuine and had been chosen to convey the identities of the composers through their style. The music itself was eternal and came from God, he said. Mr Lill had also sensed the presence of Beethoven as he played.

A new Oratorio had been received from Handel by Clifford Enticknapp. Funded by subscriptions to the Handelian Foundation, the final recording had cost

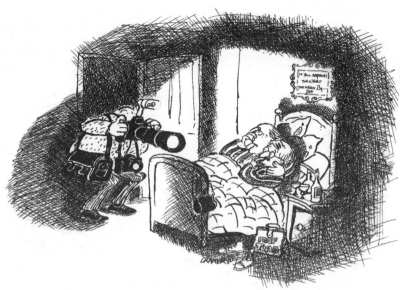

more than £10,000 and cassettes were sold at the Psychic Fair. Handel talked to Mr Enticknapp, aged about 45. 'The vibrations are much better in a place of worship,' he explained when we filmed in a church in Stanmore, where the great master had written one of his oratorios.

But when spiritual matters combine with such mundane affairs as copyright and the Musicians Union, problems arise. One was whether the copyright of the new work belonged to Mr Enticknapp, the Foundation, or Handel. 'It's not my music,' explained Mr Enticknapp. 'I don't take any credit for the music... The music is a spiritual energy, given to the earth plane through the vehicle of my flesh.'

The most profitable ghost was the nun at Borley Rectory. Harry Price did a great deal of research there, wrote several monographs about the strange hauntings – and got himself photographed in bed with Professor Joad. (Their explanation was that they were investigating supernatural activity.) The nun was reported to walk the rectory at night leaving chalk scribbles on the walls, calling for prayers and masses. Queues of earnest investigators toured the rectory with torches looking for new messages. They found them. Then it was noticed that if Harry Price was in the middle of the group nothing new appeared next time round. But when he was at the end of the line fresh ones arrived. Mysterious pebbles were thrown through the air; then pebbles were discovered in Mr Price's car boot. Doubts set in for all

but the most convinced. In spite of the famous 'cold spot' there was a fire at the rectory and the whole place burned down. That should not have mattered to the spirits, but apparently it did. They transferred to the local church, where investigators would often record noises in the dark.

I made a film on this interesting .phenomenon, which did not please locals when it was transmitted. They objected to unwelcome investigators in their church, including us. A viewer of the documentary wrote in to say HE might have caused one of the bangs on the tape we had broadcast. He had cautiously approached one night, carrying a spanner as a precaution, and dropped it in the church porch when he found the door was locked.

I met a man who spent years trying to photograph a ghost. He failed. Long sessions on a camp-bed in the dark, with trip-wires, plungers and automatic cameras had produced nothing. However, at a ghost symposium he attended abroad, to his horror, he saw flashed up on the screen a picture of an apparition he had faked for a newspaper. Wisely, in my opinion, he had remained silent before the assembled audience.

For me one difficulty remains. Ghosts are always dressed in clothes. Cloaks, socks or trousers in the afterlife present unsurmountable theological problems. There has never been a report of a nude ghost. When I hear about that I shall be less sceptical. I look forward to that – or when a Buddhist or Hindu sees a vision of the Virgin Mary.

The scourge of Sex and Nuts and Sitting

'Protein Man' waged a bizarre campaign in Oxford St for 25 years. **Cathy Ross** *celebrates a great eccentric*

Do you remember Protein Man? If you were in Oxford Street at any time between August 1968 and December 1993 the chances are that you do. Protein Man was there most days. A man with an unforgettable placard: 'Less passion from less protein: less fish, meat, bird, cheese, egg; peas, beans, nuts and sitting.' What did it mean? Was he a 'performance artist'? Was he an advertising campaign? No, he was Protein Man, London's very own superhero.

Three years after his death, he is back. His famous placard is on display in the Museum of London's new 'London Now' gallery. Not that he ever really went away. In 1995 his printing press shared space at the Serpentine Gallery with a sleeping Tilda Swinton. In 1996 he popped up on posters advertising Abbey National Tessas. There are still young people around wearing the pop group Red or Dead's 1992 'Less Passion Less Protein' T-shirts. Like all superheroes, Protein Man is indestructible.

What was 'Protein Wisdom'? Was he simply mad, or could he possibly have been right – a health and fitness guru before his time? Protein Man's campaign was not about personal health as such. Although diet was the battleground, his crusade was about the big issues of the 20th century: family breakdown, sex and violence, moral standards, the changing role of women. Protein Man's concerns were thoroughly political.

His papers, now archived in the Museum of London, confirm this. They reveal him as a fierce monitor of current affairs. Any newspaper story confirming the onward march of wickedness in modern life was cut out and filed, usually in a Sainsbury's bag or an old soap powder packet. Everything was carefully marked: 'Aids', 'Celibacy', 'Vietnam War'. Then

there were the letters. After a hard day on the streets, Protein Man would return to his council flat in Ealing and write to public figures.

Sorting Protein Man's copy letters for the Museum was a treat. Everybody who was anybody is there, from the Archbishop of Canterbury and the Director of the Family Planning Association, to the Editor of *The Times* ('Protein Wisdom would not reduce your circulation and it might increase it') and the Director-General of the BBC (denouncing the sexual immorality of *The Archers*, 'a glossy tale of easy-going people'). Politicians were favourite targets: Edwina Currie on eggs, Willie Whitelaw ('Why can you not arrange for all prisoners, wives or husbands to receive a version of my enclosed booklet?') and John Major ('Will your government be yet another that will promote sexual promiscuity among young people?').

But his most passionate letters were addressed to Mrs Thatcher, whom he often addressed as 'Ma'am'. Among the newspaper scraps we found was one from 1974 in which a political commentator had mused on the sudden softening in the then education minister's manner. What, wondered the writer, had happened to make Mrs Thatcher more 'kindly'? Protein Man had pencilled excited asterisks by this passage and noted: 'I sent my booklet to Mrs

Thatcher (in 1972)' followed by the initials 'PW'. Clearly he believed the future prime minister was in receipt of 'Protein Wisdom'.

Protein Man's real name was Stanley Green. He was born on 22nd February 1915 in Tottenham, the son of May and Richard, described on the birth certificate as a 'bottle stopper maker's clerk'. There were two swimming certificates from Wood Green School and a junior boxing medal dated 1923. He served in the Navy during the Second World War and saw active service. There was a rejection letter from the University of London dated 1946 telling Mr Green that he'd failed the entrance exam in elementary mathematics and (perhaps predictably) logic. He worked for Selfridges for a time, then the Post Office, the Ministry of Works and, surprisingly, the Fine Art Society. Among the papers were some drawings and watercolours. They were very good. Stanley's artistic abilities were confirmed by his brother Richard, who donated his papers to the Museum. Stanley had gone to classes before the war and had hoped to become an artist or illustrator. Richard Green had further examples of his work: energetic book illustrations, portraits and still lives, all executed with vigour – and passion.

Stanley was the youngest of four sons. All the others followed conventional careers and raised families. Stanley never married and never left home. He lived with his parents until his father's death in 1966, and his mother's the following year. 'Why protein?' I asked. Richard said: 'Perhaps it was something he read. He was always reading.'

Some clues are provided by his unpublished novel *Behind the Veil: More Than Just a Tale*, a surreal drama of life in

London played out by characters with meaningful names: Mr and Mrs Blissfold, Mrs Posey, old Mr Heetoff and Mrs Autella Frugally.

The author's hand is all too evident (all the women have an irresistible urge to talk about the menstrual cycle) and particularly so in the character of Mr Fallaway, a man who is at odds with the world: 'His rat-race days, before he dropped out, were mostly unhappy days, because he was on an empty strand and had no boat to push out. Now 20 years later, he was still stranded, but somehow, exactly how he knew not, he had found contentment in just living from day to day.'

He is probably best seen in the context of the social upheavals his generation lived through. He was born into a world where people knew their place; he died in a world of global awareness where stories of war, Aids and adultery tumbled relentlessly into people's lives. Did this process of change cause him to transform himself into Protein Man, with a mission to save the world?

It is difficult not to get fond of Stanley Green. Protein Man could be misogynist, intolerant and stubborn. But beneath was a mere mortal, trying like everybody to make some sense of the 20th century. One warms to his exuberant contradictions: who else could make a crusade preaching restraint and conformity into a triumph of individual exhibitionism? Who else could have plugged their own small world so successfully into the global media network? Who else could have been so funny while being so serious? 'I am trying' he once wrote, 'to help people lead happier lives.' And so he did, if not quite in the manner intended.

Dr Ross is head of the Department of Later London History, Museum of London, London Wall, EC2.

Andy Warhol

IN THE EARLY Eighties I was a chauffeur for Mercedes car hire firm in West Berlin. One day I was sent to the Hotel Kempinski to pick up four customers and take them to East Berlin. When I arrived at the Kempinski I found that one of the four was Andy Warhol, who was in West Berlin to visit an exhibition in the Martin-Gropius-Bau. The others were a Canadian author whose name I have forgotten and two tattooed leather-and-steel clad gentlemen friends of the Canadian and Warhol. At first everything went OK. We drove through Checkpoint Charlie, made a compulsory money exchange, visited the usual tourist sites of East Berlin, the Pergamon Museum, Alexander Platz and, of course, the Russian cemetery in Treptow. On our way back to West Berlin I pointed out to Mr Warhol that none of us would be able to take our East German marks out of East Berlin. Warhol asked me what we could buy with the money and I suggested going to a souvenir shop. It was agreed and drove them to a shop in Treptower Park. Warhol bought some kitsch, a replica of the TV tower at Alexander Platz. The Canadian bought something small, and the two 'heavies' purchased an armful.

The trouble started when one of the boy friends asked me to ask the shop assistant for another brown paper bag. (Should explain here that this was East Berlin, not Times Square, and that with his purchase each customer got one paper bag, and one only.) I explained the situation to lover boy but he insisted that I should ask anyway. I did and, as I knew would happen, the request was refused. I translated this for angel face and after looking heavenwards for guidance he told me to ask that 'asshole' for a 'BROWN PAPER BAG – GODDAMMIT' – which I did and was again refused. This went on for another couple of times, Warhol's friend getting progressively noisier. After a couple of 'Does she know who the fuck, she is dealing with?' he slowly sank to his knees and with his hands held high, tears streaming down his face – he shouted at the top of his voice: 'All I want for Christ' sake is a fucking brown paper bag.'

A deathly silence fell over the shop. Warhol had a half grin on his face but I noticed one assistant saying to the other 'Call the Stasi' (secret police). I said to Warhol that if we didn't get away smartish we would all wind up in the huge complex at Alexander Platz that housed the Staatssicherheitsdienst and that the least that would happen would be that we would have to cool our heels for a few hours for disturbing the peace. I reminded Warhol of his appointment that evening at the Martin-Gropius-Bau and told him we should leave immediately. The Canadian and the other fine example of American manhood dragged their by now hysterical friend back to the car. I raced to Checkpoint Charlie and we passed back into West Berlin and to the Kempinski. On the way back, the Canadian started to sing that song that Bob Hope sang in *Pale Face* – 'East is East and West is West, and the wrong one I have chose'. Everyone laughed (Warhol just grinned) and the hysterical one went back to being the lovely broken-nosed, scarfaced, sweet young thing he was before. I was glad to see them get out of the car and out of my sight.

ROBERT LOWE

From time to time I live in the foothills of the Himalayas. You drive eight hours east of Delhi, through the Terai (a skirt of malarial forest at the base of the hills) where Sikh militants from the Punjab shelter with relatives, and every now and then, shoot people. There is a section of the Terai through which you are forbidden to drive at night. Police posts guard each end. But I have driven through it, very fast, at night. All it required was a bribe, and the presence of a VIP. My hair stood on end all the way. Even so, this is one section of the Indian Himalayas that is relatively free of political violence, and now wealthy urbanites, no longer able to holiday in Kashmir, are dotting the hills with kitsch.

Once you are climbing (avoiding landslides and fatalistic bus drivers) the heaviness and sorrow of the plains begin to fall away. The air starts to effervesce, like good champagne. You could imagine yourself on a graph – the increase in altitude corresponding with a backward movement through time, into an older, less confused India. This is an illusion. You have only to look at the vistas of naked mountains, the trees gone, the water sources drying up, the terraced farms not even providing subsistence crops any more, the villages ugly and poor, to know that the chaos is here too.

The British took out most of the native oak. They introduced pine, which competes with native flora, spreading and drying and creating bush fires wherever it has taken hold. It is of no use to local people, who depend on the oak for fuel and fodder. Farmers are too poor to use alternative sources of energy. The women have to go so far now to gather wood and feed, that they are out all day. The men stay at home to work the fields, and to look after the

From her home in the foothills of the Himalayas, Australian-born traveller **Robyn Davidso**

A Goat for

children. Or they disappear into the slums of cities, to try to find work.

As usual, I park the jeep at Padampuri – a village consisting of post-office, tea shop, and a muddle of wooden houses. The ponies are loaded with luggage, and I walk for an hour and a half, straight up, to the house. I am accompanied, by Hanuman, our manager, who carries a rifle – defence against bears, leopards or wild pigs.

We own 400 acres – one of the last patches of healthy growth in the area. We are trying to protect it, taking the long term view that eventually it will be more useful as a species reserve and water catchment than as a wasteland. Local women are welcome to forage, but no tree-cutting or poaching is allowed. Hanuman is an outsider – a Rajput from Rajasthan. If we employed a local as boss, he would not be able to withstand pressure from his relatives and friends, and soon the trees would be gone. Nevertheless, we do employ many local men to work for us, and this counterbalances any unpopularity we might suffer for closing the forest. There is no other work to be had here.

The staff consists of two Rajputs at the top, some local Brahmins, including Bishan the cook, and Chandrawallab, the odd-job man. Various scheduled caste men work as carpenters and builders, or help out in the kitchen, thereby breaking ritual cleanliness taboos. The Rajputs are illiterate, while many locals can read and write. As I often spend months on my own here, away from telephone or friends, I have grown close to these men, particularly Bishan, who tries to teach me Hindi while I reciprocate with English.

When I first went there, he said, 'It was better when the British were here.' He said this partly because he thought it would flatter me, partly because he believed it. 'But the British were cruel to

you. They robbed you of the forest, and siphoned all the wealth out of the country.'

'Yes,' he agreed, 'but now we rob each other. And everything is upside down.' He was right in this sense: for every dollar designated to relieve poverty, something like five cents actually reaches the target. The rest goes into the pockets of middlemen, swelling the new middle class so welcomed by American markets, and the already obscenely bulging bank accounts of those at the top of the pile. The bottom of the pile is being, as Bishan would not dream of putting it, fucked.

The staff, I would like to think, are also friends. Perhaps this is an illusion too. I am as far from them as it is possible to be. Yet when I am with them, joking with them, I am aware of our similarities, not our differences. There are differences among them too – different castes, different levels of status. But they are united by a world view I cannot share, which is symbolized by their relationship to the temple.

NANDA DEVI TEMPLE is tiny, round and white. It sits on a plinth, under an oak from whose branches hang bronze bells, fraying flags, and monsoon lichens crusted over centuries. Forest surrounds it, but at the foot of the slope is a clearing from which the Himalayan peaks can be seen, Nanda Devi at the centre – a sight which lends existence here, for all its discomforts, sublimity. Those mountains (the shattered bones of two continental shoulders smashing into each other) place humanness in perspective – a blip of awareness in boundless insentience. No one knows when the first humans hallowed this particular place with meaning. Perhaps hunter-gatherers chose just this little rise on which to make their

obeisances before the mystery of being. Perhaps, like certain nomads in Africa, they left grass weavings in an oak to mark their passing. Now, there is a lingum here, fused into the earth by time, the bole of the tree grown round it like flesh. Another lingum, younger, is inside the temple, which was built to shelter it a hundred years ago.

The stone dome is six foot in diameter. You stoop to enter, then sit in front of gaudy gods in frames; brass incense holders; a conch for calling worshippers; clay dias holding oil and wicks; a marble statue of Parvati in her local manifestation as Nanda Devi, dressed in gold silk skirt and red glass bracelets. Everything is daubed with saffron, ghee, red dye and silver, and here and there are scattered the remains of marigolds and rhododendron. When electricity came to our house, a line was laid all the way up here, so that flashing Christmas lights could be draped over the idols. From the apex of the dome hang a bare bulb and a bunch of naked wires. A history of humanness could be deciphered from this temple – the imagined grass offerings of the hunters, the neurotic stone fixtures of sedentary folk, the discordant

ent to witness a rite of propitiation and divination almost as old as the hills themselves

the Goddess

technology of the 20th century, and the most recent footnote, I myself, who have no god to bow to.

Outside, jungle crows and magpies with long blue tails bicker in the branches. Thrushes and oreoles pour sound through the air as limpid as spring water. I've watched a leopard sprawled by the lingum, flicking the tip of his tail. Few strangers come here, but those who do climb for hours, sometimes days, to reach the goddess. It's a good place to be alone.

On this particular day, throughout India, various Hindu castes slaughter an animal, usually a goat. It is a form of propitiation to the gods, and a method of divining (and causing) the future. If the rituals surrounding the deed go smoothly, the goddess has approved, and will bring good fortune. If not, the year ahead will be filled with problems.

Bishan hints that as everyone would be taking a bath, perhaps I too should wash for the occasion, and wear clean clothes. Otherwise, there is nothing I have to do. He himself has never seen this ritual performed, and admits he is a little nervous about it. Being a Brahmin, and therefore a vegetarian (though I've seen him tuck into a plate of goat curry with those decadent Rajputs who, because they in turn had been seduced by flesh-eating Mughals,

enjoy guzzling as much meat as possible), he infers that he might have to look away when the deed is done. But his intellectual curiosity will overcome his timidity, of that I am sure.

Hanuman is to perform the sacrifice. He is a big, handsome man – the most respected man of his village. He carries his authority with quiet dignity. Usually he wears khaki trousers and army jacket with fake fur collar. Today he is dressed in white muslin dhoti, white kurta, and everything about him is crisp, pressed, clean and oiled. He has not eaten for a day, so even his insides are clean. He is wearing his pagra (turban) tied as appropriate to his sub-caste and caste. He is not nervous so much as intensely aware of his responsibility as a vehicle for a higher order of thing. Each movement he makes is self-conscious and grave. I am invited to walk with him to the temple, carrying the offerings – a brass thali filled with ghee, sweets, coconut, thread, red paste, rice grains, incense. To this I add flowers and more incense. Hanuman is also carrying a sword.

As we trudge up the hill, it begins to rain. He hands me the thali and puts up a black umbrella. For a moment I think he is doing it for me, as normally his Rajput chivalry would demand. But no, he uses it to cover the thali. Thus we proceed to the hut beside the temple, where the other men are preparing a fire. We do not hurry, and we ignore the rain which stings the cheeks like metal.

The men smile and make room for me by the fire. All of them are bathed and wearing their second pair of clothes. Chandrawallab's job is to keep the fire going, and to produce coals for Hanuman who is busy inside the temple. He comes out now, carrying a painting of Ram. Ram does not eat meat, and therefore would be offended at the sight of the killing. He is made to face the wall of the hut.

The sacrifice is only to Devi in her many forms – Kali, Parvati, Durga. Hanuman goes back inside for 10 minutes, pops

his head out, clangs the big brass bell, beckons me in.

At the foot of the plinth, a goat is tethered to a tree. It is a pretty young thing – black with brown patches, and delicate horns. It looks me up and down as I pass by. I look back at the goat. In the mutual stare there is an acknowledgement of each other's existence. But I pass on and out (I suppose) of the goat's consciousness. (Is Borges right when he says that man lives in time, in succession, while the animal lives 'in the present, in the eternity of an instant'?)

INSIDE THE TEMPLE, I sit by Hanuman as he lights the dias. Then he passes over each of the idols. I repeat the action. My flowers have been placed in Parvati's hand. A little of each of the gifts has been placed in front of her. Over the hot coals, ghee is burned, then pieces of coconut, their essence transubstantiated into food for the gods. Hanuman sings snatches of mantras. Then he takes pinches of rice and counts them in his palm. By this method, he is asking the goddess if she approves of the sacrifice. It seems that she does, because he picks up even numbers time after time, until he is satisfied as to her answer. He backs out of the temple at last, to get the consecrated red paste, made of ash and rose petals. This he places on the forehead of each idol.

The sword is the last object to be brought in – a scimitar, four feet long, curved, not, it appears, particularly sharp. Blessed string is tied round the handle. It is purified by saffron, and water from the Ganges. Then we go outside.

The goat is brought up onto the plinth and released. It charges off and I grab it automatically, not knowing what is expected of me. I am told gently to let it go. It goes straight into the temple, turns around and looks at us through the doorway, as if from its own, safe home. When it gives a shudder, a cry of delight and relief goes up. This is Parvati's ultimate sign of acceptance and on this occasion it has been perfectly clear. Sometimes this process takes hours, Bishan informs me, and occasionally another goat must be brought. Part of me feels like tipping off the goat: 'Don't shiver, you fool. Let some other goat shiver in your stead.'

But the goat shivers and is led to the killing site. One man holds the horns, another a hind leg. Hanuman stands to the side and behind the head of the goat. He gives the signal for Chandrawallab to let go of the horns. The animal gazes impassively away from Hanuman, who lifts the sword, over his head, over and behind his back, way over until it can go no further, then brings it whooshing through a 270 degree arc to strike the goat's neck, severing the spine. In one immeasurable instant, something unspeakably strange has occurred – the goatness of the goat has vanished.

Bishan flinches and gives a nervous grin. The head is being sawed through with the blunt sword, the bleeding stopped from the carotid, the head offered to Bhairon Ji – the stone guardian at the entrance of the temple. I look at the head at the foot of the idol. An ear twitches and the mouth opens abruptly as if to say 'what … happened?' Bishan puts his hand over his mouth, and rolls his eyes.

Hanuman is transformed. He has done a perfect job and he is elated. The goat did not cry out – all the shaguns have been remarkably favourable. He says that for a whole year the gods will be kind. There will be no deaths, no sickness. The blood is cleared from the spot with leaves, then the ground is washed. Saffron and rice from the temple are placed on everyone's forehead, and food blessed in the temple is eaten. We are all light-headed, as if something burdensome has been taken away.

The goat is skinned. That magical and anxious moment between the state of animal and the state of food has passed. The glance the goat gave me is unrelated to the spiced liver I am brought an hour later, which is delicious. Later, Hanuman will cook the meat – less chilli for me; a violently fiery version for everyone else.

I do not know what the goat sacrifice means to them. But to me it was a moment of profound unity, not just with my companions, but with the whole of poor, bewildered man.

The origins of the event go back further than the Vedas, or settlement, to the first self-awareness that set us apart from other species. The cat, when it kills, kills in innocence. It shares no kinship with its prey. Man when he kills, consigns life to oblivion. Man can imagine what it is like to be dead. In order to bear the guilt of killing, he had to sanctify the deed, and in doing so come to terms with what it means to be 'a sausage of angel and beast' – our capacity to kill, our horror of death, our longing for transcendence, our unique alienness, our unbearable consciousness.

Alice Thomas-Ellis

I recently asked a young – well, youngish – friend (42 to be exact) what she thought of feminists. 'Hate them,' she responded tersely. She is an editor on a New York magazine; elegant, witty, confident and acknowledging no debt to the Sisters. She reminds me of certain film stars of the 30s and 40s – Katharine Hepburn, Joan Crawford, Bette Davis etc, none of whom resemble in the least the downtrodden wimps so crucial to feminist myth. Modern Woman was coming along nicely until after the war, when Baby Doll emerged – Lord knows where from – to be counterbalanced by the Amazon who, even if she did not slice off a breast, burned her bra (which, when you come to consider it, was foolish, since if you are going in for drawing bows a little structural support in the background can only be beneficial). Disgruntled females organised 'consciousness raising sessions' and adopted other outmoded and discredited Marxist tactics, so that in a while everyone hated them, though few dared to admit it. A dreadful breed of feminist men arose, claiming to sympathise with this struggle; everyone hated them too.

Social engineering is not a good idea. Human nature just will not have it. In LA a few years ago I sat with a group of ladies round a lunch table. They wore the baffled, aggrieved expression of hyenas who cannot understand why their prey is proving elusive. They all had jobs but no men and they could not imagine why this should be so. They had done all the right things – loved and esteemed themselves highly, explained to men what chauvinist pigs they were, been to assertiveness classes and thought hard before shaving their legs. Those with an ex-husband demanded that he support them for the rest of their lives, no matter what the relative state of their salaries, and then wondered despairingly why most men appeared to be homosexual. They were unaware of the extent of their unattractiveness: their greed, humourlessness, whingeing, lack of generosity and the unsightly cut of their jackets.

Many of them still give the impression of being clinically insane. A group recently carted round a church crucifix with a female on it – not a real one – referring to the curious thing as Jesa Crista. Sheer, pure nuttiness can go no further. Never mind that it's blasphemous, it is silly to suggest that historical figures can change sex. Was General Custer a girl? Mussolini a madam? The recorded circumcision of Our Lord was used as evidence against the early heresies as proof of his humanity. It must surely also serve as evidence of his maleness.

I have another question I should like answered. What if God had chosen to send a daughter to redeem us? What would the feminists say to that? You can bet your boots – and your hat, coat and gloves – that they'd be whining that women had to do everything; men were just absolutely hopeless and never did anything useful. Here was this poor woman suffering unspeakable agonies for us and what were the men doing, eh? One 'feminist theologian' I spoke to gave it as her opinion that if Our Lord couldn't be represented as female then females couldn't be sure that they were redeemed. I know people are thick but surely they can't be as thick as that.

As long as equality is construed as meaning 'identical' we are going down skidding on good intentions to the inky bottom. The Cardinal, a well-meaning soul, has just said something about the Church 'going forward' – an unfortunate concept to apply to an edifice built upon a rock. If it starts paddling like a poodle in all directions after whatever fad or fancy is presently beguiling the 'intellectuals', it will collapse into nothing more than a pizza parlour (a nightmare predicted in the light of newly-built churches) and everyone can choke on their chosen flavour.

Ronnie Barker

picks his top six…

1 Tommy Cooper
Funny.

2 Eric Morecambe
Funnier.

3 Wilson, Keppell and Betty
Funniest.

4 Ingrid Bergman
My first love.

5 Lynda Baron
Much favoured in the Bristol area.

6 My Aunt Louisa
What a gal!

*Right: Comedian
Ronnie Barker*

WHEN I LEARNT to samba in Patagonia, the first thing my antediluvian and over-lipsticked teacher told me was to pretend I had a stick of chalk up my bum and draw a figure of eight.

Consequently I was prepared for anything when I turned up at my first belly-dancing lesson. It took place in a chilly, high-ceilinged gym round the corner from my flat in Camden Town; a flunky marched in to wash the walls while the class was in progress, fumes of Jeyes cleaning fluid standing in for the whiff of the souk and the grating of mop against pail for the swish of silken robes.

At the time, I had recently returned from five months languishing in the sepulchral wastes of Antarctica, and anything associated with heat or hot places called me siren-like to its door. When, therefore, I spotted the advertisement for these belly-dancing classes, images of sultry nights and warm exposed flesh crowded into my curdled brain and I signed up immediately. The course involved classes at 6.30pm on four consecutive Thursdays (£3 each).

No sooner had I enrolled than I discovered that belly-dancing was enjoying an unexpected renaissance in Britain and classes were breaking out all over the place. I concluded that this must be another symptom of the benign 90s; formerly written off by feminists as one more hideous symbol of patriarchy and the ritual humiliation of women, belly-wiggling has been rehabilitated because, don't you know, we're doing it for *us*. We have reclaimed our bodies and loosened our cultural moorings.

A woman signing up at the same time confided that she found the idea of learning to belly-dance liberating. 'I mean, it's empowering yourself. And belly-dancing kind of says that it's alright not being the shape of a supermodel.' I always knew there was a reason why I do not make the effort to be more like a supermodel – it's so that I could belly-dance!

Eight women turned up for the first lesson and we cowered at the back of the gym trying to make ourselves invisible while the teacher flapped around a dinosaur of a cassette player. One of the eight was a retired history teacher of 61, another an unemployed young woman called Sharon with two rings in her nose, a

third a senior civil servant.

Our teacher was a diminutive Moroccan called Leila who launched her introductory talk by assuring us that belly-dancing constituted such good exercise, both internal and external (whatever that means), that pregnant women were referred to her by doctors. After four lessons, she declared, we might consider turning professional. I thought this was an unlikely option in my case, but you never know; the bottom might fall out of the travel-writing market and it's good to have another string to your bow.

Leila distributed scarves for us to knot on our hips ('it accentuates the figure'). Mr Leila, a sphinx-like Egyptian, turned on the cassette player and Leila set about demonstrating the basic movements of the dance, a combination of steps, swings,

Wiggling for beginners

by Sara Wheeler

Sleek-headed men in Fezzes will seek to possess you.

31

thrusts, neck-slides and shimmies, the latter a kind of wobbly shoulder-rippling affair. We copied woodenly. Then we threaded all these components together and made a sequence; it was all about hips rather than belly and there was not a navel in sight. Fluidity of movement is everything and it was this that we found the hardest. 'Translate the music with your bodies!' cried Leila.

Everyone except the senescent history teacher was very bad. The Egyptian husband eventually began sniggering uncontrollably. Leila kept looking at her watch. What she liked was not teaching but dancing, and boy, could she dance! Shoulders thrust back, overflowing bosoms flung forward and eyes blazing, she was a study in concentrated provocation.

At the end of the class we were despatched with instructions to practise a series of exercises which included shutting an imaginary door sharply with our bottoms and holding a pretend stick at waist height with both hands, swinging the hips round to hit each end in turn. 'Try it at the bus stop!' suggested Leila helpfully.

Everyone came back for more. During the second session we did a lot of 'travelling', the technical bellydancing term for moving backwards or forwards or from side to side with little tippy-toe steps and accompanying hip-swings and arm gestures. Halfway through the class we moved on to a bit of North African technique; what we had been learning hitherto was apparently Egyptian (for indeed the forms of the dance are numerous) and Leila was anxious that we shouldn't get bored. The Moroccans, it turned out, place even more emphasis on the hips and shoulders, and we were equally lamentable at this new style, though by this time we had dispensed with our inhibitions and were swinging our hips around wildly at the slightest provocation.

My third lesson took place after an afternoon in the Marquis of Granby with *Oldie* contributor Jeremy Lewis, both of

> **A flunky washed the walls as the class was in progress, the fumes of Jeyes cleaning fluid standing in for the whiff of the souk and the grating of mop against pail for the swish of silken robes**

us unable to face our beckoning and treacherous typescripts.

By the time I got to the gym I was in fine spirits, and the effects lasted through the class with the result that I broke the rule I had imposed on myself at the outset of the lessons. Outside of the gym I was never, ever going to let anyone see me belly-dancing.

Tripping lightly back to my flat, a Moroccan tune on my lips and a shimmy quivering on my shoulders, I was apprehended by my downstairs neighbour, the drop-dead gorgeous and disgracefully young Ahmer, a physics undergraduate at University College. 'Hello Sara!' said he. 'Fancy a cup of tea?' One thing led to another in his basement flat and the next thing I knew I was demonstrating my newly acquired skills in front of the television set.

The dancing got off to a bad start when I trod in his last slice of pizza but I felt the situation was retrievable until I noticed that he was rolling on the sofa convulsed with laughter and calling out to his multitudinous Byronic flatmates who appeared out of every orifice of the building to watch the freak show.

After a week I was able to consign this humiliating episode to the stygian basements of memory and pitch up for the last lesson. This began with the Whole Body Shimmy. 'Imagine an electric shock all over,' said Leila. 'But you'd be dead then,' said Sharon. This was certainly a case of more jelly than belly. Other exciting new movements included the Shoulder Shimmy combined with Wrist Flexing, which was like simultaneously rubbing your tummy and patting your head, and the Tease, which involved moving provocatively forward making beckoning gestures and then retreating swiftly, presumably once the quarry was suitable ensnared.

At the end of the class we shimmied in unison across the gym and into the pub, where Leila asked us if any of us were in fact considering going professional. I said I was sticking to the day job.

AUBERON WAUGH
RAGE

IT IS A TERRIBLE responsibility to be asked to appoint an Oldie of the Year. If physical activity is to be the deciding factor, I feel the prize should go to William Deedes, the 81-year-old *Telegraph* journalist, who in the course of 1994 was parachuted twice into Bosnia, inspected starving Somalis in war-torn Mogadishu, and single-handedly refloated a school of sperm whales beached by a freak tide in the north of England. But physical activity is not enough to win this glittering award.

Sir John Gielgud and the Queen Mother are nearer the mark except for a growing suspicion that over the years they may have become one and the same person. It would not be fair to award it to either while these suspicions remain. No, one old man stands out for his service to the cause this year. Will Mr Ted Newbery, of Ilkeston, Derbyshire, please step forward to take a bow?

Mr Newbery, a retired miner of 81, is

'...£150,000... *Sold to the gentleman in the Napoleon uniform with a banana stuck in his ear*'

an active gardener. Like 60 per cent of Britain's allotment owners, he found that his allotment was repeatedly being raided and his carefully tended vegetables were being stolen. Neighbours complained that their sheds were broken into. Spades and hoes were removed, doors and windows broken. As a CID spokesman in Oxford explained: 'Allotments are easy targets, especially at night. We don't have the manpower to provide protection.'

This is a permanent refrain from the police, of course. They do not have the manpower to provide protection for public car parks, either, despite the fact that crime against parked cars has increased seven-fold in the last two years. All they would appear to be able to provide with existing manpower is nocturnal protection for birds' nests (on overtime) and illegal roadblocks to harass and terrify motorists over Christmas.

Anything else will require extra funding, more recruitment. If you are burgled, they advise you to lock up your house more carefully. If you have an allotment shed, they advise you to leave it empty and unlocked.

So it would appear that the law of the land no longer applies in garden allotments any more than it applies in public car parks. While the rest of the country whinged about this, urged that the government should do something about it, give the police more money (as if police funding had not already been increased by three times in real terms), Mr Ted Newbery bought himself a shotgun and cartridges and settled down to sleep in his allotment shed. After several nights he succeeded in surprising two would-be burglars and shot one of them – badly but not fatally – by pushing his shotgun through a hole in the wall and pulling the trigger.

Mr Newbery was immediately arrested by the police, charged with deliberately injuring 28-year-old Mark Revill, the burglar, in the course of his burgling activities. Cleared of this charge by Derby Crown Court at the end of November, Mr Newbery found himself hauled before the High Court in a civil action for damages brought by the burglar. Mr Justice Rougier (who turned out to be the son of Georgette Heyer, the great historical novelist remembered chiefly for her novels of

'I wish to enrol for the chattering classes'

the Regency period) awarded the burglar £4,003 for his injuries.

Trying to explain his extraordinary behaviour in a letter to the *Daily Telegraph*, the judge (who revealed he had been tipped off by the defendant's counsel that Mr Newbery was insured) asked what obviously seemed to him a rhetorical question: 'Is the farmer entitled to shoot with impunity the boy scrumping apples in his orchard?'

I suppose the answer must be that it depends how old the farmer is. Boys used to be hanged for stealing an apple, as Macaulay reminds us, and it would have been the earlier equivalents of Sir Richard Rougier who sent them to the gallows. We of the oldies' lobby cannot concern ourselves about farmers, but where there is no police protection for the property of old people, we must plainly agitate for a right to protect it ourselves. The question is whether, confronted by those young people who are all demented by vegetarian greed, we oldies must wait until they start stealing our

Oldies must take it in turns to go on a rampage and shoot anyone under 30 that they meet

vegetables before we are allowed to shoot them. Should not the old have an absolute right to shoot the young, at any rate until such time as the police and the judiciary get their act together?

In recent weeks we have seen the government's ruinous Disabled Persons Act concede practically every demand put before it by the disability lobby. We have also seen the Chancellor drop plans to increase VAT on domestic fuel in deference to the destitute oldies' lobby. They are terrified of being upstaged by people who can pose as poor or unfortunate.

Taking Mr Newbery as our example, it is time to agitate for an absolute right to protect our property against Shirley's children, as the generation of thieves and vegetarians is known. If that is not granted, individual oldies must take it in turns to go on a rampage and shoot anyone under 30 that they meet. No respectable jury would convict them. Some of their 'victims' may be innocent, but prevention is always better than cure.

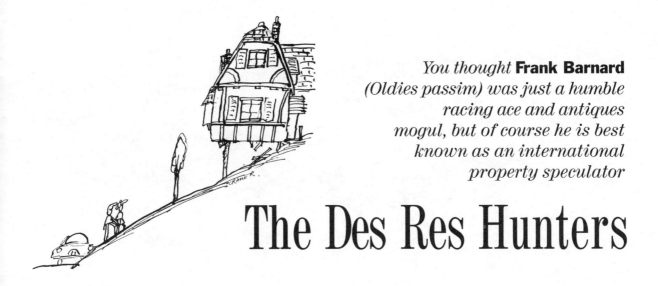

*You thought **Frank Barnard** (Oldies passim) was just a humble racing ace and antiques mogul, but of course he is best known as an international property speculator*

The Des Res Hunters

THERE WE STOOD, on the stone terrace of the farmhouse on the outskirts of Campanet in Northern Majorca, taking in the sweep of the exotic gardens leading the eye across the exquisite valley, echoing to sheep bells and bright with wild flowers, to the blue mountains beyond.

'Have a look inside,' said the venerable English dame who looked after the place for the owners. Our footfalls rang on cool tiled floors as we moved from one elegant room to another. Upstairs, as the house-sitter swung back the shutters to admit the heat and the call of crickets, Jan mused: 'So this will be our bedroom.'

'I liked the one looking over the pool,' I said.

'But here we'll have a self-contained wing and leave the rest free for the guest. We'll need a break from time to time.'

We had it all worked out. We were going to sell the cottage in Oxfordshire, buy this dream of a Majorcan farmhouse and invest whatever money was left in catering for well-heeled walkers who would sample the delights of undiscovered by-ways, led by me, and return to superb and expensive meals created by Jan. We had done our sums in the car and reckoned we could clear £60,000 a year without the pension.

On the way out I worried about the garage being big enough to house the two minibuses I was going to need to collect guests at Palma airport and ferry them around. Jan was concerned about a slight whiff of drains but the old Englishwoman said she knew a reliable ex-pat plumber in Pollenca.

We drove back down the cobbled lane flanked by vibrant hedgerows, taking pictures to prove to the family that we had our heads screwed on. This wasn't just any old farmhouse, this was a farmhouse sent from Heaven

and it had only just come on the market.

'Say it's £300,000,' said Jan. 'We can just about manage that.'

'It'll be tight for the first year,' I said, 'but then the income will start coming through. Anyway, you could be talking 200, I mean how many people would want to live this far out? Most of them want to be on the coast.'

'Perhaps 200 is too much then,' said Jan worriedly. 'We've got to sell it again.'

Back in the hill village of Caimari, where we were staying with a friend, the question of price came up again. 'I haven't got a clue how much it is,' said Nicki. 'All I know is you're probably the first people to look over it.' She gave me the London number of the owner…

'Start at £175,000,' said Jan. 'Remember the cost of the minibuses.'

The owner wasn't in his Chelsea office. They suggested I should call him in Beverley Hills. He was surprised by the call. 'I didn't know it was on the market yet.' I told him Nicki had tipped me off.

'Well that's great,' he said. 'The faster we sell the better. It's too much trying to keep five places going. So you like our little rural retreat?' Five places? Little? A certain anxiety began to creep into my bones, at about the time I started to fret about the cost of the call to California. 'I mean obviously there are a few things needing doing,' I said, resisting the impulse to mention the ex-pat plumber to try and get the price down. 'But we were wondering what kind of figure you might be looking for.' Jan mouthed 'One hundred and sixty…' from the kitchen door.

'Well after all you're the first,' said the owner, 'and if we could complete things quickly I'd be

35

prepared to talk in the region of – oh, I don't know – say £850,000? How much were you thinking of?'

Later we agreed the whole plan had been too ambitious. I was getting too old to lead walking parties and Jan had done enough cooking for other people. Then there was the ferrying to and from the airport. And the summer heat. And keeping the pool clean. And having the family descend on you for weeks on end. And anyway Northern Majorca would probably be discovered and we'd find a Best Western hotel and conference centre sprouting under our noses in the middle of that exquisite valley. A lucky escape. No minibuses to buy, no drains to sort out. In half an hour we'd forgotten all about it.

At the time though, standing in the dim, serene hallway of the farmhouse, with the fierce sun filtering through the slats of the shutters, it was attainable, it was real, it was ours. It always is…

It was real in the Lot Valley when a Souillac estate agent drove us down a one mile track to a derelict *bastide* with castellations. 'This whole space area could convert into a sitting and dining area,' said Jan, waving her arms at the immense and cavernous interior. 'Stairs running up the walls on both sides and leading to galleries. Bedrooms off.'

'Where's my study?' I said.

'You can have one of the barns,' she said. We looked at each other, apparently completely serious.

'God, the peace!' I said outside.

'What's that squeak?' said Jan.

'That's your neighbour's wind-pump,' said the agent.

'Nothing a little oil can put right,' I said.

'If he catch you on his land he shoot you,' said the agent.

On such small things a sale turns. It had been a great plan but who was going to create the stairways and the galleries and the bedrooms off? Could we really stand coming down that track with a car full of shopping? What about a phone? Come to that what about electricity? We would emerge from these episodes as from a dream.

'Well, you seemed to like it anyway.'

'Me? I hated it.'

'You told me I could have my study in one of the barns…'

'I was only stringing things along. And anyway what about saying that having no electricity wasn't a problem?'

'Well, it's solvable. But who wants to live next to a maniac who takes potshots at people greasing windpumps?'

It was also real in Sussex when we came across some abandoned coastguard cottages and I was going to throw in my job as a director of a public relations consultancy and become a warden in the Cuckmere Haven Nature Reserve. I vaguely remember that Jan was going to bake fairy cakes for the Visitor Centre and I'd do evening work on the dodgems in Brighton to earn a little extra. The estate agent from Eastbourne phoned us a few times to find out what had happened but we were always out.

It was real again in Skye where we were going to start an antiques business because there weren't any and then we started to wonder whey there weren't any and went off the idea, despite the rock-bottom price of the unconverted and entirely original crofter's cottage and cosy visions of emerging into the crisp, clean air at five in the morning wearing tweed.

And it was very real in Dartmouth where we passed an estate agent's window on the way to dinner and came back after breakfast. We viewed a *Mon Oncle* monstrosity infesting a wonderful position, going round saying how wonderful it was, admiring the kitchen fashioned from wood-grain Fablon and even haggling about the price.

We made our way through the garden of someone else's house, disturbing a tea party, to descend rusting iron ladders to what appeared to be a converted machine gun emplacement splattered with seafaring motifs like anchors and seahorses. Decaying lifebelts lay below huge, salt-stained picture windows. The rotting window frames were almost audible. And yet I stood on the private jetty and concocted an entirely plausible scheme to introduce Thames slipper launches to Dartmouth Harbour and make a killing. 'We're interested,' we told the expectant agent, 'definitely interested.'

And so we were, until he gave us details of a Gothic jewel in one of the best positions in Dartmouth. Staggering view, total seclusion… We climbed the 175 steps that led to the property. It was the only access. The villa was a delight, subtly improved, a haven of tranquillity only half a mile from the town centre. All right, much of that was vertical – but there was nothing wrong that a call to the Stannah Stairlift people couldn't put right. It was only when we were driving through Totnes, after checking to see if Stannah had a local distributor, that we looked at each other and were confronted with those familiar smirks that signalled re-entry into the real world.

We wonder, sometimes, whether estate agents circulate warnings to each other about people like us. Are they taken in when we ping through their door looking like apparently sensible human beings, or can they spot us a mile off, perhaps running their fingers down a Time-wasters Table issued by the National Association of Estate Agents?

Perhaps they put in calls, while we are on our perambulations, to Jean-Pierre in Souillac, Felipe in Puerto Pollenca and Jeremy in Eastbourne. Maybe they glean enough to discount any encouraging comments we make on our return or undertakings we appear to be embarking on connected with house sales, mortgages and removal vans; enough to know that all serious intentions have vanished from our leads by the time the door pings on our way out.

Douglas Bader

The year was 1982, and Sir Douglas Bader was to be interviewed by Michael Parkinson. A young researcher was sent to talk to him in his mews house near the Albert Hall. Within half-an-hour Sir Douglas phoned to say he was sending her back as she knew nothing about him. I was asked to go in her place. 'Do you mind?' the producer asked. Mind! I'd have paid for the privilege.

I knew all about him, of course. A biography had just been written by his friend 'Laddie' Lucas and I asked for an hour or two to skim through it. Somehow, I managed to grasp the fundamentals of Bader's views on how the Battle of Britain should have been fought, what the Duxford Wing was, why there were differences of opinion between 11 and 12 Fighter Groups, pilot shortage and Lord Dowding's strengths and weaknesses.

Nevertheless it was not without trepidation that I rang his doorbell. My hero opened the door and beamed. 'Thank God they didn't send a young researcher.' I laughed. 'Come in, my dear. I can only give you 45 minutes because I have to pick up the old duck.' I daringly asked who that was. 'My wife, Joan. And God help me if I'm late.'

I asked him if he'd be able to come down the steps leading to the TV interview area. 'No problem, my dear. If I fall down, Parky can come and pick me up. That'll be a laugh to start with.'

He said he only had a problem with his legs if he had to kneel. When he went to receive his knighthood, 'old' Dicky Gillette (everybody was referred to as 'old' this or that) worried in case he overbalanced, he decided they'd better have a rehearsal. 'Good idea, old boy', Douglas had said. 'Don't want me falling flat on my face and bringing HER down, do we?' Fortunately 'old' Johnny Mills and another chum, 'old' Neil Cameron, were also there. They both pretended they had tin legs, and fell about all over the place. Altogether they had 'a good giggle'. I soon discovered that Sir Douglas's main aim in life was to have a good giggle.

Sir Douglas didn't want to talk about flying, the Battle of Britain, or being a PoW. 'Oh forget about that. Everybody knows about it. They've seen the film and think I'm Kenneth More.' He laughed uproariously.

We talked about sport, and the joy of still being able to compete, with or without legs. He was full of admiration for the chaps who played wheelchair basketball. He nearly fell off his chair with laughter recalling a game he'd watched in Canada. The referee was unpopular, so the participants ran him down and he had to be carried off.

His philosophy regarding loss of limbs was that the younger you lost them the better! He meant that it is much easier to adapt when young. He was tremendously enthusiastic about the work he did talking to other disabled people.

Inevitably the conversation came round to golf. He'd had one of his artificial limbs shortened to improve his stroke and hit the ball much further. 'Old Henry Longhurst could never understand the principal of this. Said I'd had the wrong leg shortened. Ha, Ha, Ha.'

He secretly enjoyed a spot of fortune-telling. A couple of years later he and his wife Joan went to a fete near Banbury. Noticing a booth marked 'Fortune Teller', he popped in. The lady inside said that she wasn't really a fortune-teller, but was in touch with 'the other side'. She told him, 'Someone called Henry wants to tell you that he went to sleep for a little while and then woke up. He's now doing exactly as he wants, and he'd like you to know that the grass is a great deal greener this side than it ever was over your side.' Douglas was adamant Henry had sent a promised message.

Douglas often went to Scotland to play golf with his good friend, Jan Collins, the publisher. Jan always arranged for Douglas to have one particular caddie, Andy Anderson, a dour Scotsman. 'He's long since gone up there to join Henry, where the fairways are greener. Ha, Ha, Ha, Ha!' One day, as they were completing a round of golf at Troon, Jan told him about a lovely course called Machrihanish, over the water on the Mull of Kintyre. 'Let's go over,' said Douglas. 'I've got my aeroplane at Prestwick. It'll only take us 20 minutes to fly.' As they finished the game, he said to Andy 'I'll pick you up in the morning in my car, drive you to Prestwick and we'll fly over there.' Andy stopped dead in his tracks, and banged Douglas's bag of clubs onto the ground with a determined thump 'I'll no fly with ye, ye mad bugger,' he said, and they never did play Machrihanish.

Andy's description of Douglas prompted me to say that I'd heard his language when flying was very colourful, and that the RT had to be turned off so that the WAAF in the ops room couldn't hear him. 'Nonsense,' he said. 'I can't remember say-ing anything worse than "My eyes are hanging out like dog's balls, and I can't see a bloody thing". The girls loved it. Ha, Ha, Ha, Ha.'

I asked him whether he thought youngsters today would be prepared to fight and die for this country, as he and all his con-tempories had been. 'Of course they would. People don't change. The country doesn't change. Our parents thought we were a bunch of bums in our wide trousers with long scarves wrapped round our necks.'

I wonder. Had he lived long enough to see Channel 4's *Secret Lives*, would he have defended the odious youngsters who made it? Hopefully he would have had an opportunity to 'shoot them down in flames, old boy'.

All the time we'd been talking, Sir Douglas had been lighting his pipe, puffing it, knocking it out, or re-filling it. Suddenly he knocked it out again , without refilling it. There was a certain finality about it. My 45 minutes had gone in a flash.

'Well there you are, my dear! Can I give you a lift anywhere?' he asked. 'I'm going to Hyde Park Corner.' I was going in the opposite direction. 'Oh thank you,' I said. 'Hyde Park Corner will be wonderful.' Anything for a few more minutes with my hero.

I asked if I could use his bathroom. 'Yes, but hurry. I daren't be late for the old duck.' I'd hardly got up the stairs when I heard him revving up. 'Bang the door behind you and leap in,' he said, the Mini already on the move. The mews became a runway, and I was in a Spitfire, taking off down the narrow cobbled lane. He darted between cars on Kensington Gore – I swear we were air-borne. We screamed to a halt just in time, as Lady Bader walked up from the other direction. She took my place, and the Spitfire zoomed away.

He'd told me that, during the war, he'd been able to park his aeroplane outside his hut – no running out to it like you see on the films. So I arranged for him to park his Mini right outside TV Centre, for the programme. Vera Lynn was one of the other guests, and sang 'We'll Meet Again'. When Sir Douglas was ready to leave. I took him down to his car. He gave me a kiss and said 'We will meet again, Eve.' I was thrilled, although I couldn't quite see how. A few weeks later he died. Now it will have to be on the other side, where the grass is greener.   **EVE LUCAS**

M'LUD   **KATHRYN LAMB**

THE FACT THAT I MAY BE A FREEMASON OR MEMBER OF ANY OTHER SECRET SOCIETY, IN NO WAY AFFECTS MY MIND!

PROCEED!

Beer and Nothingness

Existentialism was alive to the mambo beat in 1950s London, recalls **Paddy Kitchen**

'MY FIRST JOB?' I replied brightly to the young man. '1952 – junior secretary in a Mayfair advertising agency. Couldn't make ends meet, so the following year I moonlighted as a hat-check girl in an existentialist nightclub.'

'You what? There can't have been any existentialist clubs in London.' But there were: Le Club Contemporain in White Horse Street and Le Faubourg in Soho. Does anyone remember them?

It came about like this. My flatmate – who also worked at the advertising agency – and I were bemoaning in the office one Wednesday that we'd run out of money. Our little brown wage packet wouldn't be brought round by Mrs Seers, who'd recently shocked us all by dyeing her hair blonde, until Friday. The tea lady overheard us, and said she'd been offered an evening job working in the cloakroom of a new nightclub but she couldn't take it on; should she put in a word for us?

I searched his jacket pockets for a handkerchief and found a gun

Next day, my friend and I went to Le Club Contemporain in White Horse Street to meet a Monsieur Fernand Calvet. I was 19, nervous and ignorant: the combination of a foreigner and a nightclub more or less signalled to me that subject dear to the *The News of the World* – white slave traffic.

Fernand Calvet was about 27, serious and good looking with a neat black beard, and spent most of the interview explaining to us, mainly in French, the gist of something he cared passionately about called existentialism, which had inspired the ethos of Le Club. We didn't understand, but nodded a lot, said 'Oui', and got the job. It was a very simple set-up. Entrance money was taken at a table in the narrow hall, beyond which was a tiny room with a half-door at which we stood to take coats. We had to promise not to let clients see into the cloakroom as there were no hooks or hangers, and everything from furs to dirty duffles were slung in heaps on the floor.

People were charged sixpence to leave things in the cloakroom, from which we were to keep threepence. Fernand could check the stubs in the ticket books to see we handed the right amount over to him. On thin nights, we barely earned enough to buy next day's spaghetti lunch. My friend soon decided that by giving only one ticket per party, but still charging sixpence per item, we could do better. Morally I wasn't sure I approved; in reality, I concurred. We were on duty from eight until midnight, took it in turns to work weekdays, and were together at weekends.

One evening when I was on my own, I fell in love. I didn't realise what was happening immediately. The cause of the strange feeling that overwhelmed me bore absolutely no resemblance to the manly English boy I fantasised I would one day meet, and who would ask me to marry him and miraculously earn my father's approval.

This man was a swaggering, plump, flirty Indian film producer with eyelashes to die for (we didn't use that phrase then). When he was in England he came to the club frequently and I began to realise I adored him.

Sometimes, when the club was quiet, he'd take me downstairs for a dance. Once he hooked his finger, through my skirt, round the bottom of my roll-on and pinged it. 'You don't need to wear that,' he said. And I never did again. The walls of the claustrophobic basement were decorated with some rather terrifying expressionist murals by Laszlo Szilvassy, the young Hungarian painter who'd recently destroyed Reg Butler's winning maquette for the Unknown Political Prisoner sculpture exhibition because he felt it insulted the memory of the dead and the suffering of the living. Laszlo came into the club occasionally and was slight and shy: I was in awe of him.

Secretly, I started going back to the film producer's flat in Maida Vale. He drove a dark blue Riley and liked to stand in the middle of his small sitting room conducting along to LPs of Beethoven symphonies which he'd bought cheaply in Eastern Europe. There was usually a generous bowl of fruit on the table. Once, when he'd gone out and I was desperate to blow my nose (the flat was stuffy and this was pre-tissue or soft loo-paper time), I searched his jacket pockets in the wardrobe for a handkerchief and found a gun. I quickly put it back and never mentioned it.

After about six months, Fernand sacked my flatmate and me for cheating him (he was too polite to put it like that). Later, when I discovered Sartre and Camus, they sort of came with his imprimatur and the hint of a mambo beat. The last I heard of the film producer was that he'd gone to live in Canada.

That excellent television programme *Brookside*, which brings such heart-warming tales of murder, drug-dealing and incest into our drawing rooms, is to take on the ultimate challenge of LEM or Latelife Exploration Malady. This is the syndrome when ordinary everyday oldies suddenly get an unshakeable desire to climb K2 or hang-glide the Grand Canyon. If one reads the casualty figures for any avalanche, tall ships, climbing or other outward bound disaster, chances are

the corpses are all over 40. 'The body of 46-year-old Nantwich chiropodist Mabel Elms still has not been completely found…' Much of Everest's main glacier is now so littered with these day-glo cadavers it gives a whole new meaning to the phrase terminal moraine.

But the greatest danger facing David and Jean Crosby as they take the Kathmandu trail is, of course, themselves. My favourite explorer C V Tillman once, sailing for India, only said two words on the entire trip: 'Hmmm… Sea' when they

cast off and 'Hmmm… Land' when the ship arrived in Bombay. To some this may have seemed like bad manners and unfriendliness verging on the psychotic. But to Tillman it made perfect sense. Ninety per cent of all LEMing fatalities are caused by murder or suicide perpetrated by LEMings who become fed up to the back teeth with each other, according to a recent survey of oldsters' holidays by the University of San Diego.

To test this out I went sailing in the Greek islands. This is a very common

Paul Pickering *experiences the danger*

form of LEMing where after a few days with a loved one or a group of close friends one wants either to jump over the side or strangle one's partner.

Matters came to a head 20 minutes after a couple and I cast off to explore the wine-dark waters around the Peloponnese. 'I don't know how to put this,' I said, as calmly as possible, a mile off the Greek island of Spetsai on our learn-to-sail holiday, 'but there are several inches of water in the main cabin and it appears to be rising.'

Our captain, an overweight accountant at the helm for the first time, went very pale. He already hated me because he had begun to talk of his problem with premature ejaculation only to find I was on deck by an open hatch and had overheard.

LEMing is often related to sexual problems but sinking so prematurely was not exactly what the LEMing has in mind. In the past four days' training on shore he had been assured that what he had been taught by his instructors equipped him for every salty situation. The

company then trusted him to go on a six-day sail with other novices, following a mother-hen lead boat. No killjoy had said anything about rising wet stuff, or that the rope pulling the front sail across the pointy end might constantly jam on a deck shackle and have to be bound up with a first aid box bandage, or that a guard rail would give way…

'Are you sure it's water?' asked my LEMing. 'Aye, aye, skip!' I answered cheerily. 'Several inches above the boards and it's all nasty and oily and smells. Don't you think we should call for assistance? Oh, and the pump's not working. Look, I'm no expert on boats, but I really don't think that several inches of oily water is quite right…'

But he was the skipper and his wife backed him up and so we sailed on for half-an-hour, below decks slowly coming to resemble one of those wave experimentation tanks. When I did manage to radio to the lead boat, which was far ahead of us, I was told not to worry about the problem below stairs 'as it would sort itself out'. I was ecstatic to hear that we were not actually sinking and our on-board paddling pool was probably 'to do with the lavatory'. I'd have celebrated, but the skipper's wife kept saying 'Alcohol is a poison' when I reached for a beer.

I would have been celebrating too soon. After sloshing about on the wrong course for seven miles the wind dropped and our skipper, bless his scowling dimples, tried to switch on the engine. The engine refused. We then began drifting rather quickly towards very sharp rocks on one of those barren, waterless islands where Greek tyrants dumped ugly spouses.

Imminent shipwreck is a tough idea for any new skipper to grasp. I knew my LEMing had heard me because his little eyes flicked momentarily to the looming cliff, or port, as we sea dogs call the left hand side. 'Look, I don't mean to be premature, skippy, and I'm not an expert or anything, but as we may hit those rocks don't you think we should try to call for help? I mean, with all the oily, smelly wet stuff that might be from the toilet sloshing down below as well?'

Reluctantly he tried to call all the other boats in the area. But due to our skipper's skill they were now on the other side of an

A Jaunt with Jonah

ndrome known as Latelife Exploration Malady

'There are several inches of water in the main cabin and it appears to be rising…'

waterhouse.

I could see there was murder in those LEMing eyes

island and could not be reached. The channel was too deep to anchor. So, defying the black looks of the LEMing wife, I decided to have that last beer before a rather long swim to the nearest bay.

Then, as gently as I could, I made a suggestion to the Scarlet Pirate at the helm, 'Look, I don't want to go off half-cock, skippy. But don't you think we should pull out the choke thingy? Yes, that. You know, the thingy you pull out to switch the engine off? No? You'd already thought of that? Good. Well, don't you think we should do it?

I could see there was murder in those LEMing eyes when we started first time. His wife took him a huge bag of sour cream and chive flavour munchies as comfort. The plain fact was that it was no use at all saying that Nelson and Raleigh probably forgot to check their engine's basic controls before the first day out. But, thanks to his wife putting out a general distress call, the VHF was alive with boats steaming to our help, who all had to be told we had found 'the choke thingy'.

The LEMing serially ate munchies until we put into port. An engineer discovered our main tank had fractured and in turn had flooded the engine and caused a fuel leak. Below deck there was oil everywhere and one expected any minute to have to rescue diesel soaked cormorants from behind the cushions. The LEMing put a munchie-filled paw around his wife's reddening neck, both still twitching slightly with rage even though the engine was switched off. Another boat was provided – to be followed by a third a few days later for another couple on the ill-fated week's flotilla. But I felt they blamed me as the harbinger of constant bad news. The LEMing skipper kept trying to sneak up

and stand on my fingers.

The instructor on the lead boat said such 'clashes of personality' were happening up to three times a week last summer. One couple had started divorce proceedings on their return to England, seven days before their silver wedding anniversary. But this summer had gone swimmingly until Jonah Pickering had put in an appearance. When we got into port the LEMing threatened murder if I got back on board and I last saw them sail off into the sunset, arguing.

Captain Oates who just popped outside for a moment into the howling darkness of an Antarctic blizzard is most often cited as the 'leading light' of all such LEMings, but this is forgetting Theodore Roosevelt and his son Kermit, the average age of whose South American expeditions was well over 50 and who had to send back several party members for losing their false teeth. Moses, however, is probably the LEMing's LEMing. Forty years wandering about in the wilderness is an achievement as yet unmatched by any holiday company.

But as David and Jean Crosby set off to what is doubtless certain and miserable death, prominent politicians on the Tory right are already considering paying half the cost of adventure holidays including hang-gliding and underwater caving 'If these people were taken out of the benefit picture, permanently, imagine the saving,' one think-tank member confessed, rubbing his hands. So in those last moments when you have cut the wife's safety rope and are just about to perish from exposure under the South Col, remember, LEMing is patriotic and in the future could probably fulfil the same role as world wars did in the past. Happy trails!

Modern Life

What is... The Toronto Blessing?

IT SOUNDS A BIT like a Glagow Kiss (which is a head-butt). In fact it is something that is increasingly going on in church. This is what happens: people go to church and sing hymns, then some of them start crying out – 'Jesus' or 'Alleluia' – then some fall to the ground, fainting, twitching, babbling, weeping and, most notably, laughing.

The 'Toronto' bit refers to the church where the phenomenon was first noticed. That church belongs to the Vineyard Christian Fellowship, a network of 500 or so churches of a markedly evangelical bent (and, back when he went Born Again, Bob Dylan's church of choice). It is a small, bare, ugly building too close for comfort to Toronto airport. The Fellowship is one of the many independent denominations that are far more common in North America than in Britain.

Their great phenomenon, the Blessing, is coming here soon, indeed it has probably arrived at a church near you. They attribute it to the Holy Spirit, who, in the New Testament, is described as having caused the Apostles to speak in tongues. People mocked the Apostles, accusing them of being drunk, but St Peter had a nice knock-down argument to refute them: 'These are not drunken, as ye suppose, seeing it is but the third hour of the day' (nine o'clock).

The date on which the Toronto Blessing was first manifested is recorded as 20th January 1994 – a more specific dating than most religious phenomena are able to boast. Within four months the Blessing had reached Putney. It is spreading.

Two preachers were there on that first Thursday evening in Toronto last year: Randy Clark, who had already seen congregations falling in the aisles in St Louis, Missouri, and John Arnott. Both had widespread contacts with pentecostalist evangelists. On that January night, Mr Arnott remembers, '80 per cent of our church were laughing and on the floor. It looked like the Battle of Atlanta.'

In Britain, the most famous place where the Toronto Blessing can be found is Holy Trinity, Brompton (ironically, one may say, behind the Brompton Oratory). This church is packed full of fairly well-off, guitar-friendly, definitely evangelical and rather weirdly susceptible worshippers, week after week. Even in 1990, four years before Toronto was heard of, they were busy speaking in tongues and sayings things like 'Jesus blows your mind'.

That is an example of the wider trend – the charismatic movement, which is principally at work in the evangelical wing of the Church of England, the United Reformed Church, the Baptists and various freelance churches. Even some Catholics show unusually charismatic sympathies. Again, the justification comes from the New Testament: 'Concerning spiritual gifts, brethren, I would not leave you ignorant… To one is given the Spirit of wisdom… to another divers kinds of tongues; to another the interpretation of tongues,' as St Paul says in his epistle to the Corinthians.

It was the business of *gifts* (Greek, *charismata*) that gave rise to the name of this brand of Christians or sectaries, or wings within established churches: 'charismatics' or 'pentecostalists' (after the day of Pentecost, or Whitsun, when the Holy Ghost came down). These people lean towards personal inspiration and against control by bishops; towards DIY liturgy and against the Book of Common Prayer or the Tridentine Mass. Some of them experience being 'slain in the spirit', a bodily manifestation, which sounds even

'I think these wild rumours that the company is controlled by some mysterious cult must be squelched immediately, O High Priest of Utter Darkness'

worse than the Toronto Blessing.

The complication is of course that the Church of England and the Church of Rome both recognise the importance of the Holy Spirit. Indeed we have been here before. Charles Wesley, who remained to his death a member of the Church of England, was possessed by a strong urge to preach in the Spirit.

But he did not achieve such effects as his contemporary, the Rev John Berridge, a Calvinist minister at Everton in Bedfordshire. During the famous outbreaks there in 1759 Wesley notes in his journal that four examples at least of uncontained laughter burst out, with others of long trances, convulsions, falling to the ground, or the agonies for hours of a

man whose 'veins of his neck were swelled as if ready to burst'.

Wesley's early co-worker George Whitfield, who went out to preach in America, found one day that 'the whole room was full of nothing but outcries, faintings and the like… the children there were very generally and greatly affected.'

In those days such manifestations were called *enthusiasm*. They might be, but need not be, connected with mass religious revival. Fits, groanings, dancing, frothing, shaking, tears, screams, glossolalia, body-piercing and writhings have been noted from time to time not only among the Anglicans, Methodists and Quakers but also among the Jansenists, Camisards, Ranters, Messalians, Beghards and such-like heretics.

It is tempting to wonder if the odd goings-on in Toronto and the Brompton Road are such a long way from the world in which the admonition was given to John Wesley (Charles's brother) by Bishop Joseph Butler (1692–1752): 'Sir, the pretending to extraordinary revelations and gifts of the Holy Ghost is a horrid thing, a very horrid thing.'
CHRISTOPHER HOWSE

Need a slogan?

Then send for a poet - or perhaps a novelist. That's what the top advertising agencies did in the Sixties, says **Christopher Matthew**, *who worked alongside Fay Weldon and Gavin Ewart*

Go to work on an egg

The best headline William Trevor ever managed to dream up for Heineken was 'Hi, Heineken'. But it didn't matter

Above: Fay Weldon's creation for egg advertising Right: one of a series of Wills cigar adverts created by Christopher Matthew during his time at J Walter Thompson

So there we was digging this 'ole
and smoking a Wills cigar

And what's so funny about that? It isn't only the big nobs who know their way round a good cigar. The men in the picture are experts too. Wills have seen to that!

Fact is that only a few years ago cigar smoking was very much a board room ritual. Wills have brought it right down to street level and in this case even below. Their strategy: to spread the joys of cigar smoking as wide as the demand goes. That means good cigars at low prices for people in high, medium and low places. And the moral: anyone with a hundred or so years of experience (like Wills) knows how to make a great cigar. But you've got to know your people too. That's why if you glance around next time you're out you'll spot Wills cigar men in the unlikeliest places.

PICADOR · TOLEDO · WILLS WHIFFS
VAN DYCK · CASTELLA · EMBASSY

**W. D. & H. O. WILLS
CIGARMAKERS-PACEMAKERS**

P70D

When he was a junior copy writer at Ogilvy & Mather in the early Sixties, novelist and playwright Nick Salaman would sit on the steps of Waterloo Bridge during his lunch hour, staring out over the Thames, muttering: 'The times are out of joint, oh cursed spite, that ever I was born to copywrite.'

I know how he felt. I'd started in advertising at about the same time – for an agency called the London Press Exchange.

In those days, most arts graduates from Oxford and Cambridge with leanings towards writing or producing tried first to get a job in television or journalism. Failing that, they went into advertising – the perfect refuge for aimless talent. A few thought of it as a career and stuck to it, but a lot – myself included – saw it merely as a useful stepping stone to something more in keeping with their real talent – writing novels or plays. For all his early youthful grumblings, Salaman went on to become one of the youngest creative directors at J Walter Thompson. I, on the other hand, could never bring myself to take the business quite as seriously as I could have done. Beginning with the copy test. Every would-be copywriter had to sit one. It was like an O Level English paper with jokes. 'Write a birthday card from one Easter egg to another' – that kind of thing.

I can't remember much about the LPE test, but after a couple of years there, I applied for a job at J Walter Thompson, then the biggest and best known agency in London. Part of their test involved composing a poem in praise of a well-known domestic product. Mine went as follows:

In a little plastic soap dish on the basin by the loo
Sits a little bar of soap called Pink Camay.
It has made the name and fortune of a girl called You Know Who
And she looks a little lovelier each day.
If you ask her if she'd rather
Use a soap that makes less lather,
She'll talk for hours about essential oil.
By the PR men who made you,
And the ad men who displayed you,
You're a better girl than I am, Katie Boyle.'

I posted it off with an invoice: to Freelance Copy Test: 75 Guineas. I got

the job – though not the fee.

Despite my early misgivings, agency life turned out to be a good deal more agreeable than I had envisaged. The people I worked with were funny and clever. You could joke about it all, but you were expected to work hard when you had to. Nobody gave a hoot who you were or whether you'd been to university or how clever you were. All that mattered was being able to do the job.

There were plenty of old hands around who knew a good ad when they saw one and wasted no time telling me when my efforts were not up to snuff. In the early Sixties, when campaigns were still waged largely in newspapers and magazines, being able to write good, grammatical English was thought to be an advantage and the agency world was aglow with real writers both budding and in full flower. Behind every partition lurked a novelist or a playwright – or, often a poet.

At JWT I was sandwiched in an office between Bernard Gutteridge and Gavin Ewart. At Ogilvy & Mather, Fay Weldon was in charge of a group full of poets, including Edwin Brock, David Wevill and the pipe-smoking Julian Orde. The copy chief at Notley's, Marchant Smith, employed so many poets the place was known as the nest of singing birds – amongst them Peter Porter, Peter Redgrove and Oliver Bernard. Also there, writing novels and short stories, was William Trevor.

Some of these real writers were committed advertising men, most were passing through, yet all were cherished and nurtured. Most got the hang of it eventually, some never quite did. The best headline William Trevor ever managed to dream up for Heineken was 'Hi, Heineken'. But it didn't matter. There were plenty of people on hand to help out and there was surprisingly little professional jealousy among 'the creatives', as they came to be known. Fay Weldon took the phrase 'Go To Work on an Egg' from the middle of someone else's copy, made a headline of it and created an advertising legend, and though I am credited with the brilliantly witty headline 'Cheese Tastes Quite Nice Sometimes', I suspect Llewellyn Thomas, Dylan's boy, had a hand in it somewhere.

Looking back, it's hard to believe that I

and others even more talented than myself should have devoted so much time and energy to the selling of fish fingers or a gravy mix. Especially given the attitude to advertising in those days. No one went quite so far as to accuse one of lying, but lips were definitely curled.

There were consolations. Most of us knew we were only in it for the money, but at least we felt we were part of that creative explosion that hit London in the mid-Sixties.

Some of the best campaigns were thought up over lunch at which prominent figures in the arts would mingle, gnaw on chicken legs and talk about their work. I don't know what they thought of us, but it did our morale good to feel that we were, if only tangentially, in the same business. And sometimes those brief meetings extended into serious professional relationships. Lindsay Anderson and Karel Reisz made films for us; Peter Blake designed whisky labels; the Rolling Stones made a test commercial for Rice Krispies.

For all the trendy sounding names, JWT still had one foot in the gentle, slightly old fashioned world of advertising as lived and described by old Benson's hand, Dorothy L Sayers. One was very aware that smaller agencies were emerging, such as Collett Dickenson Pearce where copy writers like Alan Parker and Charles Saatchi and entrepreneurial account executives like David Puttnam, were acquiring well-deserved reputations as creative hot shots. People were being encouraged to buy what they wanted rather than merely what they needed. Suddenly, images sold more than words and a new breed of writers came into the business who thought purely in pictures and never had sleepless nights over split infinitives or dangling participles. The copywriting was on the wall; it was time to move on – Fay Weldon and John Bowen to TV playwriting and novels. William Trevor to novels and short stories, Fay Maschler and I to journalism.

None of us regretted our time in advertising. On the contrary. It taught us how to handle words, fight our corners, be professionals. Of all my contemporaries, though, only Fay Weldon can claim to have devised a really famous headline – 'Go To Work on an Egg' – and to this day she is not sure whether to be pleased or sorry.

Bank Holiday Monday Island is a small volcanic island roughly half-way between Christmas Island and Easter Island. The island, measuring some seven miles by three miles, was discovered on Bank Holiday Monday, 1st May, 1831 by Admiral Ivor W Hopper aboard HMS Champion.
A full set of designs was drawn up when colonisation was proposed to accommodate overspill from Australasia, but was postponed indefinitely due to complications over draft Sunday Trading laws on the island.

The Gastric Clinic at Serone was to be depicted on the lower values of the 1938 definitives. Run by Dr Armando Kinder and his dedicated staff of Armalite nuns, the clinic was opened in 1893 and closed in 1936. 'Bechuana Tummy' was rife in the colony in the early part of the century, but mercifully the condition was eradicated by 1935.

The oomagoolie bird (*Tauraco sinegamba*) was to have featured on the 1c KUT definitive. This legless avian was, however, found to be extinct. The last breeding pair were sighted by Lake Turkana in early 1935, when the male's plaintive landing cry was heard for the last time. The Crowned Crane proudly took its place in the design.

Without doubt Jamaica's most important cash crop, along with bananas, is marijuana, known locally as ganga.

This most attractive plant was to be the subject of the 2d definitive. It was designed by Vincent Pittman, but the Crown Agents were not happy. In a memorandum it was stated that 'this weed was not a welcome visitor upon the postage stamps of the island as it encouraged lassitude and feeble-mindedness among the natives'.

The Coco Palms design of the previous reign was reverted to.

THE UNISSUED STAMPS OF THE BRITISH EMPIRE

COLLECTOR'S CORNER • DAVID HORRY

Probably the first postage stamp to deal with the subject of homosexuality, even if unwittingly. The title 'Kiwi Fruit' was intended for another design featuring the humble kiwi fruit. Due to an 'internal misunderstanding' the wrong title was applied. The New Zealand Government intervened, and this design was subsequently used for the 1937 Health issue, bearing the legend 'Health'.

One of the great stamp design gaffes of all time. The badge of the colony was the agreed subject matter, that being an elephant standing by a palm tree. Designer H L Bennett-Bigley who was 83 years of age at the time – and somewhat eccentric – submitted the design with a polar bear on an ice-floe by a palm tree. Proofs were taken from the plates. It was only then that the error was noticed. H L Bennett-Bigley died three months later – of shame, and the elephant returned to its rightful position.

Arthur Rubinstein & Adlai Stevenson

IN 1950 I SOUGHT an interview with Adlai Stevenson. He was then aged 50 and had been elected governor of Illinois two years previously by an unprecedented majority. He appeared to be a likely Democratic candidate for the White House in 1952, in succession to President Truman. I was 35, the BBC news correspondent in Washington.

Stevenson's executive secretary sent me a friendly reply. The interview was agreed, and he added that the hotels in Springfield, the small state capital of Illinois, were not very good, so the governor had invited me to stay overnight at the Executive Mansion.

I found that the only plane that could bring me to Springfield was scheduled to land at 9pm. That seemed an inconvenient time to arrive, but there was no choice. I sent my travel details to the executive secretary, with my apologies. At Springfield airport I was met by a huge state trooper who was Stevenson's chauffeur. I learned later that he had served for the past 20 years driving Illinois governors of different political persuasions. He led me outside to where I found the governor waiting in a large limousine with the number plate ILLINOIS 1.

Stevenson gave me a courteous welcome. He said that Springfield did not often have much interesting music, but Arthur Rubinstein, the famous Polish-born pianist, was giving a concert there that evening. If I did not need to go immediately to the Executive Mansion we could drive straight to the concert hall and enter during the interval. (I reflected that this remarkable governor was not only prepared to come to the airport himself to meet an unknown BBC correspondent but would even cut the first half of a Rubinstein concert to do so.)

There was loud applause when the popular governor entered the hall. Rubinstein, then 61, was in splendid form and gave a sparkling performance in the second half of his concert. As an encore he played the nocturne for the left hand written by Scriabin when suffering a neuralgia in his right hand. Stevenson then took Rubinstein and me out to supper. (This was a special treat for me as both proved to be great raconteurs.)

47

Stevenson praised the left-handed nocturne and Rubinstein commented that Stravinsky was very vain. He had said to Rubinstein, 'Before me – no music. After me – no music.'

Then Rubinstein told us how President Peron, the Argentinian dictator, had tried to force him to broadcast from the State Concert House in Buenos Aires instead of performing for political rivals in a local cinema. Peron prevented the unloading of Rubinstein's personal Steinway from the ship in the harbour, alleging customs irregularities. Rubinstein surreptitiously telephoned New York and arranged to have a brand new Steinway flown to Buenos Aires and taken direct to the cinema.

So much for the all-powerful Peron. (Rubinstein had originally perferred Bechstein pianos to Steinway. 'I was born in a Bechstein,' he said.)

At the end of the meal Rubinstein offered us excellent cigars. This was before Castro came to power and in the United States Cuban cigars were still politically correct. Rubinstein said that the entertainment world used to be divided over whether his cigars were better than those of Sir Alexander Korda, whom he had never met. One day suddenly they encountered each other in the doorway of Le Pavillon, the fashionable New York restaurant. Like duellists each immediately drew from his pocket a long cigar and offered it to the other, without saying a word.

The next morning I had my interview with Stevenson and realised why I had been invited to stay at the Executive Mansion. He was in the throes of a divorce and was desperately lonely. He had married Ellen Borden, an intelligent beauty from Chicago about whom Benjamin Jowett's quip had been adapted. What time she could spare from the adornment of her person she devoted to the neglect of her duties. She never forgave Adlai for outshining her in the public eye, and she certainly was not going to exchange the metropolitan sophistication of Chicago for small town life at Springfield.

Stevenson told me that in the early part of the war he had served in the Navy Department, supervising the shipment of American arms to the Soviet Union. One day a Russian official complained that the United States was behind schedule in delivering supplies to Moscow. Stevenson agreed, but insisted that this was because the Soviets were behind in providing a schedule of their needs. 'I have not come here,' the Russian replied, 'to talk about my behind, but about your behind.'

The governor had political blood in his veins. His grandfather, also Adlai Ewing Stevenson, had been Vice-President of the United States. He told me he was daily receiving between eight and 20 speaking invitations.

Two years later the resounding success of his welcoming speech to the delegates attending the Democratic National Convention in Chicago resulted in Stevenson being drafted to run against General Eisenhower, though I heard him plead with the Illinois caucus to let him finish the job at Springfield. Nobody, he said, needed to save the country from Ike Eisenhower, and couldn't if they tried.

Stevenson fought an eloquent campaign but was decisively defeated. He said he felt like the little boy who had stubbed his toe in the dark. He was too old to cry but it hurt too much to laugh.   **LEONARD MIALL**

'Since he's been on Prozac, he makes far fewer sudden key changes'

Donald MacIntosh *recollects*
a former employee.
Illustrations by **Robert Geary**

The name's Sperm, Magic Sperm

He had travelled far in the back of a mammy wagon to see me, and the blackness of his skin was dusted a greyish pink from the laterite clays of old Africa. He stood before my desk now, an insignificant little runt of perhaps 14 years of age clad only in a pair of disreputable khaki shorts several sizes too large for him. I had spread the word around that I was looking for a clerk to help me in a botanical survey I was about to conduct in a remote forest area. It was a job that would require a comprehensive knowledge of trees and a reasonable standard of written English. Applicants had been few; while most bush people knew their trees all right, those who had the necessary standard of literacy refused to venture into remote forests among strange and possibly hostile tribes, not to mention even more hostile creatures. Less hazardous clerical work was easily obtainable nearer to home.

'Do you know trees?' I asked.

'My father is a hunter,' he replied proudly. 'And we live in the forest. I know all the trees.'

'You would not be afraid to travel with me to far away places?'

'No sir.'

I studied him carefully. He had no tribal markings on his face, but he had the alert wiriness about him that seemed to be the hallmark of so many Ekitis.

'Can you write and count?' I enquired.

'Yes sir. I attended the Sacred Heart Catholic School in Ekiti for five whole years.'

'But can you write good English?' I persisted doubtfully. 'After only five years at school?'

'Reverend Fadders got dam' strong arm, sir,' he replied emphatically.

I had made up my mind. 'I want to see how well you can write,' I said finally. 'Write me a letter of application for this job and bring it to me in the morning. If I'm satisfied with that, you're hired.'

He was heading for the door when I called after him: 'By the way, what is your name?'

He turned in the doorway. 'My name, sir,' he informed me with the quiet dignity of his race, 'is Magic Sperm.'

I SUPPOSE his name should have given me some hint of what was to follow. But, apart from musing upon the absurdity of it and wondering how he had acquired it, I gave little thought to the matter at the time. Exotic sobriquets were common in the forests

of the White Man's Grave in my day. I already had on my payroll a Local Thunder, a Money-No-Reach and a Two-At-One-Time. Probably, I conjectured, he had seen it on the label of a bottle of virility potion in a bazaar somewhere and he had adopted it without understanding its significance.

His letter of application, when he brought it the following morning, was couched in the quaintly florid English invariably employed by those who had served time in mission schools in the African hinterland. It began: 'Dear Master, I have long admired you from afar, and now I wish to satisfy you on the ground...' and it ended: 'May God have mercy on your soul, Yours lovingly, Magic T Sperm.'

I never did find out what the 'T' stood for.

He was good at the job for which I had hired him. He was intelligent and he had an engaging personality that made him popular with everyone who met him. Everyone, that is, except the parents of nubile daughters.

The problems arose on those occasions when I had to return to headquarters, which I did every three months or so in order to compile maps and collect wages. Magic Sperm, I was soon to discover, had a low boredom threshold. He had to be kept occupied, a concept easier said than applied. He proved useless in the office, and the very sight of anything resembling physical labour made

49

**'He had nowhere
to stay so I fixed up the
potting shed behind
the girls' dorm. He seems
to like it there'**

him quite ill. Eventually, the sight of his doleful figure hanging around my office door was beginning to make *me* feel ill, I told him to keep away from the compound until it was time to go back to the forest.

As I was rarely at headquarters for more than a week at a time, this seemed to me to be the ideal solution. It was certainly so for Magic Sperm. He had found the perfect antidote to boredom. By the dawning of his 15th birthday he had impregnated more maidens during those brief visits than the King of Benin had managed to do after a lifetime of trying with his extensive harem.

Or so it seemed to me. I began to dread each homecoming, knowing that I was sure to be greeted by yet another posse of wrathful fathers, their obviously fecund daughters in tow and voices aquiver with indignation as they assailed me with their now familiar reproach: 'Massa, your Sperm Boy…'

I suppose it was inevitable that I should end up as the scapegoat in Magic Sperm's shenanigans. A visit to the area by one of the country's leading politicians – a man noted for his brutally robust responses to those who crossed him – had been unofficially marked by a night of amorous dalliance between Magic Sperm and one of the entourage, a young lady who just happened to be the Great Man's favourite niece. The resultant unpleasantness cost me a case of best gin to placate the incensed politician and several crates of imported beer to keep his bodyguards from shooting everything that moved around the compound, myself included.

When they had departed, I went in search of Magic Sperm. His room was empty. He had packed his bag and vanished, never to return.

SIX WEEKS later I was passing through a township some distance to the north and I called at the Catholic Girls' Grammar School on the outskirts. Convents are not places I choose to visit regularly and I cannot now remember why I should have been in this particular one, but I do remember being escorted round the premises by a nun of quite outstanding beauty.

Sister Mary – I shall call her that, though this was not her real name – was a new arrival on 'The Coast'. She was very young and sweetly naive. She had been given charge of the convent gardens; a labour of love, she assured me, as she had always been fond of gardening back in Ireland. She liked life in West Africa, she said, even though she was experiencing the usual problems in adjusting: the sweltering heat, the smells, the flies, the difficulty in understanding the local pidgin English…

We stopped in the shade of a mango tree on the edge of the garden. I gazed at the figure of a youth working industriously with a hoe some distance from us. 'That,' she told me proudly, 'is Boniface, one of my protégés. My best worker, and a leading member of our church choir.'

We wandered out through the garden, past the perspiring youth, but Magic Sperm did not look at us. We returned to the mango tree. 'How did – er – Boniface manage to get a job with you, Sister?' I enquired curiously. 'He came here about six weeks ago, and I felt so sorry for him,' said the Sister. 'He told me that he had been working for a very cruel white man who beat him every day with a stick. I needed a helper for my garden and when he told me how fond he was of gardening, I got permission from the Mother Superior to employ him.'

I ignored the disgraceful slander contained in her second sentence. Something was puzzling me. 'He actually told you he was fond of *gardening*?' I asked in disbelief.

'Not exactly in those words,' she admitted. 'But you know the funny ways these people have of saying things. What he actually said was that he was good at forking, and I told him that it was *my* favourite hobby, too.'

I was speechless. The good Sister continued: 'He had nowhere to stay, so I fixed up the old potting shed behind the girls' dormitory for him. He seems to like it there.'

We looked back over the garden. My erstwhile employee was hacking away at the stony soil with an enthusiasm that would have been quite unsuspected. I was the one to break the silence this time.

'Yes, Sister Mary,' I murmured. 'I bet he does.'

Miles Kington

Meanwhile, Back at the Ranch

The other night I had a dream in which someone burst into the room and shouted: 'I've discovered who committed the murder!' (I have quite exciting dreams.) This incursion produced general puzzlement, for the simple reason that there hadn't been any murder in the dream. But instead of people in the dream saying to this bloke, 'What murder are you talking about?' I had the guilty feeling that I should have known about the murder and there should have been one. And I can remember thinking, while I was still dreaming, 'Well, maybe we could stage the murder *now* and edit it into an earlier part of the dream! Then what this bloke is saying would make sense.'

You may say that it is impossible to have thoughts about your dream while you are actually having it. To stand back and view the dream as if it were a film, and even propose editorial changes to it while you are still asleep, I say is not impossible. I say this because I have done it before. I can remember the very first time I did it. I was about 11 or 12 at the time, and had been told by someone that if, in a dream, you dreamt that you were dying, you really did die. How anyone could prove this is beyond me but it obviously impressed me because a bit later I had a dream that I was walking along the landing of our house and I came to the top of the stairs.

I was about to walk down the 12 or 13 steps when I thought to myself in the dream, 'Wait a mo – this is a dream! You can jump from the top of the stairs to the bottom without hurting yourself! No need to walk! Just jump it!'

I was on the point of doing this when another thought occurred to me. 'What if I jump 12 steps and land badly, so badly that I die in my dream? Won't I die in real life too?' Which was promptly followed by another thought: 'Well, if you don't try, you'll never find out. Do it!' And I did it, and I floated down the whole staircase, and landed very softly, so softly that it felt really nice and I ran to the top of the steps and did it over and over again…

So it is not impossible to control dreams, even if you are in a semi-conscious state at the time. But my recent experience – wanting to edit a murder into a dream – makes me ask a question I had never asked before. Has mankind started dreaming differently since the invention of film?

Film does have its own language.

We all speak it. We speak it so fluently we hardly notice. But if you don't speak the language, films can be incomprehensible. I remember Peter Christie, ex-colleague from Instant Sunshine, telling me that when he was a doctor in Tanzania he sometimes went to the cinema along with Africans who had never seen films before and therefore were unaware of film language. So, if a man in the film got into a car in the country and drove off, and in the next scene was seen arriving in the city, you and I and Peter Christie would know that it was assumed he had driven two hours meanwhile, out of sight of us, but the Africans would cry out, 'That was quick! That was magic!' believing that the film was in real time. But it wasn't, it had been translated into film language.

We all have to learn this language as children. And I believe we come to dream in film language. We can skip locations, skip time, encounter mystery characters in our dreams, without an explanation being offered or demanded. We *know* about flash-backs and cuts. We don't mix and dissolve in dreams, or pan round, because that's camera language and we don't use camera language in dreams, only editor's language. And if this is so, then would it not be reasonable to say that the way everyone dreams has changed in the last 100 years? That our forefathers, not knowing about films or film language, therefore could not dream in film language and *had* to dream in some other way?

It is true that you occasionally get something very like film language dating from before the invention of film. I remember when I was reading Flaubert's *Trois Contes* at university I was struck by the one called 'A Simple Soul' and felt strongly that one passage of Flaubert's description inside a large church was written almost like a film treatment, and if I had the energy I would go and look it up and quote it, but it still seems unanswerable to me that the way we dreamed up to 100 years ago *must* have been different from the way we dream now. You couldn't have used film narrative technique in dreams before the invention of film technique. It's probably too late to prove it now but if anyone ever comes across a description of a dream written pre-1890 – or visits parts of Tanzania where they still haven't seen any films – let me know your findings.

But please, *please* don't write and tell me about dreams that you have had. There is nothing so interesting to people and so boring to others as their dreams. Unless it is their burglaries.

'Hello, we're Jehovah's Widnes'

I Was a Crazy Gang Chorus Girl

Way back when there was no alternative to comedy, **Marie Lindsay-Hogg** *trod the boards of the Victoria Palace with Nervo and Knox, Naughton and Gold and Bud Flanagan*

I can smell the greasepaint now. Leichner 5 & 9 and I've forgotten what else, but that smell...!

I was having lunch with my old friend Gai Pearl and we were reminiscing. We'd been together in *Knights of Madness*, the Crazy Gang show at the Victoria Palace in the early 50s.

'Do you remember when Charlie Naughton locked me in the loo?' said Gai.

'No. What happened?'

'I missed two numbers. I was on Punishment Call and fined! At least he paid my fine though.'

Gai and I hadn't met for years; we'd lost touch and found each other again by sheer chance. She had gone on to become a famous dancer in Italy, married, and was now big in PR for Italian fashion houses.

I'd had a husband and lots of children in Norfolk.

'Then, another time,' she continued, 'in "Dig-a-Doo" the whole row of us danced onto the stage in Zulu costume with black curly wigs – I was in the middle – and suddenly I was yanked to a standstill. My wig hooked up on the scenery and I went through all the motions on the spot for the rest of the number. Grace Draper wondered what on earth the audience was laughing at.' (Grace Draper was the solo 'Zulu', up front, unaware of the comedy behind her. Political correctness hadn't yet arrived.)

The Crazy Gang Shows had been revived after the war by Jack Hylton and *Knights of Madness* ran for two and a half years. The Gang at that time consisted of

Nervo and Knox, Naughton and Gold and Bud Flanagan – in his battered straw hat and enormous old racoon coat. Chesney Allen, Bud's partner, had retired, ill, in 1946. Freddie Bretherton conducted the orchestra and Grace Draper, Gillian Roma and Linda Lee were the leading ladies. Sundry speciality acts filled the gaps. I was one of six showgirls picked for good voices, height and looks. Together with a dozen or so dancers, girls and boys, we provided the glamour in the brilliant twice-nightly explosion of lights and colour and music and fun.

One night in the second performance, the six of us strutted onto the stage singing 'Musical Demon', a 1920's number. We wore tight black satin dresses fringed with white, white satin cloche caps and high

Most of us, most of the time, didn't have boyfriends. The audiences wouldn't have believed this and we, too, thought it odd; we were all so dishy!

heeled, cross-laced, white shoes. Except me. My plain black courts stood out like a sore thumb. Or two. Oh Lord! I almost lost my smile; the consequences would be dire.

After the number, back in the dressing room, the tannoy crackled into life. 'Miss Foster... Prompt Corner In The Interval PLEASE!' It was the stage manager speaking in C-A-P-I-T-A-L letters and he wasn't known as 'Adolf Hitler' for nothing. I was sentenced to be at the theatre at half past nine the next morning on Punishment Call. Nine thirty!

By the time I got back to my digs, had dinner and time to unwind it was nearly four o'clock in the morning! I needed my lie-in and having to get up at seven o'clock was punishment in itself.

Despite bus and train delays I was

there on time. So was Adolf (he'd had to get up early too), and what a telling off I got! I then had to sit in the semi-dark stalls until released, thoroughly diminished, an hour or so later. I was too naive and vulnerable in those days to protest. You could be forgiven for thinking that this all happened in Borstal during the inmates' annual concert.

The girls' dressing rooms were on the far side of the stage up a narrow, winding, stone staircase. We showgirls had the middle room. Mirrors stuck with telegrams and good luck cards and bordered with bright lights ranged down one wall; the long dressing table held makeup boxes, pots of cream and powder, mascots, and all the paraphernalia marking our individual places. On the opposite wall

and on a rail at the far end near the washbasins hung our voluminous costumes, cared for by Barbara, our beloved dresser cum 'Mum'. Between frantic changes she sat and knitted, listened to our woes and chatter and made our interval tea.

Most of us, most of the time, didn't have boyfriends. The audiences wouldn't have believed this and we, too, thought it odd; we were all so dishy! Most of us were virginally innocent – reluctantly, to judge by our conversation which veered from this phenomenon to the love life of whoever was lucky enough to have one. Great excitement erupted when one of us arrived, starry-eyed about a marvellous man she'd met. We'd all rush out after the show to give him the once over as he waited for her at the stage door.

Tall, elegant Frances told us one Monday that she had met Ray Milland at a party that weekend. She was surprisingly cagey and blushed a lot, confessing that he'd paid her a great deal of attention and called her a beautiful English rose. She had agreed to go out with him after the show. We were sworn to secrecy and all promised faithfully not to stare if we saw him waiting. He really was there, leaning on a lamp post on the opposite side of the road, looking for all the world like Ray Milland in a Hollywood movie, coat collar turned up and the brim of his trilby pulled down, hands deep in his pockets.

The next evening in the dressing room, we clamoured for details but didn't get them. Frances blushed even more and quietly said she'd had a lovely time. It was different in those days. Romance was the thing. Sex was still pretty private and 'the media' hadn't been invented. We read in the paper later that Mr Milland had returned to the States – and to his wife.

Fay was a different kettle of fish altogether. She was large, loud, exceptionally pretty and very white-skinned. Her steady boyfriend came and went as his job directed. One weekend they'd made the most of his return and she arrived late for the Monday evening show, wide-eyed and worried. The rest of us were made up and waiting in bras and pants ready to don our first costumes. Fay stripped off. We gasped and hooted. 'Oh help!' she moaned.

She was covered in love bites. Brilliant black and purple ones all over her shoulders, neck, arms and thighs.

'Fifteen minutes, please,' called a voice over the tannoy and we all sprang into action.

'You do your face!' I yelled at Fay. 'Come on Fran, you do that side and I'll do this.' For 10 frantic minutes I daubed make-up on the love bites on one side and Fran did the same on the other while Fay, with difficulty, struggled in the middle to do her face. She looked only slightly less piebald when we'd finished and had to brave the witticisms of the Gang and others until the marks faded a long time later.

I reminded Gai about the cafe opposite the Victoria Palace stage door. We used to congregate there before the show, dancers and showgirls and others from about 4.30pm onwards. Friendships were started here – and finished. Assignations were made, gossip exchanged and grievances aired. There was invariably a weedy man at another table ogling the girls (or the boys) but nobody minded. Those days we felt safe. No matter how late I left the theatre – and it was never before 11.30pm, I had no qualms about travelling back to my digs alone, walking quite some way in the dark from the station.

Gai reminded me about a Sunday shortly before the show folded. She'd telephoned to ask me to go with her that night to a party on board a P&O ship in East Ham Docks. I was to be the blind date of the host, the young Second Officer. I went...

Reader, I married him.

'Here is a newpaper published on the very day he was born'

Modern Life

What is... Marketing?

MODERN LIVES are being remorselessly crushed beneath the blind executive rump; its twin white buttocks are management and accountancy, between which escapes the thin mephitic steam of marketing.

Marketing men are the bogus priests and snake-oil men of modern commerce. Their trade is a shitty combination of wishful thinking, statistical jiggery-pokery and the jitters, which elements they manipulate with the glib plausibility of a street-corner three-card-tricksters, though instead of finding the lady, they find the lowest common denominator.

If you asked a marketing man what he actually did, his instincts would direct him to question 1,732 randomly-selected individuals in the target population as to what they thought he did, and present that to you in the form of a laser-printed, perfect-bound Report complete with pie-charts, graphics and outline numbering without which no marketing man can face the world. ('I'm Michael; how d'you do?' 'Ah, I'm glad you asked that. 2. I'm Chip. 2(a) I'm in marketing, 2(a)(i) for my sins; 2(b) what's your line exactly? (3) Great. Super. Cheers.')

We used to see a government or great enterprise as a ship. Now, command has been seized by deracinated 'executives' who, having spent their working lives climbing the greasy pole, possess no other skills than greasy-pole climbing, and are hiding in the Captain's cabin, swigging up the drink and negotiating to flog off the engines. The accountants – unsocialised, mole-like men who once toiled honourably in the bowels making sure the steam pressure didn't drop and there was always enough coal – have been invited on to the bridge; now they scamper from portside to starboard, tapping the dials and writing down the readings; but they do not know which one is the compass, and there's no point looking ouside because all the charts have been sold.

Some primitive faculty of imitation has shown these miserable 'men' that, although navigation need not actually be done, it should at least appear to be done. This task has been given to marketing, who perform it by carrying out surveys of the passengers, asking them where they would like to go, and where they think they might be at the moment.

The passengers' answers – unblemished by any hint of actual knowledge – are subjected to expert statistical analysis, then got up in the form of a laser-printed report (illustrated with computer graphics, pie charts, bell-curves, logos and inspirational pictograms), which are then pushed under the door of the Captain's cabin. And when the ship hits the rocks, there can be no blame, because everything that could be done, was done.

Marketing men trade in hindsight: 20/20 vision, but blurred with a curtain of fear and disabled by a great blind-spot. Hindsight is perfect for covering your back; nobody takes the blame; if

'… or I'll tear your head off and sell the rest of you for dog food. Yours affectionately…'

something worked before but does not work now, why, attribute it to blind caprice, malice, the whirligig of time bringing in his revenges. But it can show nothing of the future.

A friend who has had dealings with Hollywood once said 'Marketing men are the ones who come up to you and say: "You know that truly extraordinary, original, innovative film you made? The one that broke all the rules? That nobody ever thought would succeed? That just came out of left field and broke all the records? Well… could you make another one, exactly the same?'

Marketing men dislike originality, virtue, idiosyncracy and commitment. They prefer the levelling tendencies of the

plebiscite. A marketing man was once asked about the qualities which had given his company's lager supremacy in the market. 'It's not really that it has any particular qualities at all,' he said, with a candour rare in his trade. 'It's more that there's not really anything you can say *against* it.'

Thus, the gifts of the marketing men to our civilisation blandness, imitation, predictability… and profound dishonesty. One of the nastiest diseases of our time is the belief that if you say something is so, it becomes so; this, too, is a marketing trick. The 'mission statement,' the winsome rural label design, the tasteless cheese, the concept restaurant, the heritage theme park, the vernacular superstore: all these are the presents of marketing men to a country which knows it is being cheated but feels powerless to stop it. Blandness wrapped in mendacity: the prerogative of the marketing man through the ages.

Marketing is a trade of the deepest cynicism. It loathes diversity and difference. It is marketing that has insisted on the emasculation of our food, our movies, our architecture and our politics. Had there been a director of marketing at the Globe theatre, can you believe that even one of Shakespeare's plays would have been staged as he wrote it?

Of course not. Because the one thing the marketing man cannot, literally, afford is to give offence. And so they end by off-ending us all. **MICHAEL BYWATER**

"I'd just leave it as it is, and the public won't know the difference.'

Tied Up In Notts

Stained-glass maker **Patrick Reyntiens** *casts an acute artist's eye*
over the massed musculature at a bodybuilders' show

'TAKE MY LEOTARD,' said Aunt Dot, 'I'll wear the G-string with the sequins and the black square-cut mini-bra. That'll set the boys on fire.' 'Remember you're 65, getting on for 66: do you think that's wise?' 'One can but try…'

Actually Aunt Dot wouldn't have got in sideways at the Royal Centre at Nottingham a few weeks ago, where the cream of England's muscle was showing off to an audience of thousands packed hard into the hall. She wouldn't have got in because 80 per cent of the audience were proportioned five-by-five, jostled together like Flintstone hamsters; northern working-class lads ready to lurch and barge towards anything, seat, T-shirt, beer or bint that took their fancy. Weight-trained heavies in full fighting fig, smelling of after-shave and chumping bananas.

The show was billed as starting at 1pm but (such seems the patience of the northern British body-builder) hadn't really got under way until five. Of the 18 to 35 year olds and their molls that made up the audience, three-quarters showed evidence of long hard work in the gym. They were bulky as only Lancashire men, Yorkshiremen and Tynesiders can be when they put their minds to it.

The principles of bodybuilding had been applied consistently, with a vengeance, but not in the right direction. Most of the spectators were the result of the misapplication of bodybuilding principles. They were shapeless and enormously, solidly stout. They looked like a cross between a kebab hunk and a doughnut. And there were thousands. Poor Aunt Dot, crushed between human 40-ton lorries and bulk cement deliverers.

A fatal combination of northern pub food and beer in quantities, together with hard work in the weightlifting gym, packing bulk on bulk on bulk: the result – 3,000 minders and chuckers capable of giving the bum's rush to any number of massed special constables.

Most were wearing fanciful baggy track-suit bottoms, dyed, painted and printed in deliriously perverse patterns and all the colours of the rainbow. The visual aggression of the training-pants was, on reflection, in the same order as the wearing of the kilt at Wembley. Identity and defiance combined with definition.

In between these man-mountains of chubby and ruby flesh there were sandwiched cute little molls in body-tights and sado-masochistic boots. I saw no whips, however. I wore my Brigade of Guards tie.

But to the show! Bodybuilding shows have apparently never been able to make up their minds about presentation. It's as though a gymnasium line-up had inadvertently been crossed with a stage show. The result? A tacky mutant. As George V said on having knighted Sir Alfred Bossom, 'Silly name that: neither one thing nor the other.'

Tacky too the music of ear-splitting cacophony – humper-thumper thumper, thumper, dumb, dumb, dumb, BANG, humper-dumper. Adrenalin and blood bumped and throbbed without restraint. Then 'they' all filed in from the right to generous applause.

White identity numbers were tacked haphazardly to their posing-jocks. A line of guardsmen they were not. They turned, they faced the audience. Applause, applause, applause. The roof came off, nearly. The cream of bodybuilders.

I should explain that the evaluation of a bodybuilding competition (let's shorten the unwieldy term to BB, in spite of that French lady), consists basically of two parts. The first is a sort of gym line-up, a series of compulsory poses and exercises for the competitors, very like dressage at a horse-trial or the obligatory figures in Olympic skating. This goes on at a pretty leaden pace.

Then come the 'free' poses and exercises, a routine chosen and choreographed by the contestant himself and done to (sometimes) appropriate music. This is the most fun; nearly comes into the category of art; and, if it's fluffed or goes wrong in any way, affords the maximum embarrassment for the contestant and audience alike.

Anyway the compulsory exercises and poses got started. These set poses are very boring to the layman. To the initiate, however, they are the lifeblood of the movement. The set-exercises are heraldic. I half expected to hear 'Passant,' 'Passant gardant,' 'Couchant regardant' (a bit camp, that one, or a shade too erotic) and so on.

The poses of lions, leopards, talbots and griffins on an escutcheon could not have been more rigidly and strictly regimented than those competitors, condemned over and over to repeat the biceps to the front, turn, triceps to the side, turn, lats to the back, turn to the front, show thighs and abs (abdominal muscles)… All this to the ecstasy of the 3,000 five-by-five spectating.

Why such enthusiasm for such repetitive commonplace activity? Well, the whole year previous to the show the enthusiastic BBer has idolised certain icons of perfection in the shape of photos in their specialised magazines – of which there are a surprising number, greater than those devoted to football and cricket combined.

The 'icon of physical perfection' has been adored, defended, spat upon, execrated, argued about; a hagiography has been constructed around them by reportage and hearsay. They have been stashed on to the private iconostasis in every enthusiastic weight-trainer's bedroom. And now for the great moment, when these

57

flat icons actually come to life on stage.

It is a religious experience for those who take it seriously. The heroes are there. No matter if they are required to undergo pifflingly dull poses time after time. These dull setups correspond to the pre-formed iconic image inside the brainpan of each BB enthusiast. They are, on stage, a kind of variation on the expectancy that would accompany the Second Coming.

Evaluation by set reps is, in fact, the only way of evaluating the particular physical merits of a man's body. Then comes (after a seemingly interminable interval) the high point of the show, the 'free' exercises and poses. Each competitor comes on to the stage from the right as a solo act.

I should explain that the competitors are rigidly groomed for the part. In going in for a competition, the body has to be shorn of all its superficial hair. Pate, pits and pubes are ruthlessly depilated, as in Ancient Egyptian mourning rites. No fur anywhere. The contestant walks in and performs his 'free' as best he can do. The diminutive delicacy, not to say vulnerability and pathos of the genitalia contrasts with the vast extended slabs of integral and powerful muscle exfoliating above.

But there's a snag, for what we should be witnessing is art – the ability of the heroically formed male body to express something, to suggest something, beyond itself, beyond its own limitations. Art comes before athleticism, but does it in this case?

Most of the competitors are good athletes (if BB is athletics) but they are hopelessly deficient as artists with the material of their own bodies. Especially this is so with regard to the hands. For it is through the hands that the whole reservoir of energy and developed generosity and, yes, beauty, inherent in the human body is given to the viewer.

The music is inevitably a revelation of the lack of culture in the individual displaying himself – and it's invariably far too loud. The imbalance between gross aural stimulus, the music, and modest visual stimulus, the competitor's physique (as seen from any seat other than the front 10 rows) is too painful to be sustained for long.

Occasionally, as happened when I was there, the music announces something of such portentousness and grandeur that you sit up and take notice. Bach's great Toccata and Fugue in D, a magnificent black contestant, six foot three in height and proportionately built in bulk and definition, unfortunately got cramp on stage and in bar five had to withdraw…

So the show dribbled away. The prizes were given. Of 14 competitors at the first line-up, there were only some seven or eight left to be finally accoladed. The rest had become non-persons in the best Soviet-Russia tradition.

Dorian Yates, the proprietor of a particularly successful gym in Birmingham, whose free exercise/posing, admitedly reminded me of a funerary effigy of Rameses II attempting a saraband, was declared a winner. Physically he was more akin to a Bentley in build, a typical integral English lion if you like. His runner-up, who was American, had a physique curiously reminiscent of the best sort of Cadillac.

Odd how the human body is influenced by the rhetoric and energy-patterns of the motor-car. Perhaps not so odd in the 20th century. Better than being influenced by steam-trains.

The Life and Death of a Bookshop

Bryan Forbes *explains why he ran a bookshop for 38 years – and why he doesn't any more*

IT WAS A SMALL village store to begin with, and I was just a regular customer, the best customer I suspect and the one who kept it afloat. It was owned by a somewhat eccentric lady, Peggy Pegler, the daughter of a once-famous publisher.

In addition to being an insatiable collector of books, I had always been a frustrated bookseller from the time when, immediately after the war, I struck up a friendship with the late, and remarkable, Tony Godwin who, almost single-handed, dragged bookselling into the 20th century. Better Books in Charing Cross Road was a trail-blazing shop, for Tony was a true innovator, slightly mad, a passionate man, who only lived for books. As our friendship developed he let me serve in the shop as a happy, if unpaid, assistant during my frequent 'resting' periods between acting jobs.

Fate intervened when Mrs Pegler was involved in a car accident, sustaining injuries which eventually killed her. First she asked if I would like to become her partner, an offer I readily accepted. Then, following her death, the executors approached me to purchase the remaining 50 per cent. I took over the lease, but when I examined the books I found that the business was virtually insolvent. The annual turnover was a pitiful £8,000, and the small, eclectic stock mirrored Peggy's taste rather than appealing to the general reader.

So began the long, expensive task of making the enterprise viable. Because I was often away filming I needed to find somebody of like enthusiasm to operate the shop in my absence, and this proved difficult. I went through four managers before finding a young man named Patric Glasheen as dedicated as I was, and who has remained with me for the past 28 years. I provided the money but it was Patric's unsurpassed knowledge of and love for books that, over the years, built up our clientele.

We vastly increased the stock, refitted the shop, and made of it a small oasis of calm, where no customer was ever pressurised and no enquiry too difficult to satisfy. I made many mistakes which I had to subsidise out of my film earnings, but gradually we began to turn the corner, occasionally even making a small profit. I was content with that.

At that time my landlord was the Prudential, a company that

had always advertised itself as the champion of the small man, but after 17 years as a model tenant I received a letter from the good old Pru telling me that the shop had been sold to a property speculator.

Within weeks the new landlord hiked the rent by some 50 per cent and then, after a short lapse, served notice that I had a month to decide whether I would like to buy the freehold – at a quick profit to him, I discovered, of some £90,000. Fortunately I had an understanding bank manager and somehow managed to secure a mortgage for the £170,000 being demanded.

Today, after the recent demise of the Net Book Agreement, it is worth describing the economics of bookselling as they pertain to the small independent. When I first operated the shop the maximum publisher's discount was 33.33 per cent. Gradually, over a period of years, this crept up to the strange figure 36.63 per cent and most independents, according to surveys, were lucky if they ended up with three per cent net profit at the end of the year. To return unsold books was a chancy business, entailing that one first got authority from the publisher's reps, and then waited for the sales manager to OK it – a process that more often that not took three months before a credit note was passed. This despite the fact that booksellers were only given 30 days credit or else risked being put 'on stop'. Under licence we were permitted to hold a sale once a year.

Over the years Patric and I managed to edge the turnover towards the £150,000 mark, which proved virtually the break-even point, covering the overheads some years and allowing of a modest 'book profit.' For nine months of the year we trod water with the aid of an overdraft, only October to December provided the fat, bringing in nearly half of the yearly turnover.

We introduced computerisation, allowing us to satisfy single customer orders of any British book in print within 48 hours, and this side of the business increased every year, for it was a service that customers valued. The shop became the village pump and we served coffee, maintained a comprehensive stock of fiction and non-fiction, together with the widest range of children's books, held signing sessions, gave some shelf space to decent second-hand titles, allowed local artists to display their wares and gave special discounts to local schools and charities.

We were fortunate in that the American school, Tassis, was nearby and became a major customer. During the Christmas period we stayed open late for the convenience of commuters

We are selling pleasures that can be returned to and handed on to future generations

who wished to browse at their leisure and we gift-wrapped for free.

But none of this, none of our constantly revised efforts, proved enough when the Net Book Agreement folded overnight, for the cream went to the multiples (it does not take much skill or effort to move bestsellers).

The shopping parade itself which, when I first moved into the district 30 or more years ago, provided every daily need and was a living entity, was gradually whittled away as rents and the onerous business rate forced small traders out of business.

Instead of the widest choice we now have four estate agents, three wine shops and two cleaners. Even service with a smile and that rarity, free parking, is not enough to seduce people away from the superstores and malls, so the passing trade now passes us by. I am all for widening the readership of books, illiteracy being what it sadly is, and happy for anybody to get a bargain. But whereas the wine stores, petrol stations and tobacconists can legally sell books, the independent bookseller cannot sell alcohol, petrol or the weed, and there's the rub.

I would gladly have soldiered on had I and others like me been granted the sort of discounts offered to the big multiples, but the downturn was too immediate and dramatic. I held on to see whether the Christmas season would bring about a revival of my fortunes, but it was not to be – the turnover went down by 26 per cent and sounded the death knell.

I don't regret one moment of the 38 years I devoted to the shop, for it was always a release valve. I never lost the thrill of opening up the parcels of new books, or of being able to recommend and sell a first novel I had discovered and enjoyed, to stock a young poet, to guide a teenager towards one of the great, now neglected, books of the 20th century as well as the older classics. The function of a dedicated bookseller goes beyond making a sale and it must start with a real love of the printed page.

We are not selling our wares as just another commodity, like pet food or frozen hamburgers, we are selling pleasures less transitory, pleasures that can be returned to time and time again and handed on to future generations.

Somebody once wrote that 'A man is known by the company his mind keeps' and if in some small way, in a small community, The Bookshop, Virginia Water, encouraged a few more to discover the worth of books in the increasingly arid world of the multimedia and tabloid instant-dross, then all is not lost.

I was making a film about reincarnation and by great good fortune the Dalai Lama was visiting his headquarters in Switzerland. I telephoned to ask if I could discuss the subject with him on film and an audience was arranged. I arrived with a Swiss film crew at the Office of Tibet at Rikon, high on a slope near the mountains.

I knew he was the 14th Dalai Lama and that he must be carrying the moles on his body, markings where two of the four arms of the first Dalai Lama had been. He also had the right shaped ears and had identified objects correctly when the monks had found him as a baby, in confirmation of his reincarnated identity.

We were shown into a room and set up the equipment. Soon he came in, beaming happily through his spectacles. With him were three monks, presumably to interpret any phrases which might present a problem.

I began by asking if a person could be reborn as an animal. 'Yes,' he said, 'according to Buddhist teaching.'

'But how can you prove the existence of this, whatever it is, that hops from person to person and possibly into a rabbit?'

The Dalai Lama hesitated: 'Ah – um – for the Buddhist this is not one subject, it is many subjects. Now the main point is that you must control your mind, control by yourself... '

'Do you ever doubt the question of rebirth?' I pressed him.

'No.'

'Do you ever doubt rebirth into animal form?'

'No.' He conferred in Tibetan with his three interpreters. One of them explained: 'Once you have accepted the existence of rebirth then that matter is simple.'

'How low down in this animal scale can one go? Are we talking about amoeba? Are we talking about tadpoles?' Again the Dalai Lama spoke in rapid Tibetan to his interpreters. 'Are we talking about rabbits?' I went on, 'mosquitoes?'

'One course may create some thousands of different lives. And also, you see, our consciousness is something like – ' He said something in Tibetan, and an interpreter translated: 'A refrigerator.'

'Refrigeration,' the Dalai Lama

echoed. 'It restores millions and millions and millions of different karmic reactions.'

At that point the film in the camera ran out. I did not feel I was making much progress with His Holiness, and remarked it was a pity they did not smoke. The Dalai Lama roared with laughter. 'Of course you smoke! Please, smoke! We not smoke.' I lit up.

When the camera had been reloaded, the Dalai Lama gave me a piercing smile and off we went again. 'The reason I ask these questions is because the Buddha said: "Don't take my word for granted. Test them against your own experiences in the world. Be sceptical." Now I offer the suggestion to you that it is more likely, more *likely* that a human being dies and disappears than it is that there is something within him which goes bounding from person to person or from person to animal.'

'The manifest consciousness when we die,' he began to explain, 'that time the deepest consciousness experiencing, that level is the subtle mind – subtlest – ' Another word with his interpreters, one of whom added: 'Most subtle state of consciousness.' 'That level go,' concluded the Dalai Lama. 'Depart,' an interpreter interjected. 'Depart,' the Dalai Lama concurred, then spoke again in Tibetan.

'So it would be quite difficult,' came the translation, 'to gain the certainty of conviction just through reasoning. So the easiest proof is that there are people who actually has the experience of their rebirth.'

We continued filming, but I believed I had got the point. The proof of rebirth was knowing one had lived a previous life. Of course if that 'experience' had been caused by belief in the first place, then one could travel this merry-go-round for ever.

But it appeared that the head of the British Buddhists, Judge Christmas Humphreys, who had previously informed me that human beings could only return as humans, had got it wrong. The judge

Haven'

When **Hugh Burnett** *starte*

recalled several previous lives, including one when he had an affair with the Virgin of Isis. They had met again in this life and compared notes about how they had been discovered and everything had gone black.

I THANKED HIS Holiness for his time and trouble. In the finished film, after other people recalled previous lives, we cut to the old city of Carcassonne with waving tree tops. 'So there's the confirmation. The easiest proof is memory of rebirth, personified now by this English psychiatrist from Bath, who remembers living in the south of France 700 years ago.'

Traffic noise. Mid shot of Dr Arthur

ve met before?

oking into reincarnation, one thing just led to another

Guirdham sitting behind a table on the terrace of La Cité Hotel, Carcassonne. 'My name is Dr Arthur Guirdham. I was a senior consultant in the National Health Service. This is orthodox enough, surely. But in addition I have a clear memory of five previous lives – one beginning about 1200BC in an island off the north of Crete, another in the 4th century AD in the Roman Empire, another in 7th century Celtic Cumberland, another in the 13th century in the foothills of the Pyrenees and another which spans the French Revolution era and the restoration of the Bourbons.

'I'm here in Carcassonne where I was tortured in the early 15th century. Among the tortures inflicted upon me were thumb

screws. And they also had a very nasty trick, which I could never quite under-stand, of chucking icy cold water on you. I was tortured because I was a Cathar, in the hope that I would give away other people who practised this particular heresy. You could be burnt for being a Cathar, your goods could be expropriated.

'One of the punishments was to wear a yellow cross on your back. All this stuff was carefully and minutely documented in the records of the Inquisition. And I know what my name was. I was Roger de Grissoles. I had a brother called Isam Bernard. I had a sister called Helis and two other sisters. I died on Christmas Day – I would be difficult – Christmas Day 1243 – and I was in my middish sixties when I

died. Now you may say, how do I know all this? Well, this all sounds very romantic, but I got this in the most banal and ordinary way from out-patients at my main hospital in Bath, where I met a patient who had an obviously detailed memory of the 13th century. I didn't know this was her memory of the 13th century until I had been treating her for some time. But she produced for me a shower of medieval names. It was quite useless thinking in terms of ordinary psychiatry, sexual repression and Jung.'

But couldn't reading about the Inquisition have preceded the memory? Dr Guirdham had an answer to that. Scholarly research by French academics had been paralleled by the lady in Bath. Absolutely identical, said the doctor. She had even got ahead of the scholars with certain particulars. She had insisted the Cathars had worn blue. All the historians declared they wore black. Then a M Duverney in France discovered that in certain areas the priests had indeed worn dark blue – as recorded in the sittings of the Inquisition.

THE NEXT STAGE in the psychiatrist's story came when he suffered a coronary thrombosis. While he was recuperating, there had been a knock at his door and there was a 'big, bouncing, extrovert woman' whose car had broken down outside. She used the telephone and his wife gave her a cup of tea. After frequent visits to cheer the ailing doctor, who by this time had suffered a second coronary, he learned that she had been having recurring nightmares of being dragged towards a great pile of logs and being struck on the back by a monk with a flaming torch.

The lady had been having pains and with some reluctance Dr Guirdham examined her. To his surprise he discov-ered on her back the most extraordinary protuberances he had ever seen. 'They looked,' he said, 'just like burns, except that in the blister there was solid stuff like fat and connective tissue – which you'd expect after 700 years.'

He identified her as Esclarmon de Pereille, daughter of Ramon de Pereille, the owner of a château in the south of France where the Cathars had lived. And he was able to identify several other people within a radius of 15 miles from Bristol. 'It was a question of group reincarnation. We had seven or eight candidates.'

One lady had woken with terrible pains in her toes, spreading slowly up to her knees. A Bristol doctor had diagnosed burning. When the lady whose car had broken down came out in grooves on her wrists the French scholar had explained that this was due to the chain which was tied to a leather cord before being fastened to the stake at which people were burnt.

'You may think it strange,' said Dr Guirdham, 'that an English psychiatrist should be sitting in the Pyrenees telling you memories of his life in a château over here. But it's not a question of anybody asking me: "Do I believe in reincarnation?" I *know* reincarnation is true. On the evidence I could not possibly think otherwise. Sometimes people in

bouts of misplaced humour say to me, "Doctor, don't people sometimes think you're mad?"

'My answer to that is, I would be mad if I thought otherwise than positively on reincarnation – because in rejecting reincarnation I'd be rejecting the evidence that I've received in the last several years and which I know to be true.'

Know to be true? We adjourned to a nearby cornfield, surrounded by poppies, and debated furiously the nature of evidence. In this inquisition, Dr Guirdham remained unrepentant.

As a former Cathar, inquisitions were nothing new to him. But for me the statistical chances of a multi-reincarnation seemed to be astronomically high, allowing everybody to meet up again and compare memories. Especially with animals, mosquitoes and amoeba included – with life spans grossly out of step.

I was in deeper water than when I began. But the Buddha had never promised things were going to be *simple*, after all, for the seeker…

Sarah Churchill

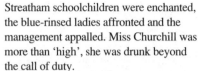

I first met Hubert Woodward when I was Carl Clopet's stage director for a tour of *Pygmalion*. It was a fairly short tour with Sarah Churchill, Sir Winston's actress daughter, in the role of Eliza Dolittle. Hubert was one of the crowd outside the church in the first scene and he was also involved with the management.

God alone knows how old Hubert was at that time, but he was fairly crippled with arthritis and got about with the aid of two sticks. He had been an actor in the time of the Aldwych farces with Tom Walls and Ralph Lynn. His wrinkled old face was a terminus of acting lines and his eyes twinkled with a wicked humour and the very pleasure of living. He was of a 'never give up' make that it is getting harder every day to find.

Miss Churchill was an actress who had gone through several husbands and a number of bottles. Sober she was a quite devastating actress and unsober a terrifying vision of unpredictable, lethal womanhood.

We were playing the Streatham Hill Theatre, a vast 2,000 seater in south London when a particularly Churchillian disaster struck. I think it was on the Thursday matinee with all the blue-rinsed ladies and genteel school parties in front, that our star changed the naughty word from its scripted 'bloody' to a less acceptable swear word. The

ACTRESS
SARAH CHURCHILL

Streatham schoolchildren were enchanted, the blue-rinsed ladies affronted and the management appalled. Miss Churchill was more than 'high', she was drunk beyond the call of duty.

In the interval between the scenes it fell to me to inform the lady that the understudy would play the rest of that afternoon's performance and to make the announcement in front of the curtain to the audience. Whilst I was doing the latter the understudy and others were getting the actress out of her costume, since there was only the one.

It was not that the management was mean, it was just that Miss C would not allow that she would ever be off and so we were forbidden to have understudy costumes at the ready. It meant of course that we had to find an understudy of the same dimensions as our star.

My announcement to the house was received with some murmuring and a little polite disbelief at my attributing her lapse to 'sudden illness'. As I returned backstage I saw our star in a state of some undress tearing across to the stairs that led to the stage door. Hubert was hobbling gamely in pursuit, saying, 'Don't worry, I'll get her!'

'You stay here, Hubert, and get the curtain up. I'll go.' And with that I chased down the stairs after her.

As well that I did. With an alarming turn of

speed she had bowled past the stage door keeper and was sprinting up the hill to the main road. I arrived at the front of the theatre in time to see her leap onto a bus that tore away towards Brixton.

There was a car, a Vauxhall, just behind the bus and I waved it down. It was occupied only by the driver, a respectable young man who was already intrigued by the sight of a half-dressed actress jumping onto a bus. 'Could you follow that bus?' I asked. 'I've lost an actress.'

To his eternal credit he caught on immediately and agreed.

'If you can catch it at a stop I'll jump on and retrieve her,' I explained. 'Could you spare the time to follow on?'

'I wouldn't miss it for worlds!'

Two stops later we managed it and I clambered aboard the bus.

'She's upstairs,' the conductress told me. 'For God's sake get her off or I'll have to call the police. She's been upsetting everyone, swearing and cursing and being most offensive.'

I climbed the stairs and found Sarah sitting in the back seat all alone. The other passengers had fled to the front to be clear of her. Gingerly I sat beside her, tight in so that she could not get her arms out to take a swipe at me. She had a hefty punch. I began to talk quietly to her, uttering soothing noises. Mostly she snarled.

Presently I said, 'The schoolchildren liked the new word.' She giggled. 'They would,' she muttered, adding, 'little bastards!' I said, 'Some of the Blue Rinse Brigade were sending out for dictionaries and others are asking if George Bernard Shaw is English.' And she laughed.

We sat for a moment or two in silence until I felt we had a feeling of truce. The time had arrived to suggest that she should get off at the next stop. I explained that I had a car following and that if she would get off quietly I would take her home to Dolphin Square. Finally she agreed, but only if I would go and join the car first, then she would get off at the next stop.

'You're never leaving her with us?' gasped the conductress.

'Don't worry, she'll get off at Brixton!' And I leapt for the car.

She did get off at Brixton but she gave me a run for my money around the back of Morleys the department store. Thank

heavens she didn't dart inside or I should have lost her.

At last I persuaded her into the car, but she would only sit in front, which scared my volunteer driver somewhat. I had a Vauxhall of my own and once she was seated I reached from the back seat and pushed down the front door lock.

In a few minutes I was thankful that I had, because she tried to get out. I held onto her though she shouted blue murder. This was an occurence that I was familiar with, so I held on for grim death and in time she sat quietly and promised to do so for the remainder of the journey.

The porter at the Square was used to her coming home in the company of a minder… One of her best and chief minders had been dear old Patrick Desmond – she was very fond of him. I do not think that she achieved more than a tolerance for me. Julia Lockwood, the gorgeous daughter of the famous Margaret, was at the Dolphin Square flat and not a bit surprised to receive our star back in her present condition. She phoned for Sarah's doctor and I sped back to the theatre.

The matinee was nearing its interval but I had hardly got to the prompt corner before being called to the telephone. It was

Julia Lockwood. Sarah would not go to sleep until I had said she could appear that evening and I had to promise to be at her flat by 6.30pm with transport.

Doubting that the woman would even be conscious at that time I duly presented myself. Sarah met me in her living room and looked marvellous except for dark glasses. Looking through the window at my unmarked Bedford van, she remarked, 'I see you've brought a plain van… How appropriate!'

That evening she went on and gave a brilliant performance, looking younger and more radiant than any other woman present. Hubert said, 'What a woman! I adore her… but I would not want to live with her!'

Dear old Carl Clopet offered me an extra fiver for keeping it out of the papers. To my moral credit I refused saying, quite rightly, that it was no more than my job called for. Carl was very impressed.

As far as keeping those sort of misadventures out of the press was concerned, there was never any difficulty with papers owned by Lord Beaverbrook, who firmly instructed his staff to be wary of printing bad stories about his friends.

TERENCE FITZGERALD

'Could you direct me to the reception desk?'

How I Met
Alastair

Claude Harris

by Naomi Sim

In 1926 my mother had rented a flat in Edinburgh and my sister and I went to St George's School for Girls in Murrayfield. In the summer of that year, when I was 12, our drama teacher, Miss Atwell, put on a production of *Love's Labour's Lost*, cast entirely from the all-female staff, but as there were no midgets among them, she needed a little girl to play Moth, Don Adiano's page. I was small for my age and just about to stagger the world with my acting ability. (I'm still just about to do

this. I do hope I haven't left it too late.) Anyway, I got the part and everyone made a fuss of me.

As soon as the Autumn term started I was approached again by Miss Attwell. She was going to produce a play to go into the annual competition of the Scottish Community Drama Association which would be held at the end of November. Amateur dramatic societies from all over Scotland put on one-act plays for this contest, which was judged each year by some well-known professional director. Miss

Attwell had decided to do *The Land of Heart's Desire* by W B Yeats and needed a child to play the Fairy Girl. Would I like to do it? Yes, please, I would, I said, trying not to turn three somersaults. She told me that we would be rehearsing every Sunday afternoon at her flat and she gave me a copy of the play.

I approached Miss Attwell's flat in Lennox Street on the first Sunday with extreme nervousness but huge excitement. Most of the actors were already there and I met the two who were to play the parents, and the rather old young man who was to play the son. Miss Attwell herself was going to play the bride. This was a surprise to me since she was round and fortyish, but I didn't know then that amateurs were unlikely to cast to type. It wouldn't stretch their talents.

Miss Attwell was telling the others that she had found it terribly difficult to get somebody to play the Priest, but only the day before she had had a stroke of luck. She had run into someone whose name I didn't catch and he had agreed to do it. He would be exactly right, and he should be here any minute.

Just then he arrived and I stood a little apart as he was introduced to the others. He was tall and gangly with crisp, black hair already receding, a lively face with huge eyes, and a very beautiful smile. About 40, I thought (he was nearly 26). The next moment, all unknown to me, my adult life began – my marvellously exciting, frequently difficult, and altogether gloriously happy adult life – for it was then that Miss Attwell called to me, 'Naomi, come and meet the man who is going to play the Priest.'

On the second Sunday Miss Attwell asked the Priest if he would like to stay on to tea after rehearsal. When he accepted, she asked me if I would like to stay too. Oh, boy, would I!

When the rest of the cast had gone, double doors were opened and someone might have waved a magic wand. Soft lights, a bright fire, a low table drawn near to it spread with a white cloth and a magnificent tea, two comfortable armchairs and a stool for me.

It appeared that the Priest never ate

cakes but I wasn't going to let Miss Attwell down. I sat quietly while my elders talked, shyly accepted cake after cake after cake, and continued my favourite occupation – gazing at the Priest. I thought Miss Attwell was being exceedingly kind to me, which of course she was, but I didn't understand at the time that I was also there as chaperone. It would have been a little difficult in 1926 for the Priest to have tea alone with her.

When it was time for us to go, the Priest said he would walk me home. He walked on the pavement while I walked on air. My mother, looking at my starry eyes, asked me, if it happened again, to bring him in so that she could thank him, and the following Sunday I watched with delight as my mother overcame her shyness and talked to him without difficulty.

I had by now discovered that his name was Alastair Sim. He was Fulton Lecturer at New College in Edinburgh, teaching budding parsons how to speak, and he also had his own School of Drama and Speech Training in Manor Place. There was no one, however, among the people close to him with whom he could talk about literature and poetry, and as my mother was in the same position this, in time, became a great bond between them.

As the day of the competition approached, my excitement became almost unbearable. If we won in Edinburgh we might go to London, and if we won there we might even go to New York. How could we fail. It seemed we could – very easily, for when the great day came the adjudicator was unimpressed. He praised me and slated the Priest and I thought he was insane.

The following day was my 13th birthday and I had made an unheard-of request to my mother. I wanted to ask the whole cast to a birthday party. I would ask the Priest first and if he didn't accept I would forget the whole thing. They all accepted. My mother gave us a superb tea and afterwards the Priest suggested that we re-enact our play, swapping over all the parts. He played the Bride, Miss Attwell's part, and was wildly funny, though perhaps Miss Attwell's laughter was a little strained. I don't remember what the others played – for me there was only one person in the room. The party had been a success although, since the Priest had given me a birthday kiss when he arrived, I had difficulty in getting to sleep that night.

I didn't meet him again for a long time although I occasionally caught a glimpse

of him from the top of a tram, as he walked from his studio to the West End.

By the time October came I was missing him so much that I asked if we could invite him to duck for apples on Hallowe'en. My mother agreed and to my huge delight he came. Again there was a great deal of laughter and when we were all exhausted, full of apples and rather damp, there was time to dry off in front of the fire and talk. He told us that once a year he hired a hall and put on a show with all his pupils, and that he was rehearsing for this now. In due course we went. There were sketches, some dramatic, some funny, scenes from Shakespeare, monologues, and wonderful verse-speaking. Some were solo pieces, some for two voices in unison, but best of all, for me, was a large choir, led by the Priest, speaking Chesterton's *Lepanto*. I found the drama of this completely intoxicating and I discovered that poetry need not be the namby-pamby thing that Miss Attwell had presented to me.

After this show we got to know Alastair well and he was often at our home. He would play football with me in the garden and clown for my benefit – a thing that never failed to astonish and delight me. In my world adults often smiled, sometimes laughed, but *never* clowned. I must have been the best audience he ever had.

He and my mother had long talks about plays and books, and sometimes he took us to the theatre or the cinema. In the spring after I was 14, he said to my mother. 'That child is learning nothing at all at school. You really ought to take her away.' To my astonishment she did. No one suggested that, instead, the child might be made to work. At any rate I left at the end of the summer term, and I still remember the joy of waking every morning to the knowledge that school was over for ever.

Of course, my so-called 'education' was supposed to continue. I was sent to English lectures at the University where I worked as hard as I had at school – not at all. I spent my time pretending to take notes, watching the other students, and wondering if the lecturer was falling in love with me. He wasn't. I also went to the Berlitz to learn French where I worked

'George! You know shellfish doesn't agree with you!'

just as hard and wondered if my rather spotty teacher was falling in love with me. No. The rest of my time was spent as a pupil at Alastair's own School of Drama and Speech Training.

A little later on he asked me if I would like to be his secretary, type his letters, keep his papers in order and so on. He would give me four shillings a week. Riches! I slowly pounded his old typewriter with two fingers and sent off letters beginning, 'Dear Sir, Further to your letter of the such and such, I now enclose etc, etc. Yours faithfully…' Before long I would have the reply, 'Dear Madam, Further to yours of the such and such, I fear that you omitted to enclose, etc, etc.' Any other employer would have fined me four shillings a week.

He entered me for a verse-speaking competition in Edinburgh where I came absolutely nowhere and guessing, rightly, that I was miserable, he sent me a charming little note restoring my sense of proportion. It was the first I had ever had from him.

One day Alastair turned up at our home in his father's car which he had borrowed for the day. He was off to Lanark to judge a verse-speaking competition. Would I like to come? My mother saw to it that I had a comb, a clean handkerchief and emergency money, and we were off. I must have been about as adult as a modern seven year old. During the day we listened to endless school children reciting Wordsworth's *Daffodils* – with gestures – and in the lunch hour we went for a walk round a ploughed field.

When we got back I was suddenly stricken. 'I've lost my purse!'

'Was there much money in it?'

'Yes, I'm afraid so. Rather a lot.'

'We'll go round the field again.'

The little purse was just the colour of the ploughed earth but after five minutes he found it with the seven shillings still inside. I should have known that there was nothing he couldn't do.

'And is this your little daughter?' people would ask him on that day and on many others. 'No', he would say with his charming smile, offering no further explanation. I was there because we were going to spend the rest of our lives together, but we didn't know that then.

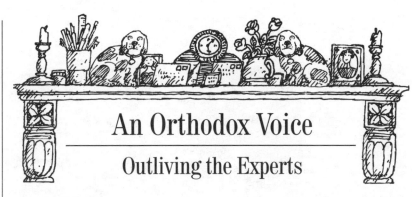

An Orthodox Voice
Outliving the Experts

AN OLD CHAP I was talking to turned out to be a former Cabinet minister. The experience had disillusioned him. 'I used to believe in science and have faith in economists,' he said. 'But then I discovered that these people are utterly bogus. Each one contradicts the other, and none of them ever manages to be right about anything. Every year the most reputable economists produce a report on current and projected trends in the world of business, and on this document the Government bases all its financial strategies for the year. Yet every such report is invariably wrong – not just inaccurate but so far off the mark that you would do better to expect the opposite of anything the experts predict.'

His final conclusion was that it was not just the economists who were always wrong, but experts generally, in every department and subject. The realisation has been a great blessing to him. It has freed his mind from worry and allowed him to spend the rest of his life in classical contentment, drinking wine and gardening.

If that is a path to happiness it seems an easy one to take. The infallible wrongness of experts is a law which you can test for yourself in any subject you care to go into. My own first glimpse of it was in archaeology, where the noble artefacts of the ancients were interpreted by experts as relics of primitive superstition. This absurd view was clearly derived from Darwin's theory of evolution, and this upon examination turned out to be no more than a myth, despite the experts' insistence upon its literal truth. On the most important subject of all, the origin of the world and the nature of life, the experts proclaimed certainties which changed so regularly and radically that they might just as well have said openly, We don't know.

So it goes on. I have just read a book, *The End of the Future*, by an astute Frenchman,

Jean Gimpel, recalling how life at the end of this century was predicted by experts in the 50s and 60s. By now, according to the highly-paid prognosticators of that period, there would be no more illness or suffering. We would live to at least 150, with everything done for us by intelligent robots. Holidays would be spent on the moon or in one of our star colonies; even the old-fashioned types who clung to Earth would be shooting around it in atomic rockets. In 1955 a 30-minute crossing of the Atlantic was officially promised within a few years.

In actual fact, says M Gimpel, technological progress has reached its end and the reverse has set in. Our civilisation is subject to the same laws and will follow the same cycle as all that have gone before. Forget the experts' babblings about time-travel through black holes, and prepare for dissolution.

Gimpel's weakness, of course, is that he too is an expert and thus as inevitably fallible as his predecessors. I read his book purely for entertainment and for yet another laugh at the experts' expense.

It really does make you happier when you see through these people. No longer at the mercy of their neuroses, you can develop your own view of the world, and if you are wise you will serve self-interest by making it as delightful as possible, basing it on the image of a God-given paradise, which is far truer and more lasting than the perverse imaginings of any expert.

So when people complain about modern education and how children learn nothing at all at school, I cannot help thinking that is not such a bad thing, after all. It took me a long time to be rid of my drummed-in fear of experts. Others in my generation never managed to work themselves free. That is why so many of them lost their money in Lloyd's.　**JOHN MICHELL**

Pin-ups

Larry Adler picks his top six

1 Sting
Sting made me revise all of my opinions (prejudices) about pop music and pop performers. I admire him for his dedication when he works for a cause, such as rain forests, saving trees, etc.

2 George Martin
How, in his business, can a man retain such calm, courtesy, kindness and charm? He never raises his voice, certainly never loses his temper. What a joy to work with such a man!

3 Jack Benny
The finest gentleman I've ever known. He made radio history when a burglar in a sketch said, 'Your money or your life!' 30 seconds of silence, 'I said, your money or your life!' Said Jack irritably, 'I'm thinking it over!'

4 Sergei Rachmaninoff
I first heard him when I was five, in Baltimore. I wanted to do what he did. I met him twice and (I don't expect anyone to believe this) I was too nervous to speak.

5 Fred Astaire
I worked with him in a Ziegfeld show, *Smiles*. That's how I learned what perfectionism means.

6 Ingrid Bergman
To know this lady was to love her. The fact that I composed film scores, notably *Genevieve*, is due entirely to Ingrid Bergman. She made me find a teacher of composition and study with him.

Grown-Up Games

Once upon a time, sex education was a rather hit-and-miss affair.
Sheila Thompson *tells how she accomplished hers*

The debate as to whether sex education should be included in the school curriculum or taught at home rumbles on, and the fierce feuds it engenders are enough to make parents wish they had not indulged in the first place and produced offspring who required an education at all. Having been raised in an era when to refer to your nether regions as a 'bottom' instead of a 'pompom' resulted in a soap and water mouthwash I was lucky to have sampled sex education both at school and at home.

My first intimation that babies did not arrive in Dr Raven's black bag came at school one day when I was eight years old. It was in Scripture class (as unlikely a place as one can imagine) when an extremely embarrassed teacher read aloud from the Bible, 'And Esau issued forth from his mother's belly.' Fifteen startled pairs of eyes were rivetted on her face but she managed to avoid meeting any of them. She was still blushing when the bell rang and 15 little girls shot past her to the cloakroom to examine their navels to find out how Esau got out. Was there a magic button somewhere? A secret formula like 'Open O Sesame'? Did one burst open?

We were caught in this act of self-scrutiny by a prefect who demanded an explanation. Defensively we explained the reason for our curiosity. She was not sympathetic, nor explanatory. She shouted, 'You filthy little beasts! Go back to your classroom!' Hurriedly we obeyed and – without any damage to our psyche – buried the mystery of Esau's exit under a welter of hockey sticks and other games of violence.

Two and a half years later my parents' separation ended in a dirty divorce during which Papa was awarded custody of all six children. Sensibly he gave back the two youngest before the ink was dry, but even then found he was hoist with his own petard.

No-one had told him how much work a mother actually did during school holidays. When she was doing it, it looked easy, but dental appointments, oculists' visits, ballet lessons, haircuts, supervising piano practice, encouraging reluctant violinists, horsewomen and skaters, are all time-consuming occupations that require patience, organisation and dictatorship – not Papa's strong points. His secretary showed a marked reluctance to relieve him of any of his responsibilities, with the result that our first holiday in his custody was cancelled.

He bribed Mama to have us for the summer. Grandly I embarked on the Golden Arrow at Victoria alone and, with the help of various Thomas Cook agents, finally arrived in Menton on the Blue Train, in time for lunch.

Mama had a semi-resident lover. Semi because in those days a live-in lover was not considered *comme il faut*. For some reason sleeping with someone at night was considered more immoral than making love to them in the daytime. But Louis ate all his meals with us.

After lunch that first day my little sister, with whom I was sharing a room, and I retired for the obligatory afternoon rest in our room adjacent to the dining room. We had no sooner taken up our books than there was a rhythmic knocking on the wall. It was regular and increased in speed and was soon accompanied by rather monotonous cries from Mama of 'Oh Louis… Oh Louis… Oh Louis… Oh! Oh! Oh…' rising to a crescendo and fading away to a loud sigh. Then there was silence.

Diana had pulled the eiderdown over her head, moaning:

ILLUSTRATIONS BY JON CRAMER

'He's killing her. I know he's killing her.' I was inclined to agree and was debating what to do when I heard footsteps in the hall – Louis entering the loo. Being foreign he left the door open, peeing being *tout à fait naturel*.

He didn't bother to wash his hands either, probably for the same reason. He called out 'À ce soir, Suchon' – Suchon being his pet name for Mama – and slammed the front door.

Obviously she wasn't dead or he wouldn't have been speaking to her, so I flounced off my bed, annoyed now that I had been frightened for nothing, and went to voice my opinion.

I entered the dining room by one door just as Mama, dressed only in her petticoat and looking rather pink and pleased with herself, was preparing to exit by the other door to go to her room.

'Mama,' I began censoriously, 'I don't know what you and Louis were doing but you made a lot of noise, and Diana was frightened.'

She looked contrite. 'I am sorry, darling, but you know what men are. They only have one trick and if you don't appear to appreciate it, and applaud them for doing it, they'll find someone else who will.'

I must have looked bewildered because she added, by way of explanation. 'And Louis is a little deaf from his years as a machine gunner during the war.'

None of this made sense to me but I battled on. 'Couldn't you go into another room?' I suggested tentatively.

'Oh, dear, no. That would spoil the spontaneity of it. Never mind, tomorrow morning I'll get Palmyre to move the chaise longue to the other side of the room. It will make a nice change. And I know I can count on you to reassure Diana.'

I was so thrilled that Mama was speaking to me as if I was a contemporary that I quite forgot to press for any further explanation. I walked on air back to our bedroom and said airily, 'Mama is fine, Diana.'

'Then what were they doing?' she insisted.

'Oh, well…' I was stuck. 'Just playing grown-up games.'

She was not fooled. 'You don't know,' she said disgustedly. 'I shall ask Pam when she arrives.'

Pam, older than me by 18 months, was the Oracle. She arrived at the weekend and had no difficulty in divining the particular activity in question, nor in explaining. At first we didn't believe her.

'You're making it up,' I said. But we were finally persuaded and suitably shocked. Mama never did find out why we kept patting her hand and saying 'Poor Mama' all through the holiday.

I returned to England feeling very sophisticated, sex education complete as far as I was concerned. I knew what 'grown-ups' did in secret.

I found out how Esau issued forth the hard way, much later.

Lost in the swells of the South Pacific is a speck of volcanic rock which should be paradise. This mile-by-mile-and-a-half island is home to 40 half-Tahitian, half-British men and women whose race, culture and country arose from a historical hiccup – the 1789 mutiny on HMS *Bounty*. Two hundred years ago, a handful of British mutineers, with their Tahitian women and followers, landed on Pitcairn seeking a haven from the gallows. Today, their island at the uttermost end of the earth is the image of escape. Each year the Pitcairners receive thousands of letters from those who yearn to live 'far from the madding crowd' on an island without cars, banks, TV, taxes, roads – with the lowest crime rate in the world.

An estimated 2,500 books and articles, and three Hollywood movies have been produced about this Garden of Eden. But if Pitcairn is the most imagined, it is the least known place on earth. It is rarely visited. Only a handful of applicants for the Licence to Land are accepted by the Island Council each year.

Pitcairn is the last British colony in the South Pacific, lying just below the tropic of Capricorn, with New Zealand 3,300 miles to the southwest, Tahiti 1,910 miles to the northwest, and Antarctica over 6,000 miles south. The coast seethes with a white ruff of surf – there are no beaches, just cliffs and craggy rockfaces battered by an untempered ocean. Steep bare ridges and deep crevices make the island sit up in the water like a crumpled sheet of steel. Less than a tenth of the land is flat. The few white houses of Adamstown, the only settlement, are faintly discernible among the banana trees and coconut palms.

The islanders are a bizarre hybrid race: tall like Europeans but with Polynesian jet-black hair; dark eyes but fair skin. Their language is a blend of 18th century English and Polynesian. They still call their guns 'muskets'. Once they wore bark cloth, but today the tribal costume is sponsored T-shirts and baseball caps which arrive from well wishers in every mail: 'Bora Bora Yacht Club', 'His and Her Tournament Chub Cay 1983.'

Like characters in a child's game, all the 24 adults on the island wear several hats. Dennis Christian, sixth generation descendant of the mutinous Master's Mate Fletcher Christian, is not only Postmaster, but Rubbish Collector and Tractor Driver Number Three. He lives in a bungalow constructed out of weather boards with a tin roof for catching the rain. His simple home is cluttered with modern appliances – a food processor, blender, electric fryer, two cookers, four industrial freezers, two VCRs. His mother Irma heats up the Pitcairn dish 'pilhi', made from grated sweet potato wrapped in banana leaves, in her microwave. Irma, an avid radio ham, has five electric kettles donated by contacts.

Bounty mania ensures that overseas devotees send a never-ending supply of often useless artefacts, as if hoping they could buy a piece of paradise with them. One charitable consignment contained enough dresses for each girl to receive 20. When an American Adventist congregation saw a video of the barefoot islanders, they shipped out 50 pairs of Reeboks.

With its hotchpotch of donations from outside and rich red volcanic soil, Pitcairn appears a land of plenty. Orange, mango, plantain, grapefruit, avocado and banana trees flourish alongside the ubiquitous coconut. Fresh vegetables are grown in small family plots scattered all over the island. The earth is rampantly fertile.

Lettuce and beans which I sowed from seed were ready to eat within two months. Breadfruit are knocked from the trees with live bullets.

But if you need a can of tomatoes, a battery, or light bulb; if you run out of writing paper; or if the clutch goes on your three-wheeled motorbike, then Pitcairn's situation is brought starkly home to you. You must wait for a passing ship.

Pitcairn lies on the Panama Canal–New Zealand shipping route, and a vessel working that passage will pass within a few miles of the island. But there is no certainty of when the next ship will call; it might be tomorrow, next week, month, or not for several months. In April 1988, 27 ships passed Pitcairn. In the same month three years later, only one ship stopped.

When a ship is sighted offshore, the bell in Adamstown's square is rung five times and the whole island hurries down to Bounty Bay to help launch the longboats, *Tin* and *Tub*. The bay is no more than a slight dent in the iron-bound coastline and provides no natural harbour. Even a few yards from the shore, the water is treacherous, and there have been accidents and deaths. One islander broke his jaw only a few feet from the jetty when the longboat hit a swell.

Island of the Saved

Dea Birkett *meets the descendants of the Bounty mutineers*

The 40-foot boat is packed with people and goods for trade. The men's baskets are heavy with fruit, vegetables and fish which they exchange with the chief steward for prized provisions – oil, eggs, flour. The women carry carvings, stamps, baskets, and Pitcairn T-shirts, which they sell to the visiting crew for US dollars. A model of the *Bounty*, copied from a video of the movie, will fetch $150.

But the islanders' most pressing shortage is not cash, but opportunity. Questions we ask our own children – What would you like to do as a career? What are your ambitions? What do you want to be? – are totally inappropriate on Pitcairn. Betty Christian's two elder daughters have left for further education in New Zealand. It is unlikely they will return. 'The more educated the children are, the less opportunities there are for them here,' says Betty. 'In most cases they move away. We're just left with the old fuddy duddies and the very young, and nothing in between.'

The vast chasm of ocean has sealed Pitcairn's destiny. There is no place where you cannot hear the crash of surf. I soon learnt of the awesome nature of this watery isolation. The long boats were returning in convoy from a trip to uninhabited Henderson Island, where the Pitcairners collect wood for their carvings. It was a rough sea and *Tin* was heavily laden with logs, but the night was clear, we had a compass to steer by, and Pitcairn was only 10 hours away. Then there was an almighty crash. A freak wave had broken over our bow and flooded the boat. The engine, submerged beneath the swirling water, spluttered and stopped. We began to sink.

Around us the dark ocean stretched for 3,000 miles, utterly empty except for *Tub*. We flashed our torches frantically towards her. There was no reply; the long boats must have drifted apart in the heavy seas. Everyone was very quiet and very still; if we moved, we might sink the boat. We sent up a flare.

The red light exploded in the sky, illuminating the black water. In the far distance, only showing when the swell lifted her higher than our boat, we spotted a tiny *Tub*. Soon we saw the helmsman's face and knew we were safe. At a service in the

Breadfruit: watercolour by Sydney Parkinson, painted on Cook's first voyage

Seventh Day Adventist church on the following Sabbath, we thanked God for our safe return. Half the Pitcairn population would have been lost.

The islanders were converted to Adventism by an itinerant American missionary in 1887, and no other faith has been practised since. The pigs, considered unclean meat, were pushed off the edge of the cliffs. Dancing was forbidden, and it became illegal to import cigarettes or alcohol. Any remnants of Polynesian culture, in which suckling pig is the favourite dish and dancing a part of life, were wiped out.

The Pastor is one of two outsiders employed on the island; the other is a Government Adviser and Schoolteacher. There are 12 pupils at his school; they cannot play a soccer match and school plays have to be adapted. 'Snow White and a Handful of Dwarfs' is a favourite.

In such a small place, the good of one is subservient to the good of all. 'Here everyone has been the same, always,' says Kari Young, whose two children attend the one-room school.

Such is the fear of creating differences, that no one person in promoted above another. Although the Postmaster has three Assistant Postmistresses, the Forester has two Assistant Foresters, and the Radio Operator has three other operators under him, no head of department will issue orders to a junior. Betty Christian, like all the islanders, believes this absence of reproach holds the community together. 'Nobody likes to tell somebody else what to do, or say "I don't think you're doing

your job right". That's a good thing.'

But, in practice, incompetence is allowed to flourish. Strong personalities can hold sway unchecked, and crimes are overlooked. Domestic violence, although well testified, goes unprosecuted. Beneath the community spirit seethes a savage undercurrent of frustrated ambitions and justice denied. Disputes are settled in unconventional, often violent ways. When one islander cut down another's banana tree, three-inch nails were in the path outside his home next morning. Police officer Nigger Brown has never made an arrest.

Social censure is expressed through an ancient, effective and most deadly weapon – gossip. One older islander did not approve of a teenage girl smoking, yet she never complained directly to the girl . When the girl came to visit, she laid out an ashtray. But behind the teenager's back, the older islander gossiped – the girl was ruining her health, her boyfriend had caught a horrible cough – hoping it would filter back. In such a closed community, rumours reach the culprit within hours.

Solitude, privacy, independence – the things we may strive for – are as foreign to Pitcairn as supermarkets and subways. Anyone can listen in to your phone calls on the party line, or tune into your radio contacts on the ham radios. They can be at your consultations with the nurse; the Dispensary is just one room. Personal business is considered such public property that the Pitcairnese greeting when you meet on the road is 'About you gwen?' (Where are you going?)

For the children of the *Bounty*, existence on a lonesome rock is not enchanting. Their country, where fewer people live than on a single floor of an average block of flats, is distinctive and extraordinary, but not as the outside world romanticises. Their lives are framed by two unrelenting and unalterable facts – the island is tiny and utterly remote. It is more crucible than melting-pot.

'There's no perfect people, no perfect community,' says Betty Christian. 'It's sort of like the Garden of Eden. There was a serpent there which ruined a perfect place.'

Dea Birkett's 'Serpent in Paradise: Among the People of the Bounty' is published by Picador.

Everyone wants their wedding preserved on video nowadays. **Kjartan Poskitt** *shows how it's done*

I came, I saw, I camcorded

'SUPPOSE I were to put five pounds in your steeple fund? I just need my tripod up here for two more minutes. Be reasonable – I've already got all the guests arriving, so can't you understand that I need continuity of shot for when the bride turns up? I'm not just a common snapper you know, this is a full weddeomentary. Look, if the steeple fund doesn't grab you, how about Christian Aid overseas or something?'

Philistine. That tomb was the perfect vantage point, and the stone angel looked rather magnificent holding my mini spotlights. I wonder where Alice has got to? If she'd met me here as planned, she could have given me a leg up into that tree. That's typical of her – she volunteers my services to some cousins I've never met, then doesn't arrive in time to help.

There's the car! Catch it in the wide shot, zoom in on the approach and – BLAST! Why did he pull up behind that rubbish skip?

'Sorry, excuse me, before she gets out could you pull back a bit? Back about three feet? Well of course it's important, this is the biggest day of her life, she wants it all for posterity doesn't she? All right, please yourself. I just hope she's happy, after all I bet her dress cost a second mortgage alone, not to mention the six hours having each hair individually lacquered. She'll be well chuffed when she sees her grand entrance stepping out from behind a pile of old plasterboards topped off with a burst sofa.'

Of course, there's two sides to every story, and so I musn't let the anxious groom feel he's forgotten. A quick dash inside while the bridesmaids arrange the dress. There he is, obviously with a haircut especially for his big day. Dear oh dear, I wonder if he knew about those boils on his neck? Oh well, that's part of the skill of making a video, you've got to catch those little details that will really

bring back the memories. Funny how the best man is always better looking. Show us the ring, son! Go on, have a bit of fun – balance it on your nose or something. That's a nice shot, trying to cheer the groom up. Poor sod, he's looking more nervous than ever. Oh I see, there's a grating in the floor. Yes, put it back in your pocket, good idea.

That sounds like the wedding march. I'll nip back and get in position for one of my specials, the bride's viewpoint as she comes down the aisle. Her old man looks a bit concerned, better put him at his ease.

'You must be the father – how do you do, Dad? I hope you weren't worried about that old sofa on the skip, I softened the focus and blended it in with the bride's hair. I think you'll be amazed at the result. Now then, you just go on ahead and enjoy the day. Ignore me – I'm invisible, you won't know I'm here.'

Oh dear, I better not leave my tripod outside if everybody is coming in. I'll just tuck it under my arm.

'Hello bridesmaids… Monica and Janet you say? Super. Don't mind me, but as you go down the aisle, I'll be between you. You just keep looking straight ahead being lovely as you are and it'll be magic. All right?'

In we go then. Obviously I want to blend in as much as possible, so I tend to stoop down as I'm walking along and hold my camera over may head. 'Actually, Janet, could you carry my tripod? Just till we get to the altar. And Dad, it's better if you don't look round. Oh, and if you don't mind my saying, try to look a bit happier. If anything you're looking a bit shirty.'

Everything continues to run smoothly. In particular I capture one of my favourite wedding sights, which is people miming to hymns that they've obviously never heard before. Dandruff, fake suntans, and outfits that have seen slimmer occupants are all included in the fun, but now we approach the main business of the day, the wedding vows. Some very delicate camera work needed here if I'm to capture the solemnity of the moment for the benefit of absent friends. That reminds me, where's Alice? Never mind, my job is to be right where the action is so it's time to bring one of my special abilities into play – the knack of being completely unnoticeable. It's something I practise at parties; indeed I find I can stand in a room for hours before anyone so much as looks at me.

Aha, the vicar is cueing me to get into position: '*If anyone knows of any just cause or impediment why these two people may not be joined together in holy matrimony, you are to declare it…*'

I rise to my feet, and at that very instant I hear a strange choking noise. Quickly panning round, I manage to catch the bride's mother on the verge of collapse. Poor old girl, the emotion of the day must be too much for her. As I walk to the front, people look a bit bewildered, but when I take my place beside the vicar with my camcorder they realise I am just as natural a part of the proceedings as he is. We are two professionals working together for a common aim, the only difference being that he's consolidating the marriage in heaven, and I'm consolidating it on videotape. Mind you, the vicar himself is giving me a funny look. In the normal way, I'd offer to sugar him with a few quid towards the brownies, but this one's already proved to be a bit strange in the charity acceptance department.

'Action!' I whisper. 'That means you can get on with it.'

The groom's having trouble getting through his lines. Poor boy seems to have a bit of a stammer. '*With this ring…*' he's said about four times, and my battery warning is flashing.

'Hold it one second,' I say with a reassuring wink. 'I'm just swapping batteries.'

'*With my body I thee worship, with my worldly goods I thee endow,*' rattles off the groom in reply.

Clunk whirr beep, we're up and running again. 'Just one more for the camera,' I smile. 'Ready when you are.'

However the vicar rather huffily turns to deal with the bride. I am just about to protest when…

PREEP! PREEP!

Luckily I have one of those old-type mobile phones that rings properly rather than plays a little melody, which could have been unseemly in the circumstances.

'Alice!… No of course I haven't missed the wedding, I'm right here up by the altar. Are you sure you can't see me? Well you know me, I'm being as discreet as ever. Yes of course I'm sure this is St Michael's church!'

'All Saints,' mutters the vicar, catching me off my guard.

'Well, St Michael has to be one of them, hasn't he?' I reply, somewhat distracted as I notice Dad is whispering to a very large version of himself, presumably some sort of brother. They are pointing at me. The brother leaves his pew and approaches, collecting my tripod from Janet as he passes.

Something about his manner suggests that doesn't intend to hand the tripod over to me in the conventional way.

I wake up to find I'm lying on something very cold. Looking down at me is that stone angel who seems to be holding some black knitting. Good grief – that mess used to be my camcorder! My body quickly sits up, but my brain doesn't. Falling off the tomb I come face to face with a pair of feet.

'Did you get him?' a voice giggles.

'Not half,' comes the reply, 'and he's in a right old state. God knows how he got there.'

What is this? I'm looking down the wrong end of a camcorder!

'Let's send it in to the telly, we could get 50 quid.'

'Lucky we were passing.'

Well! Of all the unprofessional, intrusive, callous… It's people like that who give the rest of us a bad name.

Angus and Jane

ANGUS AND JANE are married, just. Since the Maida Vale flat was sold, Angus has skulked in his Gloucestershire cottage, while Jane has bought a smaller flat near the bookshop where she works. Occasionally they speak on the telephone. More frequently, they speak to each other's answering machines.

When Angus and Jane married four years ago, their friends were delighted but surprised. Jane's first husband had been a powerful, charismatic man, with narcissistic good looks and the morals of a virus. Fatally addicted to cliché, he had succumbed to an acute mid-life crisis in his forties and run off with his secretary.

Angus, by almost comic contrast, was short and rotund, always laughing, a bit of a character. Long widowed, he had survived 35 years in advertising by being a bit of a character, by always laughing, and by manipulating and manoeuvring behind the scenes with unsqueamish ruthlessness. Jane found the combination intriguing, and was willing to overlook his less appealing physical attributes. She had been mourning the loss of her husband – last heard of in Los Angeles with his latest pregnant 25-year-old Nigerian girlfriend – for too long. Angus was good company. And after three decades at the top of his profession, he was rich enough to keep her in a style to which she looked forward to becoming accustomed. Jane was bored with genteel poverty. She still had her St John's Wood flat, the last remaining prize of her divorce settlement, but even that would have to go soon.

'But why don't you just live with him?' trilled her daughters, when she told them that Angus had proposed. Jane could see the logic of their argument, and had no strong moral objection to the idea – both her daughters lived with their boyfriends, and she had never worried about that. But like Elizabeth Taylor, she had long since decided that she was the marrying kind. They put their flats on the market, and prepared for married life.

Jane cannot remember when she first began to entertain doubts, although she now realises that the three-day honeymoon may have been a clue. Immediately after their return, Angus flew on to Hong Kong on an urgent business trip. Jane supervised the transfer of her own and Angus's belongings to the new flat. Several beloved artefacts failed to survive the move. Her cat, angry at the disturbance, urinated over Angus's favourite armchair. These were stressful weeks for Jane. In Hong Kong, Angus's urgent business trip continued indefinitely, all expenses paid.

When Angus finally returned, Jane found him less jolly and entertaining than of old. In public he remained the life and soul. At home he was morose and pedantic.

At first their differences were trivial. He liked his tea in a mug, the strength and consistency of bitumen. She preferred a pot of Earl Grey. He objected to the smell of her cat's litter. She wished he would wash his handkerchieves more often. And so on.

But more fundamental disagreements threatened. Angus now spent most of his days at home. Neither his various consultancies nor his chairmanship of an up-and-coming agency seemed to stretch him terribly hard. Even so, he still expected Jane to cook him dinner every night. Tired after a long day at the bookshop, Jane watched as Angus shovelled the fruits of her culinary skills into his gaping maw. At night, as she lay in bed, she could still hear his furious chewing, and see in her mind's eye flecks of mashed potato splashed across his fleshy lips.

The sex was unfortunate. Perhaps physical attraction would have made a difference after all. Angus's changes of mood were becoming increasingly unpredictable. When Jane bought herself a new coat he trudged around the flat as though a close relative had died. Relations between Angus and the cat declined. The cat spat whenever she saw him. Angus said she was 'vermin'.

When he came home he wiped his shoes not on the mat outside but on her Chinese rug inside. He was a hypochondriac, who became convinced that he had caught shingles from an insect bite, despite no physical evidence of shingles or, indeed, an insect bite.

Worst of all, he was a tightwad. Absurdly generous during their courtship, Angus now hung on to every penny. Before they married, they had agreed that each would be responsible for his or her own immediate expenses, and that Angus would cover the housekeeping. His income, though infinitely mysterious, was known to be by far the greater. Three months after the wedding, Angus proposed that Jane pay half of the housekeeping in the future, as she was rich, and he was finding it hard to make ends meet.

Ah, so that was it, thought Jane. He's after my money. What a shame I haven't got any. Meanwhile Angus was warming to his theme. Why did they need a cleaning woman? Why did Jane bother to work at all? He'd much prefer to have Jane at home all day, cooking all his meals, tending to all his needs…

A week later Jane ejected Angus from the marital bed. The cat developed severe bruising on her lower abdomen, and hid whenever Angus was in the room. Angus spent every weekend in Gloucestershire, alone or with his grownup children. Jane heard a rumour that he had signed over most of his assets to them in the event of a divorce settlement.

Fortunately their lawyers get on famously. **MARCUS BERKMANN**

Peter O'Toole

A man who needs no introduction…
in conversation with **Mavis Nicholson**

Portrait by Jane Bown

Peter O'Toole's study: no desk, two small butler's tables, completely bare walls, bright green carpet, yellow comfy armchair with matching footstool and settee, another settee in deep blue on which the writer sits to write his books in longhand.
I was waiting with trepidation for an ogre who hates interviews, when in sprang a friendly wizard with magical eyes who stood and ate six biscuits straight off, offering me as many if I wished.
I talked, while he had his mouth full of crumbs, telling him I knew he was fiercely private and his two autobiographies proved this, as they were not quite about him. 'I've got an answer to that,' he told me. 'When we start, remind me.'
But I began with a general question first asking him if he was pleased with the reviews of his second volume of memoirs…

I am about to remind you of what you forgot to remember. You said to me, 'The writing isn't about you.' And I was about to tell you what the whole keystone is: 'I am, I am my circumstances.' That is a quotation from a very clever Spanish gentleman whose name I have forgotten. When I came across that phrase, it gave me the ability to write, to start scratching.

Did you have to be a successful actor before you gained the confidence to try writing?
How can one know that? What is certain is that I began to scribble when I was quite young. I didn't take it very seriously then but I have in fact written screenplays and done versions of foreign plays. Though the idea of writing a book… *phaw!* The stamina…

A lot of actors become writers latish - David Niven, Richard Burton, Dirk Bogarde, Kirk Douglas…
William Shakespeare, Ben Jonson, Dryden, Noël Coward. Shall I go on? It's the ideal, isn't it? Particularly in your thirties. John Osborne, Harold Pinter…

But they were actors only briefly.
They only stopped being actors because they became bloody lazy, I think.

What made you start writing your own books? Were you frustrated speaking other people's lines?
It's true to say that it is an awfully big relief to write down my own words rather than memorise somebody else's. It takes longer to memorise than it does to write. One has of course ingested. We have been very lucky. The literature associated with theatre is super. One has had a steady diet of Jonson, Shakespeare, Shaw, Chekhov, Sheridan – you can fill in that list yourself. Even if you are only learning your own bits you are learning solidly good English.

Who is the writer you responded most to?
Different authors mean different things at different times. My first god was Maurice Walsh. For me he was exclusive stuff. All my dreads and uncertainties, he celebrated them.

What were your dreads and uncertainties?

Oh, the usual, coupled with my Irishness in Yorkshire. He celebrates the exile from Ireland and Scotland. Indeed he doesn't touch Wales. He doesn't know Wales. He was a Customs man from Ireland settled in Scotland. And his women! In one's pubescence and adolescence! This wonderful way he described a woman's breast with wine trickling down in *The Road to Nowhere*. That's like knowing the page number of – of the dirty parts! I treasured that passage. I treasured it. And I wouldn't tell anybody. He became my private property. Until I showed him to my mother who loved him too. She adored him. Orson Welles, I discovered later, wanted to make a film of one of his books.

Another book you admired later on was Geoffrey Household's 'Rogue Male'. Your first wife, Sian Phillips, suggested it to you because it was about a plot to kill Hitler and as a boy you plotted doing this, too. In your book you call her your widow. Why?
The word just happened and it seemed peculiarly right. I left it in… And then there was inevitably James Joyce. *A Portrait of the Artist as a Young Man.* I was 15, 16. I had heard that sermon. I'd heard it in St Francis' church from a Monsignor. I'd heard it and here was this chap talking about me again. Better than Maurice Walsh.

Books meant a real lot to you.
Yes they still do. I often read this description 'avid, voracious reader'. Can a tortoise be avid and voracious? If I read a book, it is slow and sensuous. I like to lie in bed and read. It's my favourite, my co-favourite thing. Nothing can be better than to lie in bed with a really good book before I go to sleep.

Being such a loving reader as a child, it must have occurred to you to want to be a writer.
Yes, but poems then. Lots of poems. Lots.

So early on, you had a way with words, didn't you?
Writing – yes.

Meaning as a talker you didn't?
Yes.

Shy?
Yes. To a point. I was never shy with older people, isn't that odd? Nor with my close mates. I have always had good friends – a solid few.

You were evacuated when you very young - sevenish. Did you understand it? Was it explained to you?
Oh yes, very carefully, and I was quite excited about going. Don't forget the mums and dads really (and with reason) were told we were going to be obliterated. According to John Keegan, if Goering had carried on the Blitzkrieg for two more weeks everything would have gone. Manpower gone, machines gone, structure gone. So yes, my mother broke her heart and my father broke his heart. Yes, it was the thing to do. Daddy was working for the Royal Navy. Mummy was Mummy was Mummy. I was very safe, very secure. I thought it was going to be great. It was an adventure. I wasn't homesick – we didn't have one at the time. I just missed my mother and father and sister. That's it. After a few months, they were fed up with it. And I was very happy when the old boy galloped into the yard and said, Come on son, let's go. And we went to the races!

And that's when you were declared a hero.
That's when I wiped the chalk board with pop. They'd run out of water. And I gave them some of my lemonade. My father's mate put me up on his shoulders and said, This is Pat's son.

Your father was an illegal bookie, like they all were in those days.
Of course. The only legal bookmakers were on the track. Then came this dreadful thing called a turf accountant. That's hardly Daddy – shut up in a barn, down an alley. He used to wear this amazing couple of raincoats. He could go through one pocket to another pocket underneath with a weather-eye for the coppers always.

In your first book, you describe getting really incensed with a

teacher who taunted you by calling you O'Foole. Why so mad?
She was a cruel woman and I've always hated cruelty. It was the war, I think, and all those things. The worries of who one was. I used to cling to our name. There was only a knot of four of us, but we were O'Tooles. My father was O'Toole. There were generations of O'Tooles. I don't like the name being messed about with even now.

You threw an inkwell.
Yes into her kisser, into her crock. Then I walked out with her ruler. You are turning me into a child, you know. The incident aroused a well of anger in me which I did not really know that I had – of determination, of vengefulness. I knew that I had to make a bloody stand.

Do you still feel your strong family pull?
Looking at my children I see mothers, fathers, sisters; I see generations; I see ancestors undreamt of. Odd moments when I am taken unaware sometimes… My sister and I were sitting in a room with my nephew, who is a lovely boy. He was only 16 – he's in his middle twenties now. He was doing this… [*wiping along his eyelid*] That was a mannerism of Daddy's.

Daddy died when my nephew was five or so. He can't have aped it. And sometimes I have found myself behaving in a way my father did. I am a bit of a hopeless father, but I think I am a loving father. Really, like my father was. Mummy was entirely loving. Happy as long as Daddy was right and we were right, and as long as she had her books and her theatre and her ciema and her bits and pieces and her mates and later her job. She began to work in the post office as a sorter and she became a boss.

As a child when you were enacting being one of your heroes (eg Robin Hood) you were, without knowing it, practising becoming an actor…?
Yes, as the sergeant major produces his role, as the condemned man produces his role, as the executioner produces his role. That actor in us, the protean, the chameleon, the shape-changer, has fascinated me since a child, still does. But the big thing I began to learn in my second year in RADA was the gulf between acting and performing. That's when one needs this massive amount of technique. And technique must be looked on as art. And it is a superb art to learn… There is a modern day practise of rehearsing in a room, which is destructive. When I began

78

we always rehearsed in a theatre. That is our arena. You start making sounds that fit a playhouse. You can't possibly gauge what you are doing in a room, for acting is speech. Ninety per cent of it is speech and it isn't a question of projecting the voice, darling. That's bollocks. It is making the right shapes to the sound, the right shapes to the body for your work on an angle on a raked stage. You learn sound goes sideways. You can look at someone that way and project that way. I use parallels with cricket. If you put your head over the line of the ball the body will follow. You learn how to move your body, you can't do it in a room.

Have you always been aware that you have enormous physical attraction?
It was brought to my attention when I was quite young, by both men and women.

Did it make you vain?
No. I thought it too. Then, the first time I look in a mirror as a young actor, a professional, in the theatre, there is this face and I can assure you there is no quicker way to disabuse yourself.

You gripped the world with your part as Lawrence of Arabia. Did you understand the man to play him so well?
No. I had a vague idea.

Something from inside you?
Y-e-s, which is what acting is all about.

Something really happened in that part, surely?
It always does. The part chooses you. You have to first absorb the words Absorb them all slowly over and over again. And then they take on. The following morning you wake up and you know how to say them. And when you know how to say them things begin to happen to one's body. It's unbidden. It's talent.

You have been called a hellraiser countless times…
Oh what a bore that is, what a bore!

Do you think you were one?
What I think we were doing was looking

'It's the inscription on dad's tombstone. He won't let mum put "miserable, tight-fisted old bastard" '

for a kind of paradise, for a heaven. We weren't looking for a hell.

You were very much a product of your times (the 50s)…
One of many, many, many thousands.

We won't see the like again, do you think?
I don't know. We were part of another culture. People have always found a device for getting blasted in some form or another. These were the people one tottered round with. In foreign parts you found a bar and knew you were with your own.

You had to give up booze, I read?
That's another myth. No, I chose to. Didn't like the effect on me any more. But to the chaps and the girls who get it right, rock on, say I.

Have you got a proudest moment in your career?
Yes. Walking up the steps of the Theatre Royal, Bristol – stone steps with an iron set of banisters – to join the Bristol Old Vic Company in 1955. Nothing has beaten that, no.

Mine was walking into Broadcasting House to do my first broadcast with Richard Baker on 'Start the Week' - and my mother's voice reminding me that I would be talking to the nation!
I walked in there twice yesterday and felt a bit special. Lovely building. And I have been back last week to where I was brought up: Leeds, the Yorkshire Playhouse, and on the platform with me, my old friend [the actor, Patrick] O'Liver. He in a wheelchair. Both of us reading extracts from my book. As we came off the stage a grumpy man came up and said weren't we going to do a question and answer session? O'Liver said: 'That is your question. No, is your answer.'

If you had your time over again would you have played it the same?
Yes. I have no regrets. Things are regrettable… I am not a French singer!

He fastens his magic eyes on me and gives a slow, loud laugh. Jumps up. Asks if I'd like a cup of tea. Yes please. He returns apologising there is no tea as there is no-one to make it. We settle for a ginger ale.

T he first time I met Geoff Hamilton – who died last summer at the age of 59 – was at, of all places, a Royal Horticultural Society flower show. He looked a bit shy and bemused, not at all the smiling confident fellow I had come to know from *Gardener's World* on television. I went up and introduced myself and explained that I'd like a chance to interview him for an American gardening magazine. After all, he was by far the most famous gardener in Britain, and most Americans – like me before I moved here – had never heard of him. He amiably suggested I pay him a visit at Barnsdale.

Given Hamilton's ubiquity in the gardening media – prime time Friday night television, up to five magazine pieces a month, half a dozen books (each a best-seller) – his almost total obscurity outside the UK was curious. Other famous gardeners – Rosemary Verey, Penelope Hobhouse, Christopher Lloyd, Stephen Lacy and Roy Strong – are known and admired in America, their books read and their lectures attended. But of Geoff – nothing.

It was partly in search of an answer to this riddle that I drove up to Rutland one dim November day a year or so ago, and found Hamilton's house at the end of a muddy and unmarked lane. (The lack of a sign was deliberate, he explained, a matter of self-defence. If he was ever so foolhardy as to hold a garden 'Open Day', 50,000 Hamilton fans might well show up.) Autumn was what passed for a quiet time in Hamilton's schedule. Broadcasts were over for the winter. He had nothing to do but prepare for *Gardener's World* and the next special series, write another book, write one of his weekly pieces for the *Radio Times* or the *Daily Express*, or a monthly one for *Country Living* or *Gardener's World* magazines, supervise the gardeners (three or four working full-time), sleep, eat… A tiger for work, Hamilton had already suffered one heart attack, and was supposedly slowing down.

We walked and talked about gardening and gardening on television. There was no mistaking his enthusiasm for the subject; he had loved growing things since he was a boy, and through years of work as a gardening journalist before becoming a television star. Yet if a man's garden is an

Salt of the earth

expression of his personality, as some would maintain, Hamilton's was a fairly unsettling mixture. The nearest thing to landscaping was a long grass alley flanked by perennial beds, with an urn at the far end. For the rest, there was a whole array of small square gardens framed by fences and hedges and little copses of trees, the horticultural detritus of many television programmes – two 'cottage gardens', a *potager*, a partially-finished 'hermitage' garden, a *parterre*. These were kept out of sentiment and the possibility that they might come in handy in a future series. Clearly, Barnsdale was a garden that meant business.

And so did Hamilton. He spent a lot of time, he admitted, trying to get the level right for his programmes and books. 'You have to show authority, of course, but you also have to appear to be learning. There are too many different kinds of gardeners, and the only thing they have in common is interest. Getting the level right is a constant dilemma. In the end, you have to make a programme for yourself.'

Anybody who spent Friday nights watching *Gardener's World* knows that this meant plenty of basic (if ingenious) how-to items from building a compost bin to tips for potting up narcissi, along with notably un-woolly commentary on horticultural practicalities. You wouldn't be likely to find Geoff wandering through Sissinghurst languidly discussing the *Rosa longicuspis* or comparing *Carya illinoiensis* with *C. myristiciformis*. On the contrary, he seemed far more at home on an allotment, possibly chatting with old George Flatt, the ancient Suffolk pensioner he found for the 'Cottage Garden' series. Hamilton's hypothetical viewer was 'a 65- to 70-year-old widow who knows a bit about horticulture and how to use a hammer, saw and screwdriver'. I suggest-

ed that this approach put him at odds with the *gratin* of British gardeners and gardening writers, what he himself called 'the Rosemary Vereys of this world'.

'Those people are great artists,' he replied. 'No question about it. But they're daunting. What worries me about them is that they give you the feeling that you ought to be able to do what they do, and make you feel bad if you can't. I want to make gardening accessible. We need the peak as something to aspire to, but I want to broaden its base.' He was cheered by the fact that RHS membership had 'rocketed' in recent years, but it was not difficult to sense an undertone of annoyance with the organisation, long identified as an exclusive club for lady and gentlemen gardeners. His own relationship with it had its ups and downs. He treasured the memory of the time one of the 'toffs' complained that *Gardener's World* had 'lost its way', because 'they were always talking about potatoes'. Perhaps better than most people, Hamilton knew that potatoes were exactly what his viewers wanted to talk about.

Ironically, given the chance, a lot of American gardeners would have probably felt the same way. The familiar problem is that potatoes and allotments are rarely associated with Britain in the mind of Americans dosed on BBC costume dramas, tales of country house life, and other anachronisms. My fellow countrymen are instinctively drawn instead to what you might call the aristocracy of the spade, after all, Americans are terrible snobs.

It's a pity. Just as the vast majority of British gardeners embraced him with enthusiasm, Geoff Hamilton would probably have 'gone down a treat' (to use one of his favourite locutions) in Terre Haute or Ypsilanti, if some broadcaster had tried. In any event this American will miss him.

*Beauty… Dacia (Winifred Allwood)
her performances captivated
audiences in 'Chu Chin Chow'*

In 1915 we were by far the least distinguished residents of Abercorn Place, north west London. On the other side of the road, for example, were the Huxleys, with their sons Julian and Aldous. ('Charming people,' my mother told her friends, 'they live opposite us in St John's Wood' – we never actually met them.)

Then on the same side of the road as the Huxleys lived the famous actor, Oscar Asche, at the time playing the title role in the record-running musical *Chu Chin Chow*. Every day his vast figure could be seen squeezing himself into his shiny car, which lurched ominously as he sat down. Opposite Oscar Asche was the home of the portrait painter Briton Riviere.

We didn't meet that family either at the time, but many years later I became friendly with their son Raymond, a sculptor,

who had the honour to be my eldest son's godfather. Most importantly of all, between the Rivieres and ourselves was Dacia.

Dacia's real name was Winifred Allwood. She lived in a small studio flat, a pretty, welcoming place, typical of 'artistic' people with little money. Stained floors, occasional rugs, divans with brightly coloured cushions. Winifred lived with her mother, who my parents knew well. (There was no evidence of husband or father.)

In the early evenings she would travel, by two buses, to His Majesty's Theatre where she became Dacia, the leading ballerina in *Chu Chin Chow*. She didn't know Oscar Asche – but sometimes he would nod in her direction.

To me, Winifred was Dacia all the time. I was five years old and Dacia was 18. She was very beautiful, graceful and olive-skinned, with an enchanting smile and black hair that had blue lights. I adored her, she filled my day-time thoughts and night-time dreams. She was a goddess, yet wonderfully human. She would take me to Regent's Park to feed the ducks and, in summer, to wander in the fragrant rose garden.

On winter afternoons when the bell of the muffin man rang in Abercorn Place, we would issue from our respective homes to buy crumpets, which we preferred to muffins, and sometimes we could go back to Dacia's flat to toast them at the little gas fire. Butter (or, I suppose, margarine) was thickly spread and would run down our laughing faces. One day I learned that my parents had booked matinee seats for *Chu Chin Chow*. I don't know what I expected, I just knew that I was about to enter Dacia's magic world.

I remember very little of the show

before Dacia appeared – huge barrels in which 40 thieves were to be drenched in boiling oil; a little shoemaker on the left side of the stage singing 'I cobble all day, and I cobble all night'. A scene of flashing silks and satins – and on came the slaves, dancing, twinkling in chiffon, and the Emperor's favourite slave, Dacia. She was a vision, I was spellbound.

In came the Emperor, Chu Chin Chow, himself a monstrous figure, in blue satin robes, wearing a little black hat and pigtail. He advanced towards Dacia, as if asking for something: laughingly she shook her head and backed away. He followed, angry, menacing. I was getting frightened – oh why didn't she do whatever it was he wanted? But now, still laughing, she shook her head 'No, no, no'. He pushed her to the centre of the stage. She was cowering, hands up to her face.

The other slaves gathered round and hid her from view. And what was this? The Emperor raised his hand and held a gleaming sword, there was a roll of drums and down came the sword. Dacia had been beheaded. I wept. I howled. Hurriedly my parents got me into the street. 'It's all right darling, she's quite all right – it was only pretend.' And they took me into her dressing room. There indeed was Winifred, quite all right, taking off her make-up and laughing. I continued to cry. I was told

…and the beast: Oscar Asche, a monstrous figure in blue satin robes

The day my world collapsed

Honor Wyatt *recalls the terrifying moment her neighbour and childhood heroine was beheaded*

much later that my father had said: 'Do you really think she would let them cut off her head every night and twice on Wednesdays, no matter what they paid her?'

But I had no sense of humour. My world had collapsed. Nothing was ever the same again. Winifred continued to be affectionate and to feed the ducks with me and toast crumpets. Winifred was very kind, but Dacia was dead.

THE YEARS PASSED as they tend to do and, in 1950, I was a talks producer on BBC Radio's *Woman's Hour*.

One day I found among the unsolicited scripts on my desk a charming piece in the first person about the life of a small bit player in undistinguished films. It had both humour and sadness and I liked it.

With the script was a letter beginning 'Dear Honor, I wonder if you remember me?' It was signed Winifred Allwood.

The editor of *Woman's Hour* shared my liking for the talk and I wrote suggesting that Miss Allwood should come to Broadcasting House for a voice test; at this time it was customary for inexperienced broadcasters to go through this ordeal.

I waited in the entrance hall at the appointed time, and in she came. I knew her at once. The slender figure and lovely legs, the dark hair streaked with grey was like a crown. Her clothes neat but shabby. She looked at me enquiringly, 'Honor?' And I went towards her with arms outstretched, 'Dacia!'

She looked at me, eyes wide and touched by tears, and said, 'I haven't been called Dacia for more than 30 years.'

She was not a natural broadcaster, but the charm of her script came over well. In due course she gave the talk on *Woman's Hour*. After the programme I went down to the entrance hall with her, as was the custom and said: 'Thank you for a lovely talk, you did it beautifully.'

She smiled and hesitated: 'And about the… that is… ?'

'Your cheque will be with you at the end of the week,' I assured her.

She nodded and put her hand on my arm. 'Dear little Honor'. And Dacia, bowing slightly to the commissionaire, who opened the door for her, stepped gracefully into Portland Place. I never saw her again.

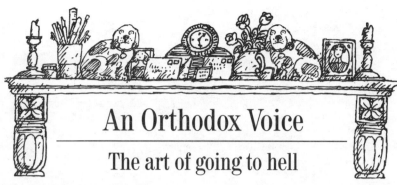

An Orthodox Voice
The art of going to hell

FELLOW GUESTS at a friend's house in Wiltshire were a couple I called the Bourgeoisie. He was plump and rosy with that oily glow that rich men often give out; she was neurotic in the way of many rich women. They were professionally involved in modern art, and it was not just their business but – in a very real sense, as we Protestants now say – their religion. They took it quite seriously and they spoke of today's fashionable artists with the reverence that was once devoted to holy saints. On a stupid impulse, or possibly to make trouble, our host showed them the little book of Orthodox Voice columns published last Christmas. With amiable condescension the Bourgeoisie glanced within it, and I suddenly realised what was going to happen. The man's face went redder, he frowned and pointed out something to his pair. He had hit upon my article about the poor Saatchi brothers, expressing sympathy for the way they have been treated by slick international art dealers, who have made them bolster the market in rubbish and have caused the Saatchis to look foolish by exhibiting trashy art gimmicks in their pretentious gallery.

The Bourgeoisie assimilated all this in a second. I knew they were going to be angry and I also knew what they were about to say. It duly followed. My belittling of the Saatchis' artwork was a sign of uncouth ignorance. Did I not know that every great artist throughout history had been ignored by contemporaries and scorned by his generation? If people like me did not appreciate the experimental art of today, that was a mark in its favour. The Bourgeoisie couple were members of the Art Elite, makers of reputations, bestowers of grants and prizes, but I was struck by the paradox that they also regarded themselves as rebels. One of their heroes was Damien Hirst, notorious artificer of pickled livestock. Applauded and reward-ed by the official institutions, he is Britain's international art star, the Gazza of our team, the Lord Leighton of our day. No one could be more firmly embedded in the 'establishment'. Yet, in the eyes of the Bourgeoisie he was a radical outsider, exciting, up-and-coming, the man to back. Only a truculent reactionary like myself could be sceptical towards his genius. They kept insisting that I was 'shocked' by Hirst's manifestations, but the shock was all on their side and it was difficult to calm them down. These people have done something very clever, having their cake and eating it, dominating the art establishment and being at the same time anti-establishment progressives. A trick they learnt from the Marxists.

The myth they build on is ridiculous. Most artists regarded as 'great' in their day – including that ruthless, egocentric communist, Picasso – were not neglected but held in honour during their lives.

As for Hirst, his colleagues and promoters, I was enlightened about their activities by a New York art critic who told me that the trade name for their movement is Media Art. The art is designed for no other purpose that to attract attention, and the more cutely original they are, the more stupid and disgusting, the more they shock and scandalise the honest public, the better they serve their purpose.

It is a dirty business and those who engage in it, as artists, dealers, promoters or curators, are thereby degraded and can never really be happy. The arts are highly influential and with that lies heavy responsibility upon those who practise them.

An artist who misuses his talents to corrupt or swindle his contemporaries is a blasphemer against the Holy Spirit. If he depicts the world as hellish he will have a corresponding experience of it, and however much flattery and riches he attracts, he will end up in hell for good. **JOHN MICHELL**

From Rebecca West in Mexico

Hacienda Uxmal, Uxmal, Yucatan, Mexico
November 24th, 1969

Dear Mrs Rowe,

I write in surroundings of positively oriental luxury, the hotel here has a wonderful palace garden in the middle of which is a swimming pool – and this I have just emerged from after 20 minutes of delight. But my failure to communicate must make you feel I don't deserve such pleasure. I have been able to do almost nothing of what I went to Mexico City to do. I can't even get to a museum that is only about half a mile away – I patronised a local travel agent who made a complete mess of this tour, and had to see her five times! But this journey has been well worth it in spite of everything.

We went down from Mexico City over a white mist that looked like a snowfield with the volcanoes shining above it, which was too beautiful, and landed in the town of Villahermosa, a farming town – and drove to Palenque in pouring rain. The drive was through beautiful country with herds of wonderful Cebu cattle (the oriental kind with humps on their backs). The village of Palenque was in a state of curious decay – everything was muted. The hotel was unbelievable – quite clean, but the rooms were like cells, the central courtyard garden, the patio, had a cottage in it which had either not been finished or had collapsed, one was not sure which, and had only a whole wall and a partition wall, so that one looked into a family lying in bed in a bedroom. There was also a wooden drawbridge suspended over a void where the floor of the ground floor had been taken away, over a cellar filled with water. The roof had also gone so the drawbridge was in the open air. It led to a door with a very new Yale lock, which however opened to nothing at all but a road. There was no food in the hotel except stale rolls and a tin of ham and instant coffee, which they made with tepid water.

The only person who tried to get things going was the official guide to Palenque tours, a grim looking man who had given up life as a sailor in the Norwegian merchant service to be a guide here because he believed the Mayas to be the lost ten tribes of Israel. We drove off to the ruins in pelting rain the next morning and could not visit all of them because they were flooded, but they were quite gorgeous – you see what seems a lot of hills covered with trees, but they are buildings that have been covered over by the jungle – only 14 of them have been excavated. They are graceful beyond belief, they seem to float, and the sculptures are most beautiful. I don't regret the 24 hours of wet and cold and unsatisfied hunger. When we went on to Meruda the journey took us hours and was wonderful. Meruda is entrancing – it is a perfect set for a comic opera, all the houses are pink and green and blue and the Merudians go about in 18th century carriages.

The hotel is as good as the best Italian hotels and a quarter of the price – the food there and at Villahermosa was marvellous, the fish is peculiarly good and most elaborately cooked. I found when I got here that all my pants but one and a slip had been stolen at Palenque and I had some amusing shopping. I was told that society ladies in Meruda often wear no pants at all, which seemed to me peculiar.

We went today to a ruined abbey close to the sea and found the well which had been the city centre and a most beautiful pool, covered with lily pads over which yellow butterflies in great profusion were flying and dipping and sunning, with some gaily suited Mexican boys skylarking. Then we had a drive here, after a very bad lunch at a restaurant which kept a zoo in the kitchen premises – an alligator, several sorts of racoon, a fox and a very large panda.

It is virtually impossible to get stamps just now, as there is a General Election and it has had the anxious result that for days the post offices have been closed! But this is a very civilised hotel and I hope this will reach you. I can't tell you what a relief it is to know you are there! Blessings, *R W*

Nothing Like A Dame

Gill McLaren Rowe *recalls her year's engagement as personal assistant to Dame Rebecca West.*
Illustrations by **Paul Hogarth**

It was through one of those 'friend of a friend of a friend' introductions that I came to be secretary/PA to Dame Rebecca West for a year or so from 1969. She had not been very worried when I confessed that I had read very little of her work, finding it hard to follow her style of writing. Her only comment had been, 'At least you're honest.' She also took it for granted that I could type, write shorthand and manage her accounts. Her main interest was in the fact that I had done the same thing for Katie Boyle a few years earlier and she wanted to know all about her.

Dame Rebecca, or Dame Cecily

Andrews, or Dame Cecily Fairfield, as she was variously known in private life, had recently lost her husband, the merchant banker Henry Andrews. She had neither the will nor, I think, the wherewithal to continue living in Ibstone House with its indoor and outdoor staff, and moved to a large, inconveniently laid out flat in Kingston House North, Princes Gate, not far from the Albert Hall and within sight of the gardens of the American Ambassador's residence – she had met the Kennedys pre-War and was very fond of telling everyone of the glory days there. Her long time companion and personal secretary had taken the opportunity to

retire and go to live with her daughter in Australia. That was where I came in.

The flat was crammed with furniture from Ibstone House, a lifetime of priceless glass, china and cutlery from years of entertaining, and pictures – pictures covering every wall of every room, mostly originals and easily identifiable as Picassos, Dufys and other, older, artists. Dame Rebecca would proudly point out which were gifts from the artists and which she had 'acquired'. I think she had been good at 'acquiring' objects that caught her eye. The fireplace in the drawing room was made of outstandingly beautiful 18th century hand-painted,

exquisitely carved porcelain, brought from Ibstone House, which she told me she had seen in a bombed house during the war and paid some men £5 to take out and carry away for her!

This amazing old lady lived her life exactly as it pleased her. I would arrive at about 10am each day and let myself in, picking up the post. She was invariably still in bed with the newspapers, a tray of tea and a pair of scissors, industriously cutting out items of interest. She would call out as soon as she heard me, going straight into a conversation about what she was interested in and leaving me to pick up the thread as best I could.

85

Although she kept an engagement diary it didn't mean much, since she would change her mind from hour to hour – but woe betide anyone who let her down! There was a telephone in every room, even the bathroom, and Dame Rebecca would wander from room to room, picking up the nearest telephone to call someone as the fancy took her and yelling at me to get off the line if I was in the middle of a call. While at home she would drink tea or coffee and eat biscuits without stopping, talking all the time and spitting out biscuit crumbs as she spoke. I soon got used to wiping out the mouthpiece when I used the phone.

Unless Dame Rebecca had a morning appointment she would take her time about getting up, having a bath, wandering around in her underwear and talking, talking, always talking. She walked with a curious rolling movement as both legs were swollen and her feet overlapped her shoes. Her hair had thinned with age and when anyone was expected, or she was going out, she would jam her wig on her head anyhow. I think it gave her a degree of confidence to feel it was there, although it looked no more natural than if she was wearing a hat. Her eyes were dark brown and deep set, and she saw a great deal more than many people realised until they read her books and articles. Her favourite scent was Hermes 'Caleche' which she used lavishly, sometimes sending passers-by reeling.

Although careless of her appearance, Dame Rebecca could be ruthless over what many people would not worry too much about. New curtains had been ordered for the drawing room as she was not happy with those brought from Ibstone House. They were hand made from a beautiful gleaming, oyster coloured silk material, stiffened and lined to hang in precise folds and so heavy that it took two men to lift each one. They had been sent back several times as Dame Rebecca found infinitesimal faults with them, but one day the men from the makers came to fit the poles and adjust the cords before the curtains were hung. The two women who had made the curtains came too, to make sure everything was alright.

When the curtains were all in place – and the windows went round two sides of the drawing room – the foreman demonstrated to Dame Rebecca how the cords worked, one to close them and one to open them, with a firm but gentle pull. Cutting the poor man short in mid-explanation, she took hold of the first cord to hand and yanked hard. Nothing happened and she yanked again. She had pulled the wrong cord and the effort she put into it pulled the pole off the bracket and the end of the curtain off the pole. Uttering one word, 'No!!!' Dame Rebecca walked out of the drawing room, slamming the door. The workmen, the curtain makers and I stood

looking at each other until her voice was heard calling me from the study. She was on the telephone to the curtain company. 'Idiots, dolts, buffoons,' she was saying. 'Send me someone immediately who can do a proper job. And they can take the curtains away, they're ruined.' The curtains were hung eventually, but not without a great deal of fuss and complaining, and all the time I was with her she maintained that they had not been put up properly!

Not many days went by without guests for luncheon, most of them well known in either the literary or theatrical world. Dame Rebecca employed a daily cook/housekeeper, a short, round, temperamental Portuguese woman who wore flowered overalls and gesticulated with knives to illustrate her point. She was not an outstanding cook, but could produce a decent lunch given enough time.

I enjoyed the lunches for the company and the conversation – not that I joined in a great deal, but it was a pleasure to listen. I remember the day the Muggeridges came. Both Malcolm and Dame Rebecca talked non stop, neither listening to the other but each pausing politely every now and then. Theatrical guests such as Michael Denison and Dulcie Grey were also present from time to time. Dame Rebecca was fascinated by Barry Humphries before he became well known as Dame Edna Everage and invited him to tea one afternoon to find out more about him.

When I arrived one morning she greeted me with the news that an old friend, Charles Curran the journalist, was taking her to see *Hair* that evening. She said she didn't know whether or not she really wanted to go and thought she would not enjoy it, but as he had been lucky enough to get tickets she felt she should, and anyway they were going to dine first. Privately I wondered what two such elderly people would make of the 'full frontal' shocker, but I should have known better. The next morning when I asked tentatively how she had enjoyed *Hair* she replied dismissively with the usual mouth full of biscuits that they had left during the interval because it was very boring, the music was not all that good and the young

She would jam a wig on her head. . . it gave her a degree of confidence to feel it there

men not worth looking at – 'too thin and scrawny'!

Although Dame Rebecca could be kind and generous to those she liked (and who conformed to her ways), she 'used' people. She did not say it in so many words, but it was obvious that she considered herself intellectually far superior to the majority of people around her. She had a number of friends, mostly widows like herself or sad elderly ladies who had never married, whom she managed for their own good. Some of them tried to stand up to her, but even they usually gave in for the sake of peace and quiet.

Then there were the ladies who were invited for afternoon tea – they were not intellectually stimulating enough for a luncheon – and brought little gifts of a book or a few flowers. It was obvious that pennies mattered to them, but although the presents were gushed over, as soon as the front door closed behind the guest they would literally be kicked into a corner with an unflattering comment. I rescued the sad little posies and gave them a place of honour in the study where I worked, which usually called forth a derogatory remark about the giver when noticed.

She also tired of people easily – her swans turned into geese very quickly, although she still gave them to believe that all was sweetness and light. Following the Spanish maid incident, related below, I heard her refer to me several times on the telephone as 'the ineffable Mrs Rowe'. To my face I was still 'my dear Gill – I don't know how I'd have managed without her in this dreadful time'.

Although outwardly contemptuous of conventional Christianity, about which she claimed to know a great deal, Dame Rebecca was profoundly interested in the Russian Orthodox Church and often attended services there, being on visiting terms with the Archbishop. The Chief Rabbi was another acquaintance who was useful for argument and discussion.

I typed manuscripts on an extremely old and unreliable typewriter, including Dame Rebecca's articles for the *Sunday Telegraph* and other publications, but there was not really much writing going on. She was fascinated by the Scottish poet William McGonagall of 'Bridge over the River Tay' fame, and spent hours in the

'More E, vicar?'

British Library researching him with the idea of a book, but this didn't get very far. Most of her thoughts were on visiting America and Mexico to gather material for her new book, subject unspecified, visit friends and fulfil outstanding engagements.

She was also on the selection panel for the Booker Prize that year and spent days in bed reading the nominated books (which I read, too). There were long telephone discussions with the other judges and eventually Bernice Rubens won with *The Unelected Member* – not Dame Rebecca's first choice by a long shot.

She decided eventually that she would go to New York and Mexico over Christmas 1969. There was no point in keeping on a cook/housekeeper, so she managed to dismiss the Portuguese lady with financial inducements. I was to manage everything while she was away and Augustina, the Spanish maid, would stay on to keep the flat clean. Visits to her solicitor, the bank, her publisher and doctor were all arranged to get ready for the trip, and tickets to New York from Heathrow were eventually settled after a good many false starts. I packed for Dame Rebecca, who had a mind above such mundane matters – and had probably had a maid to do it for her for many years – and on the appointed day drove her to Heathrow with her elder sister, Dr Fairfield, and her travelling companion, Lady Vansittart (the widow of the British Ambassador in Paris between the wars).

One of the little friends had also made the effort to go to Heathrow and gave her a paperback book of Thelwell's cartoons 'to keep you from being bored on the flight'. As soon as the friend had turned away, Dame Rebecca tossed the book into the nearest waste bin with the comment, 'As if I'd look at something like that!' I like Thelwell, so I rescued it and tucked it into my handbag, both for my own benefit and because I thought the friend deserved better. Dame Rebecca merely sniffed, but I think it finally confirmed her opinion of my intellectual level! After watching her sister and Lady Vansittart disappear towards the VIP lounge Dr Fairfield grabbed my arm and said, 'Thank goodness, that's that!' She enlivened the journey home by telling me scandalous stories about her sister's early life – which I can't remember.

Once I had cleared up the odds and ends left by the controlled chaos of Dame Rebecca's departure there was not a lot to do. I arrived at the flat each morning, opened the post and dealt with the correspondence, answered the telephone and made calls and, once Dame Rebecca's letters began to arrive, carried out her instructions. Augustina came each morning, vacuumed, dusted and polished like a whirling dervish for a couple of hours and left at lunch time. She was a little round dumpy figure dressed all in black apart from an old brown overcoat that looked like army surplus.

She spoke only enough English to communicate with anyone on a very basic level and always said goodbye to me in Spanish while taking a holey pair of woollen gloves out of her coat pocket and ramming her hands into them. She never carried a bag of any sort and stuck her hands in her pockets as I closed the front door after her. There was only one entrance to the flat, through the front door.

In the New Year of 1970, in common with thousands of others, I succumbed to the flu epidemic and had to stay at home for a week or so. I telephoned the Head Porter at Kingston House to tell Augustina that I was ill and she need not go in every day. She did not have a key, so a porter would let her into the flat and lock up after her, pick up any post and generally keep an eye on things. When I returned to work the normal routine was resumed until Dame Rebecca returned home.

I went to Heathrow to meet her and waited for her to come through Customs, suddenly seeing this almost completely unrecognisable, disorientated figure shambling towards me, completely submerged under a Mexican straw hat – rather out of place in London in mid-winter! I think she must have been jet-lagged as well as having partaken lavishly of the airline's hospitality. When I had got her back to the flat and tucked her into bed I left her to sleep off the effects of who knows what.

It took her several days to recover, but then she started to wander round the flat in the old familiar way, with one breath complimenting me on having coped while she was away and with the next complaining about the Christmas cards and presents waiting for her. (Most of the presents were dumped on my desk – 'to do what you like with them, I don't want them'. My family enjoyed several boxes of Carlsbad plums among other delicacies!)

About a week later I arrived one morning to find Dame Rebecca still in bed but surrounded by plastic bags full of necklaces – some valuable, and some downright tatty. She immediately demanded where a certain jade necklace was and I could only say I hadn't seen it. 'It's in one of the chests of drawers in one of the spare rooms,' she said, and then began a hunt through the spare bedrooms and the rooms

in the maids' quarters, all crammed with furniture from Ibstone House. Dame Rebecca demanded the inventory for the contents of the flat, which turned out to be at her solicitors. I had not even known there was one, let alone seen it. However, her memory for her possessions was formidable and when we checked against the inventory we found an incredible amount of things missing, from jewellery to pictures, linen, china and glass, pots and pans and other sundry items. Naturally, the police were called and I felt completely responsible for the whole thing, although Dame Rebecca said she didn't blame me. There was absolutely no sign of forced entry into the flat, but as the only people who had keys apart from Dame Rebecca were the Head Porter and I, we both felt we were prime suspects!

Augustina had been 'let go' while Dame Rebecca was recovering from her journey, as she had decided she couldn't stand the sight of the small black figure around the place any longer. The police were interested to hear about her and got her address from the agency which had supplied her. When they went there they found an Aladdin's cave. All Dame Rebecca's possessions were there, crammed into the room in which she lived together with innumerable items from hotels, etc, where she had worked in the past, including a dozen brand new rubber hot water bottles, hundreds of salt and pepper pots and piles of linen.

Nothing she had taken had been sold. She was a compulsive kleptomaniac. I think she was deported back to Spain, where she was also wanted by the police. But the mystery remains – how did she get even the small things out of the flat and past the porters, let alone large items such as pictures, when she never had even a shopping bag? The police found the old brown coat she always wore, suspecting poacher's pockets, but there was nothing.

D ame Rebecca gradually came to realise what I had suspected for some time, that although she would carry on writing her *Sunday Telegraph* and other articles, it was very unlikely she would produce another book. She was old and tired, and everything was becoming an effort. Several times I took my car to work to drive her to Windsor (a favourite place) to do a little shopping, but she was even losing interest in these outings. Each afternoon I left her settled in the drawing room with a tray of tea – and biscuits! – in front of the television watching *Crossroads*, which fascinated her. One day she asked me if I wanted to continue and I confessed that I had been wondering how much longer it would be worth coming. She said that the daughter of some old friends lived just round the corner off Exhibition Road and would be glad to come for a few hours whenever she wanted a little typing done. We agreed it would be best for everyone.

I was sorry to leave, despite all the ups and downs, but we parted on good terms. From time to time she would telephone me 'just for a chat, my dear Gill' – usually at *the* most inconvenient moment, the 'chat' turning into a monologue that went on for a very long time!

'Hang on! Somebody's not cheating!'

90° South

Direct from the igloo of our own Antarctic Amazonian, **Sara Wheeler**

It's just one damned thing after another in an igloo. You struggle out of the sleeping bag to solve one inescapable problem and a battalion of others queue up for recognition. Only one week in and I'm already plotting revenge on the Inuit race.

To come clean straight off, I don't actually have to live in an igloo; there's a perfectly good mountain tent lurking in my kit. But, hell, I'm in Antarctica, and I spent two days building the igloo, though I admit to a ton of help from the team of testosterone-laden seismic geologists with whom I'm camping, the weather having temporarily buggered up their chances of setting off bombs. Building work has the dangerous side-effect of creating a false sense of security, however, as carting all those ice-bricks around means you get dead hot, and the igloo feels pleasantly cool for a brief and treacherously agreeable spell. The truth is that it was 10 below centigrade when I turned in each night and shot up to a tropical eight below by the time I forced myself out of the bag in the morning. 'Ah, yes,' say the legion of bearded Antarctic igloo-fanciers one stumbles upon in these remote camps. 'That's because you're alone. You need to get at least one other person in there with you.' A few nights of quiet frozen desperation and I started looking at The Beards in a new light. I had a party in the igloo one evening, sacrificing my only bottle to the cause. Nobody stayed very long because you couldn't move without brushing your head against the wall, precipitating a rush of ice crystals down the back of the neck.

The other thing, or one of the other things, is that you have to take so many items into the bag to prevent freezing that there's barely room to get in yourself. Down here you always need your water bottle in with you, but on the West Antarctic ice sheet it's pretty parky, and in crowd the babywipes (the polar substitute for washing), batteries for the tape recorder, camera, underwear for the next day and any odd scientific equipment that happens to be loitering in the igloo. It's like sleeping in a drawer.

Having said all that, when I crawl out each day and blink up at the Hockney-blue lid of sky and the ice-crystal sundogs shimmering alongside the high sun, and when I walk up my ice steps to the fluttering Union Jack The Beards made on my first day, and crunch onto the Welcome mat carved in the snow, and when I look out over the dazzling plateau and scan the 360-degree horizon, and I see the curvature of the earth, as if I were in space, then, at that moment each day, I thank God out loud for bringing me to the most heartbreakingly beautiful place on earth, and I forget about the cold and the endemic discomfort of Igloo Life.

Like all jobs, being a travel writer in Antarctica has its pros and cons. It's nippy, you don't get to put on clean clothes much and you have to pee in front of assorted Beards. It really isn't suitable for the venerably aged as it involves a lot of hard physical work, and also Steradent freezes. But you get to see stuff that makes you realise you never really saw anything before. I believe the rest of my life will be preoccupied with getting over Antarctica, or at least assimilating it.

I arrived at the South Pole 82 years to the day after Amundsen, and hung around there until after Christmas as a guest of the small American scientific community based at Amundsen-Scott Station. At 90 degrees South I discovered a blow-up photo of Elvis standing on the snow and a large arrow indicating Graceland, and at the Geographic Pole a compass with every point showing north had been drilled into the hard ice.

Oldies contemplating a brisk visit to the South Pole take note: any official guests considered past their sell-by date are followed around by a doctor carrying oxygen tanks and cardiac paraphernalia. If the Americans had been here in 1912 they would have been on Scott's back, no doubt. And he was only 41.

Talking of Scott, I made a pilgrimage to his Cape Evans hut, occupied by the *Terra Nova* expedition between January 1911 and January 1913 and then two years later by Shackleton's wretched Ross Sea party. This is an oldie Nirvana, replete with an array of domestic products guaranteed to stimulate a Proustian rush, from Fry's cocoa tins, blue-and-orange Huntley and Palmer

biscuit barrels and striped Atora suet boxes to stacks of Findon haddock. In the fly of a cracked book (Kipling, of course), inscribed in a wistful inmate's spidery hand, I read Milton's 'When will the ship be here / Come sing to me'. Was it the half-spent candle, the hole in the toes of a boot, the slipper carelessly tossed aside? I almost turned around to see them tramping back, the clapped-out dogs at their heels and lofty aspirations in their hearts.

At Cape Crozier I found the remains of the stone igloo built by Birdie Bowers, Edward Wilson and Apsley Cherry-Garrard on their epic journey to collect Emperor penguin eggs in 1912, described later by Cherry in *The Worst Journey in the World*. A 25-knot wind was blowing there in the saddle of the mountains, and when I lay down in the igloo I thought of them: it was night all the time during their five-week trip, the temperature was 40 below and the tent blew away. 'But we kept our tempers,' wrote Cherry later, 'even with God.'

One day, a shiny red ship appeared in the sea ice off the Ross Ice Shelf. It was an American icebreaker circumnavigating the continent, and the captain sent a helicopter over to get me (ah, the advantages of being the only travel writer for several thousand miles!). When I landed on deck the crew had just been granted ice liberty and I watched them run down the gangplank, whooping,

and mark out a football pitch on the ice. It was a gratifying moment: in 1911 Herbert Ponting filmed Scott's men doing exactly the same thing, a charming scene he immortalised in his documentary *90° South*, recently released on video.

I often see exactly what Ponting so poignantly describes to us in those familiar images, and it is that timeless immutability that elevates Antarctica to the status of a symbol: it represents all that we are not in our sloughs of misery and fickle concupiscence. It gives us hope; it is the perfect tabula rasa for our vision of what lies beyond it all.

This is what it has become for me in the brief four months I've lived on the ice, though I believe you can experience that, and come here, without taking off your slippers or leaving your plump armchair.

Shackleton, perhaps the greatest polar explorer of them all, wrote in his account of his *Nimrod* expedition to Antarctica, 'We all have our own great white south,' and after all, the land of the imagination is the most beguiling country of all.

Sara Wheeler's book, Travels in a Thin Country, a journey through Chile, is available in paperback from Abacus. Her Antarctic adventure, Terra Incognita, is published by Jonathan Cape.

Video
Larry Adler

Dead Poets Society *(1989)*

Call me a cynic (Lawrence Cecil Cynic) but I cannot see a similar film being made today. It is mainly about academic idealism and the glory of knowledge for its own sake. Robin Williams gives an astonishing performance as a teacher of English in a boys prep school, eager to have his pupils express themselves, to see and understand the beauty of poetry. 'What is the purpose of language?' he asks. 'To communicate,' replies one student. 'No,' says Williams, in his role as the teacher, John Keating, 'it is to help you to think for yourself.' This especially appeals to me because I have tried to instil in my own children three principles:

1. Think for yourself.
2. Guilt is personal.
3. Where is the evidence?

Of course, if my rules were followed rigorously, it would be destructive to religion, prejudice and the advertising

industry. The film won Tom Schulman an Academy Award for his superb script and there were nominations to Robin Williams and to the director, Peter Weir… But it has a plot weakness that bothered me a lot. Keating's insistence on his pupils striking out against orthodox teaching, his individual help to one particular pupil dominated by a tyrannical father, mars an otherwise perfect film. This particular pupil wants to act, he achieves the lead in the school play against the express wish of his father, who thinks acting is for sissies and who wants his son to become a doctor.

'Holy Moses? I'm Gordon Bennett'

He grudgingly lets his son play his role on the first night of the play but then insists that the boy withdraws. He tells Keating, 'You stay away from my son!' He takes the boy home, telling him that he is withdrawing him from school, sending him to another and later to Harvard to study medicine. That night, the boy commits suicide.

My dilemma is that I admire everything that Keating has taught his students, I was moved by their enthusiasm, yet I see that, by encouraging the boy to defy his father, Keating was the catalytic factor that led to the suicide. The drama was perhaps needed in an otherwise one-mood film but what a mood and what a film! I wish I could disregard this macabre touch but I can't, it returns to haunt me whenever I think about it.

With this important caveat I would nevertheless entreat you to see this film, to have your children see it, though if they do they may never obey your orders unquestioningly ever again. I know I shall never forget this picture and, I am sure, neither will you. I lack the language to express my admiration for the golden nuggets it contains. A masterpiece.

Shrine of the Grimes

*Aldeburgh doesn't need a Britten statue, says **Robert Tear**, for there never was any love lost between festival and town*

There seems to be no easy answer to the vexatious, not to say monumental, question facing the Aldeburgh town council. Nevertheless, they have come to a conclusion. They would prefer a birdbath to a statue of Lord Britten. Make no mistake, here we are delving into the murky soul of moral philosophy, where a wrong decision taken for the right reason is no answer, and neither is the opposite. So much ink has been spilled in this half-cocked debate that I think a dim light from the Sixties might throw gentle illuminations on the argument.

As far as my creaky memory has it, Aldeburgh, since the setting up of the festival, had found itself in a similar position to that of Oxbridge when the universities were founded – the town hated gown, gown floated haughtily and continued its esoteric, and to the town's eyes, useless exercises.

There is little doubt that the people who lived in Aldeburgh found the influx of the middle-class bourgeoisie, represented especially by the dominant tweedy matrons with their imperious 'Charles, do get a programme', very hard to stomach.

It is as well to remember that although the early Sixties are said to be the start of artistic liberalism, this metropolitan *laissez faire* had not yet reached the ears of Mrs Ling, who thought that because her friend came from Saxmundham, or was it Campsea Ash, she was 'not from these parts'.

I remember scooting my bike up Aldeburgh High Street and being arraigned by a copper who said, 'We don't like you Londoners down here.' A visit by the English Opera Group to the Cross Keys would empty it in the shake of a curlew's tail. The Brittenry was held responsible for this collection of oddities. However many photographs may have been taken in fishing boats, talking to old tars, and of being understanding to the sons of the same, there was little acceptance in the community.

With the flight to America, plus the homosexuality, went the possibility of assimilation into the general life of the town. Peter Grimes's problem in a nutshell.

The alienation didn't stop at the Moot Hall. Those artists who were not satraps, were treated cruelly. A well-known but hostile critic was told in Wild West fashion to leave the town before sundown.

When the first Maltings burned to the ground there was a vicious *schadenfreude* abroad and tales of arson, an offended parent, stories of indulgences being sold and beggars offering charred wood from the True Maltings as far away as windy Norfolk.

The Brittenry, King, queen, academics and handmaidens, were not the most natural inhabitants of a small fishing town. That this same town, its atmospheres and characters, became a seminal impulse for one of the greatest musicians of this century is by the by (as is Monet's garden, Van Gogh's mysticism). It is, after all, the particular eye and soul that creates the

place. That such obsessional works of glamour and sadism would not endear themselves to Mrs Ling was not a surprise. So the history of Aldeburgh since the delivery of the festival is, I believe, one of hostility to the incomers.

The problem was that the musical genius of Britten never encompassed the genius of goodness. To say that is, however, a mite unfair because after all a composer dedicates his life to music and a saint to goodness. I mention it only because the atmosphere of the Brittenry, one of intrigue and shallow darkness, lack of care and love, was so obvious to any who was not a paid-up member of that bourgeois élite. So I well understand the council's dogged refusal.

As to statues, who needs them? Most are of leaders or good examples (and if you need either I suggest you should ask yourselves some painful questions). There is a Henry Moore (a figure, not a statue, it must be said) sitting in the green Eden of the Dart Valley that has all the charm of a turd in a punchbowl.

However, should a statue be *de rigueur*, which it is not, my mind races to a Michelangelo *pietà*. I find it hard to visualise a sculptor who might make my vision manifest, but I nominate David Wynne – because he's good at birds and sea creatures. Here is my solution. Elizabeth Garrett Anderson sits with the dead Lord Britten draped across her lap. He holds a book: Crabbe's *The Borough*. On Britten's head stands a seagull. If this is too fanciful, why don't we invite necromancers or even ouijaists to a séance and let them ask Lord Britten whether he would like a statue or not. The answer, I believe, could be revealing.

BARON BRITTEN OF ALDEBURGH OM·CH 1913 1976

Missing the Midnight

A Short Story by Jane Gardam

On Christmas Eve, when I was 20, long ago, I was sitting in the London train on York station, waiting for it to start. I was in a first class carriage. I had been pushed into it. The rest of the train was packed. This compartment must have been unlocked at the last minute, like they sometimes do. Maybe it was because I had so much luggage. I was very glad to be alone. The compartment was sumptuous, with grey and pink velvet cushions and arm-rests and white cloths to rest your head against. I'd never travelled first class.

Just as the last doors were slamming three people came into the compartment, but they looked as if they were there by right. They sat down two and one, the young man and the young woman side by side across from me, near the corridor, the old man on my side with the spare seat between us. I kept my face turned away from them but I could see them reflected in the window against the cold, black night. I had my hand up against my face.

I had my hand up against my face because I was weeping. The tears welled and welled. There had been no sign of them when I was saying my bright goodbyes to the friend who was seeing me onto the train. I had waited to be alone. Now they rolled down my face and the front of my dismal macintosh, and they would not stop.

I was leaving college a year early having failed my exams and because the man I loved had told me last week that he had found someone else. I was going home to my family, whom I despised and who had never liked me and were about to like me less. I had told them everything. Got it over in a letter. I hadn't yet told my mother, though, something which would cause her deeper distress - she was always in shallow distress - that I had also lately lost my faith.

Anthropology had been my subject. I had just come to terms with the fact that it had destroyed my Christianity totally. It had always been on a fragile footing on account of my mother's obsession with it. All she had seemed to be thinking about last night when I rang her was that if I was catching this late train I would miss the Midnight.

'But you'll be missing the Midnight,' she said, 'I'd have thought that the least you could have done would be to come with me to the Midnight.' Then she said something nauseous and unforgivable to a daughter lost, 'All the mothers will be there with their college daughters.' Oh, my God.

All my mother ever thought about was what the neighbours might say, just as all my father ever thought about was how my achievements might improve his image at the bank where he had been a desk clerk for most of his life. My father drank. He drank in the greenhouse at the end of our long narrow garden in Watford. The greenhouse was packed with splendid tomato plants in summer and with heavy-headed olde-English-sheepdog

ILLUSTRATION BY PETER BAILEY

chrysanthemums in winter. Under its benches, all the year round, stood several pairs of wellingtons and in every wellington stood a bottle. The bottles were never mentioned. They changed from full to empty to full again, invisibly. When my father came out of the greenhouse he would go upstairs to bed and cry. Then my mother would rest her head against the sitting-room mantelpiece and cry, too. Then, as she also did after she and I had quarrelled, she would fling on her coat and dash to the church for comfort.

And she always came back much better. I would hear her feet tap-tapping briskly along the pavement home as I sat in my bedroom doing my homework. I used always to be doing my homework because I so wanted to get to college.

After the church visits my mother would sing to herself in the kitchen and start preparing a huge meal for my brother. She always felt forgiven after her prayers but she never came up to see me. Her life was my brother. He was my father's life, too. He was supposed to be delicate and he had been long awaited. When I was born, eight years before him, there had been a telegram from my father's family saying 'Pity it isn't a boy.' My brother was in fact far from delicate. He was surly and uncommunicative and had the muscles of a cart-horse. He detested me.

The only time when I had been happy since my brother was born was last summer when I was in love. It was amazing how much better they'd all been then, too. Much more cheerful and nice to me. My mother had gone round saying 'Esther's engaged to a graduate.' There was another thing my mother didn't know and neither did I at this time, and it was that I was harbouring a point-of-explosion appendix. I was thinking that the pain was anguish and my green face sorrow. Nobody ever looked so unattractive as I did that Christmas. So I put my hand to my face and the tears rolled.

But I could not ignore my fellow passengers. The smell of them was so arresting – the smell of beautiful tweed clothes, shoe-leather, pipe-smokers' best tobacco and some wonderful scent. There was a glow now in the compartment. Even in the glass there was a blur like a rosy sunset.

It was the young woman. She had stood up – we were on the move now – to go down the corridor. She drew back the glass door and drew it back again outside, turning back and looking down through it at the young man. I felt for a handkerchief and took a quick look.

She was the most lovely looking girl in a glorious red coat. Her expensive hair was dark and silky with shadows in it. Long pearl swing. Big pearl earrings. Huge, soft Italian bag. The hand that rested on the door latch outside wore a huge square diamond that looked new. Shiny red lipstick. She smiled down. He smiled back up. They were enchanted with each other and enchanted because they felt their families were enchanted, too.

I was astonished. There she stood. My mother always said that you should not be seen either entering or leaving a lavatory,

yet here was this goddess, unhurried, waving her fingers at a man on the way.

The fiancé leaned comfortably back and smiled across at the man opposite who could not be anybody but his father. He had the same lanky ease, though he was thinner and greyer and was wearing a dog-collar. This old priest now looked across at me, and smiled.

The trio seemed to me to be the most enviable human beings I had ever seen. It seemed impossible that anything could harm them: easy, worldly, confident, rich, blooming with health; failure, rejection, guilt all unknown to them. And how they loved each other at this wonderful point in their lives! When the girl came back they all smiled at each other all over again.

I could see that the girl did not belong quite to the same world as the priest. I knew she thought him just rather an old duck and that she had no notion of his job. I don't know how I knew this, but I did. And I saw that the son had moved some way into the girl's world, and would go farther into it. He'd got clear of all the church-stuff. But nobody was worrying.

Was there a mother? Dead? What had she been? Cardigans and untidy hair and no time for anything? Or well-heeled, high-heeled bishop's daughter? Was there a sister. No, there was no sister. I knew the old man would have liked a daughter. You could tell by the loving look he was giving the girl who was to become one to him.

Soon the fiancé fell asleep. Maybe all of us fell asleep, for suddenly we were going through Peterborough and I was listening to a conversation taking shape between the girl and the priest who, now virtually alone with her, was sounding rather shy.

'We shan't be in until after 10 o'clock I'm afraid,' he said, 'Of course it's much quicker than it used to be.'

'Oh, much quicker.'

'I suppose we'll be able to find a taxi. Christmas Eve. It may be rather difficult.'

'Oh yes, it may be frightfully difficult.'

'Andrew is very resourceful.'

'Oh, he's absolutely marvellously resourceful.'

'I'm afraid we shall miss the Midnight.'

'The Midnight?'

'The service. The midnight Christmas Eve service. Perhaps you don't go?'

'I'm afraid I don't usually.'

'D'you know, I don't blame you. I don't greatly enjoy it either, unless it's in the country. In London people come crashing in from parties. The smell of alcohol at the altar rail can be quite overpowering.'

She looked bewildered.

'I should leave it till the morning if I were you,' he said. 'It's quieter. More serious people.'

Her red lips smiled. She said she would ask Andrew.

> **The trio seemed to me to be the most enviable human beings that I had ever seen. It seemed impossible that anything could harm them: easy, worldly, confident.**

'I don't really care for Christmas Eve at all,' he said.

He had removed his glasses to polish them. His eyes looked weak, but were still bright blue. 'Now, I don't know what you think, but I believe it must have been a very dark day for Our Lady.'

She wriggled inside the fuchsia coat and slowly began to blush. She lifted the diamond-hung hand to her hair.

'Think of it. Fully nine months pregnant on that road, Nazareth to Bethlehem. Winter weather. Well, we're now told it was in the spring. March. But it can be diabolical in the Mediterranean in March. I don't know if you've ever been to Galilee?'

The shiny lips said that they had never been to Galilee.

'Can be dreadful I believe. And the birth beginning. Far from her mother. And the first child's always slow. Contractions probably started on the road. On foot or on a mule of some kind. One hopes there were some women about. And the birth itself in a stable. We're told it was an 'annexe' now, but I prefer stable. But think about it blood in the straw. The afterbirth. . .'

He was totally unaware of her embarrassment. She had no notion what to say. She was the colour of her coat.

At last – 'We always have a family party on Christmas Eve. Absolutely lots of us. Terrific fun. I'm afraid we're not exactly churchgoers, any of us.'

'You will be having a church wedding though?'

'Oh, golly yes.'

'I'd very much like to marry you,' he said, lovingly, 'if that were possible.'

She looked startled. Then slowly it dawned. 'Oh – yes! Of course. Actually I think Mummy has some sort of tame bishop, but I'm not sure.'

'Perhaps I could assist?'

'Assist? Oh yes, assist. Of course.'

He hadn't got there yet. The chasm was still just under the snow. He noticed me looking across at him and at once and unselfconsciously he smiled. I turned quickly away to the night trying not to hear my mother's voice saying, 'I don't care what you say, Esther, there is a difference. Being a Christian does show.'

'You might just be interested in this,' I heard the priest say to the girl. He had brought out of his pocket a leather pouch, squarish, like a double spectacle case and he leaned towards her, elbows on knees, and opened it. She made a little movement forwards. Her hair brushed the fiancé's shoulder. 'How pretty. What is it?'

'I'd very much like to marry you,' he said, lovingly, 'if that were possible.' She looked startled. Then slowly it dawned. 'Oh – yes! Of course.'

Had she expected jewels? A family necklace?' 'What dear little bottles. Sweet little silver thing.'

'It's a pyx. A "viaticum", the whole thing's called. And something called an 'oil stock'. It's for taking the Sacrament to the sick in an emergency. I like to have it with me. It's an old fashioned thing to do nowadays. It was a present from my parishioners. Very generous.'

She touched a little flask. 'Is it all right to touch?'

'Of course.'

'What are these?'

'Those are the oils. For Holy Unction. We anoint the dying.'

She jumped back. 'You mean - like the Egyptians? Embalming fluid?'

'No, just oils. Very ancient idea. Long pre-Christian, I dare say.' He knew that I was looking across again and he turned towards me and said, 'Wouldn't you, my dear?'

'Yes'.

How did he know me?

'It's for people on their last legs,' he said. 'Last gasp. In extremis.'

'Can it bring them back to life?' she asked. 'Is it sort of magic?'

'Well yes. It has been known to restore life. We don't call it magic, but, yes – it has been known.'

He was looking at me.

When we reached King's Cross they were quick at gathering up their luggage. I took much longer to assemble mine which was mostly in parcels spread about the overhead racks. My two great suitcases stood outside in the corridor. I had no money for a taxi and I wasn't at all sure how I was going to get all this to the Watford train. There might just possibly be a porter, but I had no money for the tip. I let them go ahead of me, the girl first, still smiling, Andrew behind, touching her arm, then the priest winding a long grey soft woollen scarf round his neck. A present? From someone he loved? Someone who loved him?

I had no presents for anyone this year. Why should I?

They wouldn't care. There'd be none for me, or maybe just a token. I didn't care, either. Home in shame. A grim time coming. 'God help me,' I said automatically, in my heart.

The priest turned before he stepped out of the train. He smiled at me again. He still held the leather pouch. He lifted it in his hand in blessing.

They had all three disappeared by the time I had got myself together and started to shamble after them down the platform. There was a tremendous queue for taxis, so Andrew must have been at his most resourceful.

I didn't need a taxi, though, or a train or anything else because both my parents and my brother were at the platform gate.

Still With Us

Tom Lehrer

'NEXT SUNDAY you'll see / Why don't you come with me / And we'll poison the pigeons in the park / And maybe we'll do in a squirrel or two…' From 'Poisoning Pigeons in the Park' to 'The Masochism Tango', the cult of Tom Lehrer continues to thrive and so does the man himself. Next month he will celebrate his 68th birthday and he is still playing the piano despite not having performed any of the famous songs in public since 1965.

He will hate this article for being far too nostalgic. When I called to ask if he would be willing to take part in a BBC Radio 2 documentary about his life he recoiled saying, 'I hope this won't be a "where is he now?" I hate those, and anyway, I don't know where I am.' He did finally agree, after admitting that he could find no noble excuse, 'so unless I get lucky and a close friend dies, I guess I'd better do it'. He hates being interviewed: 'I think it's intrusive – you only need to give interviews when you have something to sell or something to publicise and as, thank God, I have neither, I don't really see the point.'

Lehrer started writing songs as a 15-year-old mathematics undergraduate at Harvard University. His first song, 'Fight Fiercely Harvard', was written as a parody of the Glee Club songs of the times ('back in the days when we had glee') and he is much amused to hear it now played in all seriousness at Harvard football matches. After a while writing and performing songs for his friends at parties, he was encouraged to offer his services to record companies. They all turned him down.

Eventually, in 1953, he recorded the songs himself, handling labelling and distribution from his college rooms, and a cult was born. American radio stations found his songs 'unsuitable' for airplay but the BBC had no such qualms and by the time he

brian bagnall

'We have what I describe as a nimiety of scurrility with a concomitant exiguity of restraint. In my youth there were words you couldn't say in front of a girl; now you can't say the word "girl" '

made his first appearances over here in 1958 he was a huge hit – amongst a certain few. 'Everybody who liked those records I think felt, 'Well, we appreciate it, we privileged few or happy few or intelligent few appreciate it, but the masses… would certainly not' – and that helped it along a lot.'

Many of his songs were take-offs of popular tunes, including those by his idols Gilbert and Sullivan, Cole Porter and Noël Coward, as well as the traditional songs which were starting to become popular in the late 50s during, as he terms it, 'The Folk Song Scare.' The songs were complex technical jokes with musical references to the form they were taking off. 'Alma', a jolly number about Frau Mahler's sex life, has musical quotes from Mahler's music throughout.

Lehrer thinks that most of these references will be lost on younger listeners: 'People don't know enough, they don't have enough history any more – I'm not talking about Charlemagne, I mean that young people don't have the past that even we had, so a lot of the references are lost.'

Lehrer counts himself as one of the few remaining American liberals. Some of his songs reflected his political views although in a typically offbeat way. His contribution to the debate over pornography was the song 'Smut': 'I never quibbled / If it was ribald / I would devour / Where others merely nibbled.' The song caused a storm of outraged complaint when it was released, much to Lehrer's amazement – he aimed to amuse and entertain and not, he says, to shock. 'Of course today anything goes, at least in this country, and so it has definitely led to a decline of humorous standards, I find. I don't know that that song would even make any sense now that we have what I describe as a nimiety of scurrility with a concomitant exiguity of restraint. In my youth there were words you couldn't say in front of a girl; now you can't say the word "girl".'

After sellout tours of the USA and Britain, Lehrer retired from performing in 1960 and returned to Harvard to teach mathematics. In 1965 he contributed series of songs to the American version of *TW3* and recorded them during a residency at the Hungry

I club in San Francisco. This collection contained his most controversial song, 'The Vatican Rag', which, horror of horrors, satirised the Eucharist: 'Two, four, six, eight / Time to transubstantiate…'

This was his last LP of satirical songs, although he recorded two educational numbers for the children's television programme *Sesame Street* in the early 70s. After that he went back to his career as a lecturer, teaching at Harvard, MIT and now the University of Santa Cruz in California. People still come to him with suggestions for topics for more songs, but 'I have turned them away by saying usually, if it's a serious issue, "That's like asking a resident of Pompeii for some humorous comments about lava".'

So why did he stop? At the time he said that he retired after Henry Kissinger was awarded the Nobel Peace Prize, which was a joke beyond satire. Now he says he was planning to retire as soon as he started. 'People get the idea that this was a career: there were 37 recorded songs and that was over a 20 year period, and I don't regard that as a prolific output of any kind… I could have prolonged it, but for what reason? I had done everything, the only thing that prolonged it was the chance to go to new places and underdeveloped countries, like England.'

Not only did he stop performing but he also stopped writing songs altogether. Even he isn't really sure why. 'That would take years of therapy to bring out; and I've never had therapy so I cannot say. It just stopped.'

Tom Lehrer now divides his year between summers in Cambridge and winters in Santa Cruz. He no longer teaches maths (or math as he would insist) but instead gives a course in the history of the American musical where he initiates his students into the delights of Broadway's golden era, accompanying all the performances himself on the piano.

He is reluctant to talk about his private life but is fit, relaxed, genial and seems entirely at ease. 'When at home I shilly a little in the morning leaving some time to shally in the afternoon.' Who could ask for more? **ELEANOR GARLAND**

'And here's one I made earlier'

Between your doctor saying 'let's send a bit of that vesicle off to the lab', and 'you've got shingles', to whom will your crusty scab be entrusted? To someone like me. There are 21,000 registered biomedical scientists in the UK, working in the NHS, the Public Health Laboratory Service, universities, research institutions and private and commercial laboratories. Augmented by trainees, scientists and medics, those of us who work in hospital labs are specialists in a particular discipline. Mine is virology.

An apprentice microbe hunter straight from university, my first job was in the microbiology department of a busy London hospital. Before letting me loose on viruses, I first had to gain some experience with their larger cousins, the bacteria, a huge number of which are found in the human gut. Down in the lower reaches of the colon, up to 1011 bacteria per gram of faeces enjoy the wide range of amenities provided, in happy co-existence with the host. The hooligan element bent on disruption includes campylobacter, salmonella, and shigella, and these are among the organisms most keenly sought when the intestines are in a state of flux. However, for the microbe willing to travel from the teeming shores of this cloacal Costa Brava, the urinary tract is a quiet oasis ripe for colonisation. When the bacterial count in the urine is more than 100,000 per ml, you have a urinary-tract infection. About 80 per cent of these infections are caused by the handsomely named *Eschericia coli*. Before I could deal with range, I had to have focus. Thus was I assigned to the urine bench.

I had never seen so much wee. Rack upon rack of clear, plastic Universal containers filled with urine awaited processing. As the sunlight streamed golden on to these golden streams, I gawped at this mass of micturition and realised with apprehension that each sample represented a patient. Complete strangers were giving me *carte blanche* with their body fluids. Assuming that I did not lose, spill or get a sample mixed up with someone else's, I would even have a role in determining if there were bugs in it or not. Happily, I was thrown in at the shallow end to assist, and learn from Josie.

An attractive, petite Filipina, Josie was a supreme technician. Prior to viewing a sample microscopically, a sterilised platinum wire loop was used to transfer a small drop of urine into the centre of one of a series of squares marked on a plain glass slide. If memory serves correctly, eight samples on one slide was about the maximum that experienced technicians could manage. Josie routinely did 12. Holding her loop like a paintbrush, her exquisitely deft, confident movements were almost a background to her stream of happy chatter, pausing just as she touched the loop on to the slide. Under Josie's tutelage I was eager to learn but keen to impress. Before I moved to my next bench, I proudly demonstrated my ability to place six spots of urine on a slide without one running into another. 'George,' said Josie, smiling inscrutably, as I sat surrounded by urine samples, 'you are an artist'. At the time I took it as a compliment.

With urine, fluidity of medium allowed uniformity of technique, or in Josie's case, style. However, the samples which graced the faeces bench comprised a diversity of form and consistency which demanded the adoption of a range of skills, not least of which was that of Opening the Container. The importance of

Handle with care

George F Winter *explains the art of hospital lab work, and why caution is advised*

this was emphatically underlined to me on The Day Of The Exploding Faeces. The standard faeces container was a screw-capped three-inch long aluminium cylinder.

As the contents remained a mystery until the lid was unscrewed, it was customary to release it gently while exerting slight downward pressure to allow the controlled escape of any gaseous accumulations, yet not too much pressure so that unwanted aerosols might form. My colleague on the bench was John; experienced, but, more importantly in this context, the owner of a big black beard. It was high summer, and the containers in the sack at the back of the van had been given a bumpy ride as London NW10 was trawled for specimens. Anxious to be of assistance, the donor of this particular specimen had successfully endeavoured to pack in just as much as he or she could. The inside of a small, hot metal container was no place for a true transient, given to exploring the highways and byways of its own particular environment, before accepting that its destiny lay out in

the open. It was not surprising, therefore, that simmering resentment and gas under pressure were accumulating rapidly as the van screeched to a halt outside the lab.

In retrospect, John knew that something was wrong when he found that the top was screwed on more than finger-tight. It was almost a warning. The slight easing of pressure was all that was needed. Standing with my back to the action, the bang of celebration as the faeces found freedom was eclipsed only by an instinctive yell. I spun round in time to see high-speed faeces embedding itself snugly in John's beard. As he hurried to the sink he repeated between clenched teeth the one, the only word which was both emotive and fully descriptive.

The little of what remained in the container was tested and found to have no significant bacteria present. The fall-out lasted for days and it was probably around this time that I acquired the technique of breathing only through my nose... very slowly. Was it too late for a career in forest management? Yes, I was hooked!

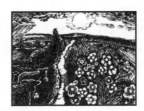

Country Life

Richard Mabey

One of the hidden costs of buying a wood is that you become prone, ever after, to attacks of custodial anxiety. You worry about doing too much, or too little, or about having the impertinence to be there at all.

I blew my savings on a patch of ancient woodland in the Chilterns 15 years ago, and ever since it has been a source of almost unalloyed pleasure and excitement. The village people are walking the tracks again, the frogs have come back to the pond, and barely a week goes by without something prodigious turning up, like a 90 million-year-old sea-urchin fossil *inside* a tree stump. The one thing I hadn't banked on were the fits of tunnel vision the place encourages. Even on glorious days when all I want to do is lie under a tree, I catch myself peering obsessively at the leaf-canopy to see if we're letting in enough light, or scouring the ground for nibbled bark, new saplings, nuthatches fallen out of nests. I blame the work ethic. Simple lotus-eating is increasingly scowled on in the countryside, as a sure badge of incomers who haven't been properly 'summered and weathered' or who haven't laboured deferentially enough, faces turned down to the soil.

At least late summer lets you off the hook a little, since there isn't much tinkering to be done. It is the flat top of the year, a brief (and probably illusory) moment of calm. So, in one of the last warm spells, I just let myself potter, and drifted across a glade nibbling wild raspberries that grow back in sheaves wherever we've done a little thinning. Around me, also on a foraging spree on the late bramble flowers, were clouds of butterflies. It has been a spectacular year for them, especially the painted ladies that migrated in from southern Europe in headline-catching numbers in early June. Maybe the influx was the consequence of freak winds, maybe of global warming. Either way, this spangled Mediterranean incomer, normally just a scarce treat on the buddleia, was the commonest butterfly in Britain for most of the summer. I saw 20 at once on one bush in my garden. Maybe a few of this vast constellation will even be genetically capable of surviving our winter, and we will have them in the spring too.

Dithering over the brambles, the residents were obviously having a bumper year, too. There were ringlets, tortoiseshells, skippers, peacocks, gatekeepers, holly blues, brimstones. Butterflies' names are a feast in themselves. None of them are truly grass-roots or folk-based in the way that the common names of birds and wildflowers are, but were coined by 18th- and 19th-century naturalists who, clearly relishing effusive christenings (they were mostly clergymen in their day-jobs), called themselves 'Aurelians'.

Their taste for ornamented language still has echoes. The other day I heard an unsentimental scientist use the word 'nectaring' for the meandering quests of butterflies among the flowers. I like the idea of nectaring. It has a deliciously effete, indulgent feel which describes exactly what one should be doing on a summer's day in a wood. I shall try to remember it whenever I am nervously tempted to take a light-meter into the dapple.

INSIDE EACH OF US, someone different is trying to get out. I think we should encourage it, if only because, as Roy Strong says, the way to stay young is to have a new career every 10 years.

I am a writer, but inside, there's a market trader. It's inherited. My mother ran a small company manufacturing children's clothes, and designed and hand-made posh frocks for Yorkshire ladies. I grew up surrounded by pins, patterns and pinking shears, and sat under sewing machines reading. For, to my mother's chagrin, I was bookish, the only child in the handicraft class whose hemming had to be unpicked *four* times. But I loved the workrooms, and even more, the business paraphernalia, the order and invoice books, with their flimsy blue carbon inserts, the ready reckoner and the appointments diary, the packing room, with its huge rolls of brown paper and tissue.

But the embryo businesswoman got buried under the books – though when I came to write them, I followed their progress eagerly from manuscript to shop, taking in printers and bindery on the way. Something stirred when I read about my heroine, the Duchess of Devonshire, starting a successful farm shop at Chatsworth. There she was, I thought admiringly, just making good use of what she found in the larder at the time. Then I found something in my own larder. Between novels, I always used to write short stories. Then I stopped. Odd how these things come and go. But, after a life and near-death crisis last year, four stories surfaced from my sub-conscious, or larder; not enough for my usual publishers to make into a full-length book though, so I was about to shove them into a drawer, when I chanced to read, in Virginia Woolf's Diary: 'We have printed off the text of "Kew Gardens" and got an estimate from McDermott for printing Murry's poems... we supply the paper and cover. Possibilities are opened up, I think.' Possibilities indeed. If she, my other heroine, a genius of a writer, could also help run the Hogarth Press, be a publisher, even to the extent of doing some printing... No sooner was the thought thought, than I had decided. I was going to be a publisher, beginning with my own new stories.

I phoned some friends in the trade and

The publisher within

Susan Hill *thought she was a writer. Then she discovered bubblewrap*

discovered that it would make perfect economic sense to do a small-format paperback. In one bound, the business-woman was free. That night, I looked across the garden at the long stone barn, in the converted granary loft of which I work. 'Long Barn Books,' I said.

Next day, I read in Virginia Woolf's Diary: 'Just back from three days with Vita, at Long Barn.'

As my mother would have said through a mouthful of pins, 'it was meant'.

Which is how I found myself returning from taking my daughter to riding, one August morning, shopping bags full of dog biscuits and cabbages, to grab the ringing telephone in the kitchen, remembering in time to say: 'Long Barn Books, good morning.'

'This is the XYZ Bookshop here. I'd like to order 20 copies of Susan Hill's *Listening To The Orchestra*, please.'

Drop carrier bags. Search for pen. Where do kitchen pens go? 'Would you just bear with me a moment?' (Well, all telesales girls say that). Race upstairs. Find

pen and order book. Race down again. But now the bookseller wants the book's ISBN number. ISBNs are not memorable and that file is at the top of the house. Race up. Get number. Race down. Hear kettle boiling over below. Race further down. Remove kettle. Race back. Give ISBN to nice bookseller, who then asks, terribly politely, if there might be any chance of speaking to me, as it were.

'You are. This is. I am me.' 'But how extraordinary.' 'I'm sorry?' 'I imagined there was a staff of 20 ... not just you, running up and down stairs.'

But so much is it just me running up and down stairs that my daughter invented a telephone routine for me: 'Good morning, Long Barn Books, which department – Management, Editorial, Production, Design, Accounts, Publicity, Sales and Marketing, Post Room or canteen?' 'It'll

all be you, Mummy, but they're not to know that.'

Being a small publisher is delightful. It is also remarkably straightforward and I have demystified a lot of things, though it helps to have been in the book world for so long and know such a lot of helpful people. I don't have to print myself off the kitchen table either, like the Woolfs. The new technology has made my new career possible. It *is* a new career, too; I am publishing other titles next year, and also producing Private Press fine limited editions, with wood engravings, a beautiful area of book publishing in which the new technology plays no part.

I am still a writer first. I go alone, into the silence of the Long Barn, to work on a new novel, which I won't be publishing myself. But, back in the house for coffee, I can't resist running up to check the fax machine for orders. I wonder if Virginia Woolf ran up and down stairs all day... I wonder if the Duchess of Devonshire does... (some stairs)... Virginia Woolf called the Hogarth Press a hobby... I bet the D of D doesn't say that of Chatsworth ... Virginia Woolf wouldn't have said 'bear with me' either... I have negotiated a further 5 per cent discount on bubblewrap... the Long Barn is full of books... and bubblewrap ... I have finished another chapter of the novel... I have to go and fetch my daughter from riding...

'Good afternoon, Long Barn Books...'

Here comes a van, laden with bubble-wrap... Help... inside this writer was a publisher who just got out... Inside this...?

'That's what I love about this city – everything's so close together'

ILLUSTRATION BY PETER BAILEY

High spots in my week

Nell Dunn *relishes the stories she hears when she picks up her pension at Mr Patel's*

I collect my pension every Monday from a small sub-post office in South West London. There, a little queue forms behind a notice which reads STAND BACK AS PEOPLE MAY WANT TO CONDUCT THEIR BUSINESS IN PRIVATE. While we wait we chat and get wised up to what's happening. There are plenty of tips on how to get a grant to insulate your roof or meals on wheels or the loan of a bedpan

for a fortnight. This morning it was frosty. The common was shrouded in mist with frozen spiders' webs hanging from the trees. But it was warm in the post office, the queue was extra long and excitement was high. The burglar alarm was ringing and the safe had automatically locked, so nobody could have their money.

Mr Patel had to stay behind the counter in case the police arrived or the safe suddenly opened. He daren't go upstairs to

turn off the alarm. So we waited and talked. A lady was worried because she had to be at St George's Hospital later and might miss her appointment unless the safe opened soon. Someone told her to take the train and not the bus because it would be quicker, then the gentleman behind me offered her a lift if he could move up in the queue. Somebody else said hospital transport wasn't as good as it used to be and so the conversation turned to politics and at least they didn't force you to leave your own home if you were ill ... full time nursing was available if you were on income support.

'If your husband dies you can get the widowed mother's allowance. That's new too,' said a young woman with a pushchair and twins.

The safe suddenly opened and there was much rejoicing in the queue.

A man behind me is getting impatient and spoiling things. 'Are you in a hurry?' the young mother asks him as he jostles her. 'Yes. I am trying to get a tax disc for my car and this is the second time I've been because of a silly rule you can only buy the disc a couple of weeks before the last one runs out.' 'I don't bother with a car,' she says. 'If I need to go anywhere I just hop on a bus.' 'What, with that lot?' someone says. 'Why not?' she says.

The man at the head of the queue is taking a long time because he can't hear what Mr Patel is telling him. He drops his stick and the young woman with the twins picks it up.

Now it's my turn and I pass over my book. 'How are you?' says Mr Patel. 'I'm well, thank you, and you?' I ask him how he manages to be so patient with us oldies and he points to a Hindu calendar with a picture of Sai Baba. 'He is my teacher.'

I collect my money (£62.90), get a book of stamps and move to the side shelf to stick them on my letters. An old lady beside me is sticking in her gas stamps and her TV stamps. We get into a conversation about managing money. 'I never have any debts but I haven't got no savings either. I don't believe in savings, I believe in enjoying my money. If that rainy days comes I'll just have to get wet.'

Everyone joins in on the 'save or not to save' theme. 'My grandmother saved all her life, under the mattress. When she died my mother never found it.' 'The undertaker probably had it.' 'Wouldn't surprise me. Anyway, you don't get your rent paid if you've got savings.'

A woman has brought in her neighbour's book. 'Not well enough to come herself. I'm going to get her bit of shopping. All right, Mr Patel?' 'All right, dear.'

Mrs Patel is at the sweet and cigarette counter so other conversations are going on there. Suddenly in walks a young man.

'What are you doing here?' shouts his mother.

'I waited a bleedin' hour. It was freezing. He never turned up.'

'Well, get on your bike and go back and see if he's there now.'

'He won't be there.'

'Go back and see if he's there.'

It turned out the young fellow had got a job with a building firm and when he turned up for work at 8 o'clock this morning the site was deserted. Anyway he went, and the rest of the queue commiserates with his mother.

'Did you enjoy your holiday?' says the old man with the stick to the young woman with the twins.

'It was all right. Turkey. Nothing to see but the people were lovely.'

The DSS would like to send our pensions directly to our banks, but I resisted this. I want to make it an occasion. A weekly ritual. I want to stand in the queue with the other pensioners to remind myself I was now a pensioner too, although I still felt only seven and elated that I could ride my tricycle. (It was a dark shining red Raleigh and I got it for my seventh birthday.)

The line between life being intolerable and life being sweet is very thin. This is specially true for us pensioners.

'He has an unfortunate manner...'

Music
Richard Osborne

IF YOU HAD asked me 30 years ago who were the two greatest Yorkshiremen ever to work in tandem, I would have said Brian Close and Raymond Illingworth. Seven county championships in 10 years was no mean feat, and though it was Close who palpably led the side, barely an over was bowled duriong those now all to dimly remembered summers when that shrewdest of cricketing lieutenenats was not at his side.

There had, though, been another, perhaps more enduringly valuable, twinning of Yorkshiremen some years before that; the Bradford-born Frederick Delius (a cricket-lover, too, in his youth) and a brilliant young self-taught musician from Scarborough, Eric Fenby who for six remarkable years acted as amanuensis to the blind and paralysed composer in his French rural retreat of Grez-sur-Loing.

As musical amanuenses go, Fenby, who died in February, 1997, aged 90, was probably without equal, for as well as helping nurse a man who was slowly dying, he helped draw from him a rich body of late work: *A Song of Summer, the Songs of Farewell*, and more besides. In an article in the *Evening Standard* in 1927, Delius' friend and greatest advocate Sir Thomas Beecham had compared Delius' plight to Handel's. 'Unless the gods intervene to restore his sight,' he wrote, 'the voice of this sweet singer will now be mute until the day of his death.'

Well, the gods did intervene. It was shortly after that, in the middle of the night, that Fenby received the 'call' to Grez, not telephonically but spiritually; a fact that later led Sir Malcolm Sargent to describe Fenby's summons as being every bit 'a vivid and real as that of Samuel'.

Had it happened in our own times, Fenby's work with the crippled composer would have been the subject of a hundred mawkish newspapers articles and a score of 'caring' documentaries on radio and television. And how both men would have hated it! Delius with his Prussian reserve,

Fenby with his instinct for privacy and quiet. (As a young man, he seriously considered becoming a Benedictine monk.)

Happily, Fenby did write his own classic memoir, *Delius As I Knew Him*, first published in 1936. It is a wonderful book, brief, but in the late Christopher Palmer's phrase 'with the quality of radium'. When he first read it, Palmer said he was reminded of Arthur Machen's writing about Swinburne: 'The book was positively strewn with the fragments of shattered altars and the torn limbs of kings and priests. Clearly, this was a terrible, a tremendous fellow, an earth-shaking, heaven-storming poet.'

Delius' atheism and moral iconoclasm certainly shocked Fenby; as surely as he had been thrilled by the sheer zest of A Mass of Life and touched by the exquisite finish of all those timeless nature-inspired fantasies: *On hearing the first Cuckoo in Spring*, *In a Summer Garden*, and *Summer Night on the River*, works inspired in part or in whole by the garden, orchard and river at Grez.

Fenby had been particularly shocked by Delius' Requiem, the 'Pagan Requiem' as Delius sometimes called it, which has just been recorded by Richard Hickox for Chandos (CHAN 9515, coupled with) with soloists Rebecca Evans and Peter Coleman-Wright. Delius wrote it between 1913 and 1916 and later dedicated it 'To the memory of all young Artists fallen in the War'.

As a work, it has suffered an even more ignominious fate than Elgar's great elegy, much admired by Britten, 'For the Fallen'. In Elgar's case it was perhaps the works' larger title *The Spirit of England* that misled a depressed and spiritually exhausted public. In the case of Delius' *Requiem*, it was the text that offended: the idea that life was to be lived, that death was a blind alley, and that religions are, indeed, the opiates of the people. (At one point the Christina 'Hallelujah!' and the Islamic 'La il Allah' are mixed and derided by the chorus.) In later years, Fenby came largely to accept the work. In 1971 he wrote:

'In no other work by Delius is his character as a man more clearly revealed – betrayed even – than in his curious Requiem'. Fenby himself took the view that any religion is better than no religion. In Emily Dickinson's words:

> *The abdication of Belief*
> *Makes the Behaviour small*
> *Better an ignis fatuus*
> *Than no illume at all.*

For Delius, though, man is finite; only Nature is eternally renewing. It was belief he held to passionately which is why the final movement of the *Requiem* is a hymn to spring and why it contains some of the most achingly intense and astonishingly beautiful; music he ever wrote. 'The snow lingers yet on the mountains,' the chorus sings, 'but yonder in the valleys the buds are breaking on the trees and hedges'. And the work ends, ecstatically: 'Springtime, Summer, Autumn, and Winter. And then comes Springtime. Springtime!' One knows the feeling.

Hell
on Wheels

Christopher Hamilton
looks back on his brief but character-forming spell as a mini-cab driver

'Drivers required. Clean and respectable. Collar and tie work. Company car provided.' It was the last sentence that did it. I was practically down and out. If they gave me a car, I reasoned, at least I could sleep in it.

The interview was brief. Once convinced that I could drive, the Controller handed me a carrier bag. In it was a radio receiver, map, petrol card, a David Frost clipboard, dockets in triplicate, a rule book (thick) and the company tie.

'Remember to hand it back at the end. If you don't you won't get paid. We don't want you cowboys passing yourselves off as genuine Consultant drivers after Christmas. We do a lot of BBC,' the Controller went on to explain. 'Respectable. And advertising agencies. You will wear the tie at all times. So they know who you are.'

'You're one of them Christmas drivers aren't you?' sneered one of the old hands as I went downstairs. He was loitering on the landing with his colleagues in a malevolent gauntlet, smoking and waiting to be paid. Their company ties were undone, miles shinier than mine.

'Yes I am,' 'Wanker!' 'Wanker!' they shouted after me as I walked downstairs. 'Christmas plonker!' A piece of gob flew by.

On reflection, I think they were right. The Christmas drivers were wankers. One had been cashiered from the Signals Regiment, another looked as if he had been living rough for some time. I had come from Wales. Practically nobody knew their way around London – few could read a map. The Inuit from Northern Canada found things particularly trying.

He was one of a group of 12 misfits when we were taken in the drizzle to the forecourt of a shady car dealer in Hemel Hempstead. There we were to collect cars in various states of disrepair, which had been hired to the Consultant Car Company for the season. After some navigational inexactitudes, most of us made it back to base in the West End. Not so the Inuit person. His car was eventually discovered near the Scottish border, facing North, its tank empty, with a note saying 'Sorry' stuck to the windscreen. He was never found. I can only assume he made it back to Canada on foot.

'804... 804 where are you? Bloody Christmas drivers!' The prefix 8 was reserved for us so that everyone on the circuit could shake their heads and enjoy the vigour with which we were bollocked over the airwaves. Our Controllers had long since abandoned the Nice Guy, Nasty Guy routine. They had Mr Nasty (the Fat Controller), who worked by day and Mr Really Very Nasty (the Obese Controller), who did nights.

'804, where the *f**k* are you? You're where?! What are you doing in Ilford?' It was Mr Nasty. 'Be at Broadcasting House for three o'clock. DO – YOU – KNOW – WHERE – THAT – IS?!'

I mumbled 'Roger' and wrote the name of the passenger on a chit. A battered fleet of Consultant cars had already clogged up the main entrance to Broadcasting House in Portland Place. They were all on waiting time. Waiting, it seemed, was more profitable than driving. Later, in one of my many idle moments, I calculated that my car alone had so far accounted for five license fees.

Some of the runs were quite legitimate. The man from Harrow who ran catering at Television Centre, for instance, had to leave home at 5 o'clock on Christmas Day, to prepare turkey for a BBC skeleton staff of 600. They were all hard at it, broadcasting warnings about drink-driving, about the weather and the fact there is never any news at Christmas.

All night, cleaners, telephonists and shift workers were ferried to and fro in

limousines to destinations in the green belt. For reasons best known to itself, the BBC does not permit employees to share cabs, even when they are heading for places as distant as Walthamstow and Sevenoaks, unless they work in the same department. In consequence, that afternoon, a large part of the Consultant fleet was bound, with one passenger per car, for the same part of North London.

At three o'clock on the dot, a BBC mandarin fell, tired and emotional, into the back of my car. He closed his eyes in silent meditation. Bearded, supreme and thoroughly pissed, he conducted the trip in silence. The mandarin lived in Dulwich Village. Though I wondered what weighty matters he had lately been considering, I discovered only that the Birtist lackey penpusher did not tip. How different from the World Service.

My first World Service man came out of Bush House at 2am. He had just finished broadcasting in Hindi. When I

'Could you run that one by me again?'

asked him about his audience ratings, the man was modest. The Hindi-speaking population is 900 million,' he said, 'My audience is relatively small – about 25 million.' I drove on to find that the man who knocks *Coronation Street* into a cocked hat every night of the week, lives in a box under a main flight path near Osterley. Now that's what I call commitment to public service broadcasting.

By the middle of Christmas some of the more experienced drivers had turned to blagging – illegally picking up fares off the street for cash. Some would target pregnant women laden with Christmas shopping and three children under five, others went for the elderly and confused. I didn't have the enterprise to do this, so I lay up outside Saatchi and Saatchi instead.

Saatchi and Saatchi were popular. Waiting times were legendary. Some drivers had spent days and nights on the leather sofas in the foyer, eating Saatchi's pizza and drinking the client's coffee, waiting for pissed Creatives. All for a very respectable £7 an hour. When you are earning £2.55 for driving, this is such stuff as dreams are made on.

Another agency asked me to deliver home an incoherent account man. He had been celebrating the billings on the current 'Who Says One More Little Drink Never Hurt Anyone' campaign. Advertising executives can be entertaining when their mouths are propped ajar by the grape. And revealing. The more bibulous of their number can be generous too. Thanks for the fiver, Mrs Miriam Keane of the tights account – your secrets are safe with me!

Pin-ups

Clare Short picks her top six

1 Pope John XXIII
A brave reformer who understood the loving aspect of Christianity, unlike the present incumbent.

2 John Smith MP
Who was so confident of his own views that he treated all others with respect. He was a joy to work with and would have been a great Prime Minister.

3 My Mum
Because she still spoils me and looks after me and is one of the joys of my life.

4 Mikhail Gorbachev
Who brought down the Communist regime and tried to replace it with Social Democracy – which would have been much better than what they have now.

5 Mary Robinson
Whom I would not have supported for President because her views were so Unionist but who has proved an inspiration in symbolising the end of bigotry and dogma in Ireland.

6 Nelson Mandela
Who lost his freedom for most of his life and remains generous and constructive. The political giant of our time.

Right: Clare Short MP

Miles Kington

Keep Britain Untidy

I got a note the other day from someone on the committee to the effect that our village was now in the finals of the West Wiltshire Best-Kept Village competition, and that if any children like our son wanted to submit a poster design on the subject of 'The Preservation of Wild Life' then what a jolly good thing that would be.

I don't think I've ever been so near the heart of a Best-Kept Village contest before, and I found when I looked into my soul that I had formed no neat, ready opinions on it at all. One's first reaction is to think, yes, what a good idea to keep the village tidy, but when you think of what it involves, you begin to wonder…

The village I grew up in was Gresford in North Wales, in what was then Denbighshire, and it was the site of one of the Seven Wonders of Wales. These seven wonders were not really all-Welsh wonders, because they were restricted to parts of North Wales, so I was not overwhelmed to learn that the bells of Gresford Church were among the Seven Wonders of Wales, even though it gave me a sneaking regard for their booming sound. My father thought quite otherwise.

Our garden was less than 100 yards from the church, and Sunday morning was not only the time he liked to garden, it was also the favourite time for bell-ringing practice; from time to time my father would stand at the bottom of the garden, driven mad by the booming, shaking his fist at God's house and shouting: 'Bloody bells! Bloody bells!' It is one of my most touching memories of him. It is also my inauguration into the feeling that a village may not be best served by fame.

The more I think about it, the more I don't want our village to be best-kept if that means having it neurotically spring-cleaned. While my father was gardening, my mother was usually spring- cleaning, which went on all the year round. She was obsessively tidy. Once, when I threw a bit of paper into a waste paper basket, she said: 'Oh, Miles, don't put that in there – I've only just emptied it…!'

It's true – people do come in two kinds, those that tidy things up and those that leave things to pile up. I am of the second sort. I accumulate. I like hoards and secret nooks and crannies, and lumber rooms, and old envelopes marked

'Are we allowed a feel good factor?'

'Interesting Correspondence from 1988 – not too late to answer…' I may like the idea of best-kept villages but not the reality. I like lawns and flowerbeds, but I like unkempt ponds and knee-deep meadows better.

There are other people in the village – in all villages – who feel differently, those who want to root out the nettles, the weeds, the tall decorative plants that spring out of the walls, and make the whole place look like those overgrown streets in 18th-century prints of half-maintained Italian towns. I worked for one of these people once; he was called Mr Pyke and he was the resident gardener in Ladbroke Square in Notting Hill in the 1960s. Mr Pyke, being a proper gardener, always called wild flowers 'weeds'.

'Always wipe your spade shiny clean before you finish digging, that was what I was taught,' Mr Pyke told me. 'That's in case the bit of earth on your spade has any seeds in it which might find their way elsewhere, and germinate.' My mother would have approved. I think she would have also agreed with Mr Pyke about wild flowers. Wild flowers had absolutely no justification in his view. And I could respect that, because he had been trained as a lad on large estates in Norfolk where there were still head gardeners who had an almost Victorian view of the craft.

But if you are on the committee of a best-kept village, you don't have that sort of justification. You just have a sort of manic tidiness to support you. And it is ironic if you are also commissioning posters on the preservation of wild life, because to be best-kept you have to extirpate as much wild life as you can lay your hands on…

There are two things in our village which I find stunning. One is a redcurrant bush rooted in the stump of an old ash tree, 12 feet above ground, and gaily producing quite different foliage and flowers at twice head height. The other is a clematis which has climbed out of control up a telephone pole and is now spreading in five different directions along the wires that meet at the top.

I am not sure whether either of these things would survive long if we had a chance of winning the Best-Kept contest. What we need, perhaps, is a Worst-Kept Village Competition. Meanwhile, I hope nobody finds out about the bats who are about to produce their babies in my bike shed. That might seem really untidy.

R S Thomas

After a lifetime as a priest in remote parishes, the poet R S Thomas was mooted for a Nobel Prize for literature. He talked with **Naim Attallah** *about God, poetry and his beloved Wales*

Portrait by Jane Bown

Is there a sense in which you can compare the idea of yourself as poet with your vocation as a priest?
Oh yes, I've never had any difficulty with that, because I think Christ was a poet and the New Testament is poetry.
The parables are metaphors really, and I'm very keen on metaphor. It was obvious that the disciples didn't always understand what Christ said to them. He was asked to explain, just as some people might ask a poet to explain.

And yet your own entry into the priesthood seems to have been less of a calling and more to do with the fact that your mother believed it was the road to a good job. . .
Not so much a good job; it was more that she had been brought up by a relation who was a cleric so that she acquired an admiration and fondness for the priesthood, and she obviously had these secret ambitions for me. I was at a malleable stage in my teens and I didn't raise any resistance. God moves in mysterious ways.

But it was not really a true vocation. . .
Well, what is a true vocation? Take the story of Samuel. The Lord came and called, and Samuel didn't understand – he had to be told three times that the Lord

was calling. So I'm not to be drawn on that one.

But had you not become a priest, what road would you have chosen, do you think?
I would have been in prison I expect. I would have been adrift. The devil finds work for idle hands.

How would you describe your feeling for your country and its language? Is it just an extreme form of patriotism, or is it much more complex and far-reaching that that?
We have a very old literary tradition. It's an older tradition than the English one, and I am fired at this. I just love my country, and when English people accuse me of being fanatical or extremist, I say to them, 'I am a patriot and I love my country as you love yours.'

Was your love of Wales something that was born and bred in you or was it acquired gradually?
I was brought up in Holyhead, which is a terrible little town, but all around was the sea and in the distance were the mountains of Wales. When I started my ministry, I had to go to the English border because I didn't speak Welsh. There was a kind of vacuum. Although I was glad to leave home and gain my freedom, I realised that

I had lost my native background, and from that moment I began a gradual return to Welsh Wales.

What makes you love Wales so much?
In a world where the big men have so much say, it is a small country, and I agree with Schumacher: small is beautiful. I always champion the small man, the small country. It is a country of extreme beauty – the industrial south has spoiled it of

course but for its size it's a lovely little country. And I love it in a way that possibly many other Welsh people don't.

I read somewhere that you have always been rather uncomfortable with Anglicanism. Is that true?
Not the Anglican communion, but I do realise that there are truths in other religions, Buddhism and Hinduism and Taoism. I wouldn't wish to say that the only gate into the kingdom is via

Anglicanism. Of course the Church of Wales is disestablished and disendowed and it sometimes lands you in an entanglement to try to explain to Welsh people in Welsh that the Anglican church is not English.
The Church in Wales is a part of the Anglican communion, and on the whole the tendency is to follow Canterbury, but we have our own prayer book, and our own governing body which means we can make certain doctrinal and other

constitutional amendments.

Have you ever experienced anything which might be called a crisis of faith?
Continually. The crisis is ongoing. Obviously you come up against problems, and things happen which are very testing. For example, a little girl was murdered the other day. If I were still with a parish, no doubt some of my parishioners would ask me how I equate a loving God with this

The Oldie Interview

sort of thing. But I never cease to believe in God.

How would you answer your parishioners in the case you mention?
Freedom is the only answer. God has taken the great risk of freedom rather than compel people to be good. He has chosen to risk their not being good, freedom being more important than compulsion. We have free will. The man who murdered the little girl has misused his God-given freedom.

Do you believe in heaven and hell?
I don't believe in heaven and hell. I leave it to God. God will decide. I try to be humble in this, I'm not going to say I'm sure that I'm going to heaven, or I'm afraid of going to hell, because it's out of my hands. I leave it to God. And that is faith – at least that is my faith. Trust is a better word; I trust that this great presence in the universe, if He so disposes, will assign me an appropriate destiny, whether it's oblivion, or whether it is a continuing existence in some other form. I can't do anything about it.

In your collection 'Counterpoint', you address some of the dilemmas caused by an ancient faith in a modern world. Can you tell me something of the difficulties as you see them?
I dare say I would have been burned at the stake in the old days because many of my views are heretical. I dislike hymns intensely, I dislike the revisions that have taken place in the liturgy. I've been a country priest all my life, dealing with semi-educated or uneducated people, and so my conception of the priesthood is rather different from what it would have been if I'd been among sophisticated and educated people.
I deplore some of the changes that have taken place under liturgical revision, and as you know there are all kinds of lunatic fringe Christians these days who believe in a godless Christianity. In my poems I rather deride that kind of thing. Where I talk about the creed, and write 'I believe in

'Say Ayatollah Rafsanjaneeeeeee'

God the Father Almighty,' and put in brackets, 'Is he married?' – this is not because I'm an unbeliever but because I resent some of the misinterpretations that have been put upon Him and the narrowness of theologians. Being a poet I naturally claim a certain amount of latitude.

But do the poems help you to resolve some of these problems?
In some of my more abstract poems I follow the argument to see if I can resolve it in some way, but to be honest I sometimes end up with a different answer like many other poets. I always say my chief end is to make a poem; I don't set out to write a Christian poem, an orthodox poem, just a poem, and if I am more or less convinced that it is a good poem then I'm satisfied.

As you look around the world in the late 20th century, are you very much aware of God's presence? Do you see him in the former Yugoslavia for example?
This is why I am such an enemy of technology and the machine in my poetry because people are very greedy, they clutch at all the latest technological inventions, they will have all these things. The result is we are flooded by news from all over the world as it's gathered, and this news is based mainly on sensationalism. At this moment somebody somewhere is almost certainly doing a very fine and self-sacrificing act, but you hear nothing about it on the media. But if somebody does something evil or nasty we get to know about it, and in this way we are being browbeaten into thinking that it is a godless world, that God is not at work. The noise that is being made in Yugoslavia and other parts of the world is drowning out the still small voices.

Your declared pacifism would seem to sit uneasily with your widely reported support for the sometimes violent campaigns against English settlers in Wales.
I'm not on record as ever having supported them. I've never incited people to be violent in Wales; I have said that I understand why it happens, but if I am reported to have supported violence then I have been libelled. I have never given my support to violent campaigns because

violence breeds violence, and this is inconsistent with pacifism.

Yet I understand that at a meeting of the Covenanters of the Free Welsh in 1990 you told the audience: 'I deplore killing, but what is the life of one English person compared to the destruction of a nation?' Would you still defend that sort of remark today?
Yes, indeed.

But isn't that tantamount to inciting people to violence?
I don't think so. It's being quite reasonable. We have to be on the defensive in Wales because we are a small country of two and a half million people living alongside an English nation of 55 million people. When we talk about the death of one English person, we mean a physical death. But Christ said, 'Don't fear those that have the power to destroy the body, fear those that have the power to destroy both the body and the soul.' And when you're dealing with a nation, you're dealing with a spiritual concept, and there's no doubt that the soul of Wales, the identity of Wales, have been eroded and are being eroded further all the time. That is why I said that.

I understand your wife was English. How did she view your attitude?
She was a painter and more concerned with other things. It wasn't her problem, it was my problem, and I didn't expect her to go out campaigning with me. We discussed it of course, and in all fair-mindedness I have to say there are good English as well as bad, but I resent terribly the takeover by England of a small country like Wales. My wife was more concerned with her own identity as a painter. Painters and musicians are not challenged by these things; they are not dependent on the language the way writers are. Now I'm living with somebody who is Irish Canadian. Her language is English, and she's able to speak to everybody, it's no problem to her, whereas I feel under a certain restraint from having to speak English to all these people who come flooding in at this time of year. She's being more Christian than I am, but she hasn't got the problem I have.

'Is there a way to adjust the escalator's speed?'

Moving on to poetry, T S Eliot, a poet whom you admire, said that genuine poetry can communicate before it is understood. Do you agree?
Yes, but he really didn't know what that meant. With poems it is really an argument of despair. In my case it's a result of my having ministered in so many of these less educated parishes, to simple people. I've always tried to make myself understood and this has stopped me from being a bobbydazzler as a poet. But at least you are on the side of people who say that great art is simple at heart.

I imagine you are unhappy with labels such as 'the best living religious poet', or 'the greatest living Welsh poet'. How would you prefer to be described?
I'm against any use of the word 'great'. My aim all along has been to write a good poem. I don't resent the description 'religious poet' because I think my work has grown more religious as I've got older, but I'm not in the stakes of being put up as the best poet now writing and all that sort of rubbish.

Despite the literary labels, the fact remains that you are not widely

read as a poet, and your reputation seems to rest more on your controversial character rather than your literary output. Is that a source of irritation to you, or disappointment perhaps?*
Poetry is unfortunately a minor art in the present century. There are a whole lot of new art forms blossoming in the late 20th century and we just have to be patient and let things work themselves out and maybe the poem will come back into its own. Poetry has been the glory of English cultural life, it has been a very great art form, as it was earlier in Wales. I deplore the shallowness and trickiness of contemporary English poetry, and I think possibly poets have asked for the contempt with which they are treated.

You have attracted a lot of enemies in your time. Does that bother you?
Well, I never meet any. It is shadow-boxing. I would expect to have made enemies, because I have been trying to stand up for a misjudged and abused nation. On the other hand, in all fairness I have also received letters from English people who say they agree with me and understand my point of view. It's always nice to be praised and unpleasant to be castigated,

The Oldie Interview

but you can't spend your time worrying about these things.

Is it one of the felicities of old age, do you think, that you stop worrying about these things?
No, I think it's the felicity of being a poet. A poet is one of the few free people that there are. I'm not a politician, I don't have to worry about my standing in the polls in case I lose the next election or do damage to the party. I am a free man, and I suppose this partly arises from having been a priest. The church offers a certain amount of freedom; as a priest I wasn't responsible to anybody, I was simply given a stipend and left to be the priest in a certain parish, and to preach the gospel as I saw it.

You say that you have always been something of a loner. How important was marriage and the companionship of a wife?
I am an old man and my time in the church was before all these economic messes and group parishes where the poor priest is rushed off his feet. I belong to the generation that had one church and a little congregation, so I was able to proceed in a leisurely way. Both my wife and I preferred the quietness of the country which small parishes offered. The need for a wife's counselling and comforting didn't really arise to the same extent as if I had been a busy town priest. And her vocation was to be a painter, so we went our own separate ways really. She preferred to stay in and paint, whereas I used to like to go out and wander about. These are the differences which arise from the pattern of life one has lived. The lone element is obviously there in me.

Would you have been able to live without a woman?
Probably not. I think poets are quite erotic. Female beauty naturally appeals to a poet, so I would have certainly ended up with somebody, I daresay.

Where do you stand on the business of women priests?
I can see no practical or philosophical or theological objection, but it doesn't seem to work out in practice as far as I'm concerned. Most of the women I know don't want them. Of course I'm speaking out of very narrow experience, but certainly in the country parishes the people would not want a woman priest. I would lose an argument with a well-trained defender of the woman priesthood, but there is certainly a gut reaction which is not happy with it.

Is your religious faith becoming stronger as you get older?
I can only say that I never lose my faith in God. I don't think atheism is a sustainable creed, so I'm never really tempted to become atheistic in any way. I'll not say my faith is deepening but I hope I have acquired a kind of acceptance, a resignation really, in the face of the enormous questions that beset us. God will dispose as he sees fit.

Looking back over your life, do you get a sense of a job well done?
Oh Lord, no. One is tinged with the pessimism of poets like A E Housman. There is a kind of life-denying part in one's makeup, a kind of nihilistic approach to life. But I don't think it is a permanent thing; it comes now and again, and the whole thing seems a ghastly sort of bungling in some way. And one recognises that one has been part of this bungling.

'My wife doesn't understand my computer…'

Epistle from Paris

IN THE EYES of the world there are three symbols that represent France: the Eiffel Tower, General de Gaulle, and Brigitte Bardot. Well, the Eiffel Tower is the oldest, the General is dead, his memory firmly imprinted as a political way of life, but Brigitte Bardot is still very much alive and capable of outselling current best-sellers and swelling a TV audience to one of its largest ever.

BB's autobiography *Initials BB* published by Grasset at the beginning of October, sold at the rate of 25,000 copies a day over the first 10 days. After just two weeks their sales department reported 450,000 copies sold in France alone. On the day of publication, she pulled in an audience of nearly nine million viewers for an hour-and-a-half interview programme which was interspersed with guests and film-clips.

Not bad when you are celebrating your 62nd birthday, when you haven't made a film for 20 years and when you are now usually photographed with dogs, cats, seals and donkeys rather than lovers.

Brigitte is a phenomenon. She was a sex symbol who never really liked acting: 'I wasn't very good except in a few roles but I went along with it because I was too involved to do anything else. I enjoyed singing and dancing, that was my pleasure.'

Bardot had grace and style, and still has. Dressed in a black trouser suit with a rose in her hair as the only adornment, she looked terrific. The hair was artfully streaked and face lightly made up. The voice hadn't changed and neither had her way of saying what she thinks.

A surprise guest was former President Valery Giscard D'Estaing. She leapt up and hugged and kissed him as he walked on stage. 'VAL-ER-EE,' she cooed. Giscard took it in good part and kissed her warmly.

In her tell-all autobiography, Bardot had recalled Giscard, when he was Minister of Finance, taking part in parlour games at one of her parties. Suddenly, he disappeared into the kitchen, she said, and came back astride a broom with a dish-cloth on his head, and leapt and ran round the room. He was acting out *Les Sorcieres de Salem* (The Witches of Salem/Arthur Miller's *The Crucible*). Grasset had wanted to cut out some of the passages of her book involving well-known people in case of trouble over her sometimes crude accounts, but finally all was left in.

Back to the TV screen with Giscard recalling how he had bumped into Bardot on the ski slopes in Meribel and they had both fallen down 'on our bums', giggled Bardot.

'And you escorted me back to your chalet where one of your malevolent dogs bit me.'

'On your behind,' said Bardot.

'On my right calf,' said Giscard firmly.

'Oh, I remember, it was a bit higher,' and Brigitte, 'however, I painted you with Mercurochrome.'

'And made it better,' said Giscard.

He also recalled carrying her bags for her when they were both boarding the same aircraft at Nice. 'Next day,' said Giscard, 'I was all over the front page of the papers – you in front, me carrying bags and the headline "Co-incidence or not?" I treasure that cutting.'

The other surprise guest was Lech Walesa whom French television had brought to Paris on a specially chartered plane to appear on the programme. When Walesa was President of Poland on an official visit to France, he had requested two things he would like to do unofficial-ly: go up the Eiffel Tower and meet Brigitte Bardot. He did manage to go up the Eiffel Tower but when he should have

been meeting Bardot, she was looking after a sick dog.

So this was the meeting. Bardot clasped him in her arms. He gave her a red rose which she stuck into her *décolleté*. His eyes misted over as he sat down and said that communist countries had admired Bardot too and that he had carried her photograph around in a pocket mirror.

'You had no right to stop,' he said, 'to deprive us of your presence.'

'But I haven't,' she said, 'I've just done something else. And you also have deprived us of your presence.'

'I too, Madame, do something else,' he smiled.

Bardot's book doesn't gloss over any-thing in her life. She says she regards childbirth as God's punishment to women.

She had one son, Nicolas Charrier, now 36, who was brought up by his father Jacques and who now lives in Norway with his Norwegian wife and two children. 'We only got to know each other when he was grown up,' she said, 'I made the right decision. The rackety life I was living and the stress was not the way to bring up a child. His father married again and Nicolas had a stable home life.'

She doesn't spare his father, though, who she says was 'bourgeois even to his balls' and who she maintains beat her up.

The great passionate love of her life was Serge Gainsbourg, the French song writer. 'Perhaps it was so perfect in retro-

'It's a take-over bid'

spect because it didn't last long!'

She bears no ill will towards Gunther Sachs although she says he only married her for a bet! 'While it lasted it was a fun world of millionaires and riches which wasn't my world but something I would never have experienced except for him.'

Grasset gave her an advance payment of five million Francs (about £600,000) which isn't a great deal when you think what they are going to get out of it, not only in French speaking countries but with translations.

At the Frankfurt book fair Grasset was jubilant. One of the editors at Grasset, Jean-Claude Fasquelle, said the French edition would be sold in 10 different coun-tries and they were looking into two offers from Russia. About a dozen translations are already under way.

But they will need to be carefully done to catch the natural tone of the book which she says took her about 20 years to write. At one point she let five years go by with-out writing a line. She jotted down things as she remembered them and finally gave the three-volume manuscript to a journal-ist friend, Patrick Mahe. 'He didn't do anything to it except get it properly edited and presented.' She said. The journalist agreed. 'A bit of correcting here and there,' he said, 'and that was it.' 546 pages at 140 francs a copy.

Most of Brigitte's share will be going to her animal foundation and she's already back in the saddle of her second career with a blistering letter addressed to the French Minister of Agriculture who recently authorised the sale of kangaroo meat in France. She called it 'scandalous'.

JOAN SMYTH

'Remember, you're accused of witchcraft so try not to cackle... and lose the hat!'

T he late Lord Goodman, legal plenipotentiary to VIPs in trouble with the Press and Writ-Server-in-Chief to *Private Eye*, made two injudicious observations during his 82 years on earth. The first, enshrined in his autobiography *Tell Them I'm On My Way*, proclaimed: 'There is probably no career that gives one a more rounded view of the human race than that of a solicitor.' Pause for canned laughter. Offhand, I can think of several, including a chief constable's, a cruise liner captain's, a journalist's and a bordello madam's. The second indiscretion: 'I have the deep-seated conviction that women are intellectually inferior to men.' The life-long bachelor did not disclose the method or depth – except that it was deep-seated – of his research, or whether his inquisitions were conducted before, during or after lunch or dinner.

My own 83-year study of the other sex, which still occupies a good deal of my time, has led me to the deep-seated conviction that the essential disparity between the sexes has little to do with intellect. The distinguishing characteristic is woman's claim to, or assumption of, infallibility.

Arnold Goodman was too busy dispensing wisdom to notice the re-emergence of the female infallibility virus since a remarkable woman named Margaret Hilda Thatcher became Britain's first female Prime Minister in 1979. Her performance as a formidable 'Presidential' leader is already established; for good or ill is for the historians to assess. What has not been acknowledged is the influence for good or ill the Iron Lady has exerted on the social demeanour of her own sex, including millions who expressed their personal dislike of her stridency in over-the-garden-wall chatter and supermarket asides as well as regularly in opinion polls.

Margaret Thatcher did not invent infallibility, agreed, but there is no doubt she stimulated its rampant revival in the formerly United Kingdom. The Infallible She is now part of the Establishment, with the Baroness T as the high priestess of the cult. Shall we accept the OED definition so, at any rate, we don't fall out over details? 'Infallible. Not fallible. Not liable to be deceived or mistaken; incapable of erring... sure, certain.'

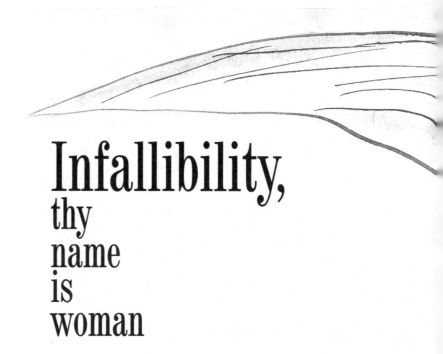

Infallibility,
thy
name
is
woman

Margaret's creed at No 10 was 'No, no, no' to Cabinet colleagues as well as to stupid foreigners. 'My view must prevail,' she told her Chancellor Nigel Lawson the day he resigned. Geoffrey Howe says that in her final years of power she regarded criticism of herself as unpatriotic. Pressed by David Frost on whether she had made any major wrong decisions, she replied: 'Goodness me, David, I think I was wrong on a number of things, but I cannot think of anything immediately.' The chapter on foreign missions in her memoirs is entitled 'Putting the World to Rights'.

There was fresh evidence recently that The Great Dissenter's penchant for correcting mere males, including other Prime Ministers, has not waned since her departure from Downing Street. The *Sunday Times* reported on 1st October, 1995:

'The Prime Minister (Mr Major) chanced his arm in his speech about Baroness Thatcher during the party for her 70th birthday at No 10 last week. He recalled an occasion when she stopped off at Honolulu in the dead of night – 2am – and was met by an admiral who suggested she go to a small apartment to rest. But

HMS·INFALLIBLE

moment of suspense, wrecking it further-more on a matter of irrelevant fact. They may not have the courage to admit it, but all men endure this torture.

The audience is spellbound by your fluency as a raconteur, your RADA char-acterisation of the principal parts ('You should have been on the stage'). You have set the final scene of the anecdote in shim-mering detail as all present assure you again they haven't heard the story before and press you to continue. And then a voice you instantly recognise as the one you have heard every day and night since it first said 'I will' shatters the tension with: 'It can't have been the Friday – that was the day we took the retriever to the vet because you thought it had hardpad.'

There are still minor matters on which the male view is allowed to prevail without challenge: which team won the Cup in 1953, which horse twice won the Derby, whether the new gents' urinal is on the left or right of the old town library. But as the party moves into top gear the last word on most other questions, especially Who, When and Where, is blasted off in soprano or contralto: *coitus interruptus* now has a wider connotation.

Let us discuss the issue in a gentleman-ly fashion with no umbrage, but I'll tell you this in confidence: men are swallow-ing their pride in the interests of domestic bliss. Bliss! The fact is they are simmering with stifled rage. The more house-trained cool off by stamping around the garden kicking stones and dead-heading daffodils, but don't be surprised if one of these fine days they blow their top, the lot of them, simultaneously, in one mighty insurrec-tion. I have no wish to raise my voice and make matters worse, but women are always assuming they are bloody right and that the man (father, husband, brother, son, or live-in lover) is always bloody wrong!

The interjections are not usually protests against the stupid fellow's inter-pretation of events, or bias, or calumny. They are merely corrective on some piddling chronological cock-up, or mispro-nounced name, or on whether the family's pet hamster was Tim or Tom, or whether in fact it was a guinea-pig and not a ham-ster at all. It isn't a deliberate attempt to sabotage the tale and drive a man mad: oh no, it is simply the need for perfection,

she demanded instead to see Pearl Harbour – the place, she said, where democracy had been saved.

'Maggie recalled the occasion. No, John, it was not 2am but 5am. She had been met not by an admiral but by a gener-al. Correcting him again, Thatcher said that on being told that a small apartment had been prepared for her to rest, she had replied: 'Rest... we're not here to rest where the flower of freedom was so nearly snuffed out,' and so on. When she was told that it was too dark, she reached into her handbag and produced a torch – the

one, incidentally, she has had with her ever since being plunged into the dark after the Brighton bomb. But why couldn't she have waited till first light? 'The Japanese did.'

The trouble is that one woman's ego-centricity has become contagious as another form of mad cow disease, embrac-ing womankind. Fiancées, wives and mis-tresses are no longer content to smile and suffer in silence on social occasions with-out outbursts of omniscience. I refer to their urge for a walk-on or talk-on part in their escort's finest party piece at its the uncontrollable passion to demonstrate, as I said rather crudely earlier on, that they are Bloody Right and the man is bloody wrong. We have all heard and seen it happen. We all know those joke-strangling, blood-vessel-bursting interjections that might well have resulted in an open-and-shut case of wife murder on the spot:

'But darling, he was short-sighted until he was 63.'

'It's the chameleon that changes the colour of its skin.'

'I told *you* that, *you* didn't tell me.'

'Can't have been pissing down, as you say, because that was the famous rainless August.'

'No, it can't have been hers in the casserole. She still had her own teeth.'

'It was a guppy. The cat had had their Siamese fighting fish the week before.'

The victim, who has a long-standing pact with his wife never to bicker in public, says, 'Yes, darling, of course you're right,' as he picks up the fragments, laboriously re-sets the scene and re-launches the story, presiding over its doom. Everybody except The Infallible She knows what he is muttering under his breath: 'Stupid bitch. What has somebody's sodding guppy got to do with it? I could strangle you with my bare hands.'

Anecdotal assassination should be punishable by 100 days' community service in a Trappist monastery, but he knows that this serial anecdotal assassin will be with him until death do them part. When, for God's sake, did veracity raise a laugh, or the truth, the whole truth and nothing but the truth have them rolling in the aisles?

The incident which forced me to break my silence and pen this protest occurred at a recent dinner party. It was an occasion bereft of hilarity on a wet Sunday night; nobody's fault – blame the weather, which was exhaustively discussed. Another guest's pointless story about a blind physiotherapist deepened the gloom. All I wanted to do was to get home to continue my diatribe against the ghastly Sunday tabloids, but a beseeching glance from the hostess emboldened me to intervene.

'Which reminds me,' I said, breaking the spell of another lull, 'of a story a blind physiotherapist told me about a woman who lived in a cottage on a lower slope of the Snowdonia massif in North Wales' –

adding with a mood-changing chuckle that it probably wasn't the same blind physio, or was it? (No laughter, even canned.)

It didn't matter, honestly, whether I had been told the story by a blind physiotherapist or a long-sighted lesbian all-in wrestler. There was surprisingly no helpful interruption at this stage correcting the identity of the mountain range or questioning whether the cottage was on the lower slope or upper slope, so I proceeded confidently to lift-off.

Well, the physio and his wife arrived at the nearest station, Llanbryngarwestbednerchwellygaer (still no fine tuning from my vigilant accompanist) and taxied to the cottage for their annual autumn hols with Gwynneth and her beloved Dai. She was there to greet them at the rickety wooden

gate, but Dai wasn't. (I was expecting an interjection here on the lines of how did I know the gate was rickety, or wooden for that matter, but she was holding her fire.)

The jolly question 'Where's Dai?' was answered with a downcast glance and a tear. 'Dai's gone. I've lost him. It was a month ago.' Dai was a keen gardener, veg rather than flowers because of the climate on the lower slopes etc. One day he'd said to Gwynneth: 'I'll get a cabbage for lunch, luv, at the bottom of the garden. Back in a minute.' And…

And then I heard a voice: 'The top.'

'Pardon?'

'The *top* not the bottom,' said The Infallible She.

'The bottom,' I repeated.

'No, *the top*. It wouldn't have

happened if the cabbage had been at the bottom of the garden.'

I began to speak in italics myself: '*It doesn't matter a bloody damn if it happened at the top or bloody bottom of the bloody garden. The point is it happened.*'

Noticing that several of the other guests had now opened their eyes or cleared their throats or moved their elbows from the table, I continued with the narrative to explain what *had* happened. When Dai failed to return with the cabbage after five minutes his wife went down to the *bottom* of the garden and found Dai lying in the cabbage patch. Dead. Heart failure.

'Good heavens,' cried the blind physiotherapist's wife, 'how awful! Whatever did you do?'

'I went back to the kitchen,' said Gwynneth, 'and opened a tin of peas.'

When nobody laughed and another lull set in, I added: 'I think it was a tin of peas. Of course, it could have been beans or Italian tomatoes, or sweet corn…'

'Cheese before or after sweets?' chirped the hostess. 'Charles and I always…'

'…or *bloody asparagus*,' I concluded, targeting the remark. 'Of course it's more likely a man would collapse with heart failure after walking *up* a sloping garden than *down* a sloping garden. Any fool knows that. But in this case…'

As we moved towards the front door, the first to leave, I heard a voice say: 'Do ask us again when they're here. It made the evening.'

It was all explained to me as I fell asleep while she drove us home. 'It is *not* interrupting and it is *not* ruining the punch line.' Zzz–zz… 'Don't you see, if somebody notices you have a fact wrong, they assume the whole story is a pack of lies? It was obviously the *top* of the garden.' Zzz–zz–zz… 'Sometimes when telling that story you say that Dai went to get some peas, but it would have taken him longer than five minutes to pick peas…'

Wasn't it C P Scott, the editor of the *Manchester Guardian*, who said: 'Comment is free but facts are sacred'? Or was it Sir Walter Scott, or Scott of the Antarctic? And did he say 'Comment is free but facts are sacred' or 'Comment is priceless but facts are up for grabs'? God bless Baroness Thatcher, that's what I say.

The Smallweeds

THE SMALLWEEDS live in a commodious residence in Ewell Village. Needless to say, they are a most respectable couple: Mrs Smallweed sings soprano in the Sutton and Banstead Early Music Chorale, and Mr S would have been made an associate director of the insurance company from which he has recently retired, Mrs S suggests, had it not been for the jealousy of a certain highly - placed colleague.

The Smallweed children have grown up and gone away now: to African agricultural aid programmes and East European consultancy projects. Mrs Smallweed writes them long punctilious letters. Mr S's little weakness is old detective novels, and he can tell from the merest inspection of a book's final pages whether he has read it before, and if the butler did it. In fact the Smallweeds are a pattern of newly-retired citizenry: hale, modest and Godfearing. And yet tradesmen quake in terror as they wander up the Smallweeds' front path (bordered by the neatest beds of lobelia), the local police sergeant hesitates to return their phone calls, and Mr Magg the village newsagent has stopped delivering their morning copy of the *Daily Telegraph* on the grounds that it 'isn't worth the trouble.'

Why is this? I had dinner with the Smallweeds not long ago (Mr S is a connection of my father) in a trattoria in Reigate: the Smallweeds don't patronise their local restaurants. It was an eventful evening. First Mr Smallweed sent back a half-pint of lager on the grounds that it infringed the requirements of the Weights and Measures Act. Then Mrs Smallweed complained of the number of olives – three, I think – in her Salade Nicoise. The main course passed without incident – though I could see that Mr S sighed wistfully over the rawness of his steak. When the bill came – and the manager himself brought it with a nervous little smile – Mrs S got out a pocket calculator and sat grimly adding up columns of figures, while Mr S examined his chequebook with an air of the most awful gravity. What didn't they do to that bill? They queried the total, of course. They bullied the drinks waiter into admitting that he might have supplied them with a supernumerary bottle of mineral water. They questioned the number of side-dishes (and I believe that Mrs S did finally avoid having to pay for a rogue bowl of soup). Mr Smallweed struck off the service charge with a fierce jab of his pen. I think they left a tip of 50 pence.

You might have thought (and I confess I thought it) that the Smallweeds would be downcast by this series of misfortunes, particularly as the meal commemorated some tender anniversary. Not a bit of it! In the taxi on the way home, while Mr S kept a vigilant eye on the meter, his wife read me the most comfortable little lecture. 'Of course,' she said demurely, 'nobody likes to complain. But there is such a thing as knowing your rights. Why, if it hadn't been for me looking at the bill for a second time those people would have charged us for your glass of tap-water.' The way Mrs Smallweed said those people was quite magnificent.

The Smallweeds, then, are genteel middle-class people who 'know their rights'. Woe betide the village shopkeeper who sells Mr Smallweed a packet of six shortcake biscuits in which the sixth is somewhat dispersed around the packet, or the greengrocer whose two pounds of apples is actually a paltry one and fifteen sixteenths (Mrs Smallweed takes all her fruit home and re-weighs it immediately). I heard a fine story about them in connection with the council tax. The Smallweeds have a substantial four-bedroomed property and there are but the two of them. Mrs S, though, suffers from migraines, and by maintaining that these frequently caused her to occupy an additional room, and by addressing the council, her MP, and finally the Ombudsman, she had the taxable value of the house reduced from band G to F.

But the Smallweeds' finest hour came a month ago. A quarter of a mile up the hill from 'Jalna' (such is the pretty name which Mrs S has bestowed on the house) is a patch of waste ground currently being transformed into a row of town houses by a property developer. Planning permission for the development was only granted after the liveliest and most tenacious struggle between building company and residents, and involved the most fearsome proscriptions with regard to noise, disturbance, working hours, frequency of site traffic, etc. Naturally the Smallweeds were the most vociferous of those opposing the plans, and their MP grew quite to dread opening his morning post (Mrs Smallweed writes to him at his private address, as it 'saves time'). A week after the work

Robert Geary

began a contractor's lorry passing Jalna at a steady 15 miles per hour deposited perhaps eight ounces of concrete mix on the Smallweeds' driveway. Mrs Smallweed was on the phone to the developers' head office within the hour. She had a letter of apology a day later. Two days after this a cleaning company arrived and at the developers' expense actually valeted the Smallweeds' car! (Mrs S maintains that they broke a ventilation duct, but this could never be proved.)

There are rumours that Mr S is the less committed of the two. I was with him once in a pub when he ordered a glass of ginger beer. 'Now what might that be?' Mr S wondered in his diffident, retired person's way, indicating a tiny speck of ambiguous matter floating near the rim. Mr S not only got the landlord to replace his drink, but emerged victorious from the conversation with a different kind of drink, alcoholic even, and certainly more expensive than the first. I watched Mr Smallweed as he drank it, looking for some slight sign of embarrassment, some faint shame at having made such an exhibition of himself. On the contrary his face wore a look of extraordinary rectitude. The worst of it is that these attitudes are contagious. Later that afternoon I am fairly sure that I complained about a dirty beer glass and, on my way to post a letter at 5.28pm, may even have remonstrated with a zealous postman whom I found already locking up the box. **D J TAYLOR**

'You spoil that dog'

Video — Larry Adler

Caesar and Cleopatra 1945

I could use some help from Gerald Ratner in writing this review. First, let me list the incontrovertibles. This was the most expensive British film ever made at the time. It cost more than £1,250,000. It took two and a half years to make. The producer actually took sand to Egypt to get the right colour. It achieved the incredible effect of making Claude Rains seem an uninteresting actor. It won one Academy nomination – John Bryan, for the sets. It made a joke of Flora Robson's performance. It proved, as if that were needed, that Vivien Leigh is beautiful. It got a rave notice from George Bernard Shaw: 'It is so wonderful as to make my other films look naive.'

Well, for me the film was crap, glorious crap. No actor was believable. It had lots of good actors I couldn't recognise, among them being Leo Genn, Stanley Holloway, Jean Simmons and Esmé Percy. I'm sure they were there, you just can't prove it by me.

Claude Rains, capable of stealing a film from Humphrey Bogart and Ingrid Bergman, as he did in *Casablanca,* here seems like a bored booking agent. This is Caesar? Georges Auric, a fine film composer, here succumbs to the tackiness around him and contributes a corny score. I'd love to know what was in Gabriel Pascal's mind when he planned this Epic of Epics. By the way, there are some shameful stereotypes of Negro slaves… no, not Blacks, I said and I mean, Negroes. They run about shouting and grimacing with dumb expressions in a way that makes you yearn for the stern realism of Stepin Fetchit. This super-crap should have been cut. Even in those days you didn't portray Blacks like that. I ploughed through this one, trying to watch the whole thing for your sake. You have no idea what I go through for you. Well, I couldn't do it. This film gives new and richer meaning to the word 'boredom'.

'Whilst you were out, the government revived our flagging fortunes'

Change for a tenor

Robert Tear *strikes a light philosophical chord on the trials of ageing and opera*

AS I STRIDE towards my dotage, noting on my way that those joints which once helped me to skip like a spring lamb are now squealing in protest at the sight of stairs and those eyes which could decipher the tail of a quaver through flickering candlelight cannot now decide whether print is too near them or too far off, I'm nudged to question whether there are any epiphanies, or even one, in this swift passage to new nappies and cheap caskets.

The physical side is all disaster. This is plain. Forking a little deeper on the philosophical side I do see a glimmer of light. This turns quickly into a walking epiphany that whispers into my ear. 'Have you considered that you seem to have more time for life, that you have less haste in your loins, that when singing a difficult aria you don't rush it, you consider from a distance, then you sing? Old age should bring a certain wisdom with it, an ability to see from a different perspective, a new dimension.'

So it is out. There is a blessing and I am a singer. Alas, as seems to be the case with all things, every cloud has its grey lining, there is no unadulterated pleasure, no perfection without a little alloy.

This is made dazzlingly clear to me when I work with conductors and producers (or stage directors as they now prefer to be called). From always being the youngest in my company, I am now inevitably and suddenly the oldest. There was no transition – it happened overnight, and whereas I perhaps have achieved a modicum of wisdom, sitting as I do in my eternal dimension, the young souls I work with are simply not old enough to sit chatting with me on my bench and to gaze wistfully at the setting sun.

I have to endure from each new talent, that not only have they spotted all life's problems, but they also have new and radical solutions.

I worked with a young conductor the other day who was performing his first Beethoven Ninth. He came up to me and explained that if these bars were phrased like that and those like this then the whole piece would be seen afresh, blindingly new. As he was talking to me I could hear gross laughter in a passing cloud and saw a white mane being tossed about in helpless mirth. At the performance the work sounded disturbingly familiar.

Directors, too, are the strangest bunch. they come with most of the psychological problems known to science. First there are those so anally retentive that a pin couldn't be inserted even in early June.

These same have a problem with control. I'm reminded of an opera I was performing in Austria, a kind of lamb's tale from Salzburg. I'm playing a shepherd, the rehearsal period is two months. At the first rehearsal I'm presented with a woolly, skittering, slippy-hooved creature just approaching adolescence who I'm supposed to carry about my neck. She is heavy. In my innocence I mention the fact that in 56 days this madonna of the bleat will be a monster sheep. The director pronounces with deadly seriousness: 'It vill not grow.' How comforting. I thought.

Then come those who need to exorcise their childhood fears, their misogyny, their terror of cupboards or the masterpieces of musical literature, most on the dartboard of the Ring, it must be said. They vindicate their infantilism by calling their antics the 'theatre of the absurd'. They also think their labour quite original, forgetting that the 'Merde!' of Alfred Jarry had happened about a hundred years earlier and that Beckett in his sad, empty way had already sucked the cardboard orange dry.

I have been told through Goebbels' pupils, 'Do not countermant mein orders,' and was once informed that if I should bring out my handkerchief again, 'I bill leaf by ze next plane.' I did and he stayed.

I recall, too, the Austrian conductor Josef Kripps saying to me (when I was almost a baby, and he should have known better): 'I can nefer forgif you for vat you dit to our vimmin in ze war.' I refused to accept the national guilt on this one.

Now before you think me a completely cantankerous old curmudgeon I must say that at this moment I'm working with the kindest, wisest, most gifted director. I'm convinced he made up the eternal bench in one tea-break and has been sitting on it waiting for me to arrive. His name is Peter Sellars. One three hour session in such visionary company is enough to convince me that not only is the job I do worthwhile after all, but that epiphanies are out and about and wearing boots to kick their way into my consciousness should I become wilfully hubristic.

John and Myfanwy Piper conducted all aspects of life with artistic precision, recalls **Patrick Reyntiens**

The art of living

Myfanwy Piper died on 18th January 1997, with economy, precision and style, just as she had lived. After a moderate lunch, getting her strength back following a bout of 'flu, she leaned back in her chair, took a deep breath and expired. It was the end of a perfectly conducted life.

There was nothing sentimental about the Pipers' outlook on life, least of all towards themselves. I don't think I ever heard less complaint and self-pity. Their tart observations extended to friends and foes alike but were never purely malicious and were based on unvarnished and unblinking truth. They knew instinctively what was phoney and what was not. But this was not in any way allied to an unfeeling, unsympathetic outlook. No one could be kinder and more understanding on a personal level.

Life at Fawley Bottom Farmhouse, near Henley-on-Thames, was of a peculiarly complicated and all-embracing character. On a domestic level, everything had to be in apple-pie order. No bed was ever left unmade, no meal ever went unwashed-up, no clothes were left strewn across the furniture. But this careful regime was not for its own sake; it was seen as the necessary condition to be able, efficiently and economically, to prosecute more important matters.

The domestic world of cooking, making, gardening and sending children to school was dovetailed into running their joint and separate professional lives. Myfanwy had a study overlooking the garden, which housed her books on either side of the chimney breast. The fire was always lit – there was no central heating – and there was a typewriter, a comfy chair and a fat, complacent marmalade cat purring away by the fireside. It was here that her articles, *libretti* and other writings were tapped out. Both Pipers worked from 9.30 to 12.30; lunch, cooked by Myfanwy, lasted from 12.30 to 2.30, and they worked

on till 4.30. Thereafter there might be any number of things to be done.

Preparing supper was of prime importance. There was something almost French in their concentration on *le repas*. For 40 years Myfanwy kept up the highest standards of cooking in England. It was not spectacular or extravagant, but it was of the very best and most original character, reflecting a fine appreciation and understanding of English, French and, to a certain extent, Italian cooking. The mode of cooking was unique to Myfanwy – John tended to be bottle-washer, salad-dressing maker and, occasionally, sub-baker. The kitchen, which led straight out of the farmyard, with a door at right angles to the living-room, was in many ways the pivot round which the household circulated. It had an all-inclusive and elaborate dresser at one end, a large Aga in the middle wall opposite the door and a massive sycamore table, the *mensa* of which was a brilliantly polished black Aberdeen granite slab some 5ft by 9ft and 2in thick. It had originally been put in place by a team of tombstone-makers or undertakers, and had never been moved since. On this sacrificial slab were set out bottles of wine, freshly uncorked, newspapers, the morning's post and other items of interest and importance. By now, John had come in from his studio, on the other side of the dresser. The conversation round the kitchen table ranged from darning socks to the provision of garden manure, from the latest scandals in the newspapers to pictures to be delivered to London galleries, from the goings-on at Aldeburgh or the architecture of Venice to the novels of Gustave Flaubert or Ted Hughes's latest book of poetry, and how disgusting and horrible so-and-so was.

Not a minute was wasted on inanities. John used to say 'I may have many faults; but one thing, I'm not lazy.' How right he was. His main attribute as a painter was diligence. Like Poussin, it could be said of John Piper that 'he had neglected nothing'. The Piper family were originally lawyers from the home counties and John had been articled as a lawyer before he rebelled and got into the Royal College of Art by sheer persistence and hard work.

This legal training, combined with his natural cleverness, made John a formidable enemy and a reliable and

Myfanwy Piper (left) turned the interior of Fawley Bottom into a work of art, combining domestic artefacts with the designs of husband John. Far left: Coventry Cathedral stained glass window designed by Piper, executed by Patrick Reyntiens

trustworthy friend. He urged one 'never to have an unresolved relationship with anyone. Either you are a friend, in which case you must always behave as a friend and be dead loyal in everything you do... or you are an enemy and then you know where you stand *vis-à-vis* this other person, and you've only yourself to blame if you let your guard down.' This was good if bleak advice and it seems to have served him well.

The Piper sense of economy was sometimes brought into play to end ridiculous time-wasting or boring situations. On one occasion 400 arties and smarties had been invited for pre-lunch drinks to inspect the huge tympanum of varied blues designed by John for Coventry Cathedral baptistery window.

There were still a few people left when the clock struck two. 'Right,' said Myfanwy, and went straight up to Sir Evelyn Shuckburgh, our ambassador to the UN at the time, and Lady Shuckburgh: 'Aren't you going? We want our lunch!'

Did nothing go wrong? Yes, perhaps it did, occasionally. One of the drawbacks was that Myfanwy couldn't or didn't or was forbidden to drive, and John was on no account to be distracted from his work in the studio in the mornings: with an important luncheon to devise and no transport, Myfanwy used to telephone the local taxi rank in Henley and soon a taxi would roll up to the door carrying prime fillet steak or half a salmon or a haunch of venison. Just in time. The garden was important, because most of the vegetables in Myfanwy's cooking came straight from it. She loathed anything out of season.

Much time was spent discussing shows and special trips abroad and routes round France, because the Pipers visited a different part of France every year. These trips – during which John would always paint and draw – were often related to the pilgrim route from Paris to Santiago de Compostela: all the major romanesque monuments of France, with their incomparable sculptures, were associated with this pilgrimage and its different routes. John was very bad at languages and couldn't speak French to save his life. But Myfanwy could, and they got what they wanted out of France.

Then it was back to work in the studio, with visits from dealers, buyers, patrons, producers, publishers. John dealt with these as he did with everything else; with courtesy, humour, patience and speed. His activities were evenly divided between his own exclusive *oeuvre*, and what might be described as 'delegated art'. It is almost inconceivable now, such is his prestige, to imagine him compromising his particular poetry by delegating any manual work. But John was completely unphased by such 'delegation' – which explains why his activities extended to etching, silkscreen and lithography, ceramics and stained glass, theatre and scenic design, fireworks and the 'public works' associated with Battersea Park at the time of the Festival of Britain. Such industry demanded delegation.

John didn't care what he wore – all his clothes were bought off the peg by Myfanwy. She had a good eye for what was what, and John looked all right. But there was a slight hiatus – call it what you will – between the man and his clothes, such as happens when someone is consistently supplied with clothes bought to someone else's taste. Myfanwy, on the other hand, was intensely interested in clothes and took them very seriously. She managed to get model clothes through contacts and friendships in the rag-trade. 'Look at this; isn't it super; so-and-so got it for me; I think it's marvellous.' And usually it was, because she had an eye.

And she always wore a piece of fabulous Sandy Calder jewellery. The Pipers were great friends with Alexander Calder, and he left three of his early mobiles about in the yard and house at Fawley.

John played the piano extremely well, from jazz and swing to Mozart and Busoni. There were two pianos in the living room, a grand and an upright, so visiting musicians could play duets; no doubt Benjamin Britten felt at home. John had a collection of about 3,000 records.

In her introduction to a collection of *Sea Poems* she published in 1944, Myfanwy wrote: 'Here there is not a single "row, sailors, row", not a Lady of Spain, not a bosun's mate, not a comb, not a glass; scarcely an oilskin or a Drake or a Trafalgar.' Vintage Myfanwy. It could not be bettered.

Happily away with the fairies

It's great to be gaga, says **Paul Pickering**, *whose hallucinating grandmother is still in fine fettle*

A CANADIAN FRIEND rang me very worried the other day. 'I don't like to admit this even to myself. But my grandmother is losing her mind. We are convinced it's Alzheimer's. My sister went over there and found grandma had cooked her purse in the microwave.' Even allowing for the fact that a purse is a handbag in Toronto, this did not sound at all serious to me. I tried to reassure my friend with an account of my own sprightly 96-year-old grandma and the evening bomber.

Most evenings at dusk my grandmother, who lives on the Winter Hills looking down into the Don Valley, Rotherham, more or less where she did in the War, sees a Heinkel bomber of the German Luftwaffe make a low level turn over the Roman Ridge to begin its attack on the steel works. The Germans wave at her and my 14-year-old mother, who has defied her father, is going off to a dance. Both point to the rosy glow in the distance where my grandfather can be found. Later, after a near miss, my grandfather and uncle come home for rabbit and potato pie and a row with granny. My mother has laddered her stockings in the black-out falling over a Pole.

The point is that my grandmother is quite at home with these hallucinations.

My granddad comes home for tea more than he did in real life. She sees and talks with family members alive and dead that most of us have forgotten. She smiles and is determined to go thus gently into that great good night. She is happy to give the lads in the bomber a smile and a wave, probably in the hope that this time they will score a direct hit on her beloved.

The general, and official, hysteria at any perceptual change is very worrying. Granny seems to be conscious of this as she avoids as much as possible talking to doctors and social workers, who simper things such as: 'Isn't it wonderful she still has her pride at 96'. When she had ulcers on her leg and had to go into hospital the ambulance crew more or less had to lasso her and strap her into a stretcher to carry her downstairs. She never said a word in the hospital, although later told me granddad came to visit.

If she had mentioned her bomber to the staff, chances are, she would have been diagnosed as suffering from senile dementia. She would have been ruled a 'danger' to herself, deprived of her independence and sent to a geriatric Gulag. Possibly she would be in the type of chemical straightjacket that would preclude pleasures such as cooking granddad's tripe and onions. Before her son died recently, the visiting nurse decided his behaviour was odd – he joked about playing golf again – and filled him with doses of morphine that would be considered eccentric in the heroin film *Trainspotting*.

We all conspire to a climate of fear that says any perceptual change means the individual is a complete basket case. We all maintain we'd rather be dead than 'gaga'. But there can be advantages to the gradual diminishing of the senses. A few years ago I was privileged to have lunch with Malcolm Muggeridge and his wife Kitty – given by the Collins publishing family. At lunch Muggeridge told how he had presented a boxer dog to the German Consul's wife, whom he had an affair with, in Laurenco Marques, Mozambique when he was working for MI6 because he could not find a British bulldog to annoy her husband. Afterwards, on the sofa, he had his hand firmly on Lady Collins's knee when Kitty said to my wife: 'My dear, the good thing about getting old is

that you see and hear much less...'

The brain is pretty awesome. A leading psychologist recently compared the complexity to that of the known universe. We can lose large chunks without tragic effect as the cognitive systems repair themselves. A friend, the photographer Tim Page, followed a sergeant out of a helicopter in Vietnam. The next thing he knew he was in a black, slimy bag and had to cut himself out with his Swiss Army knife as, pessimistically, body bags do not have zips on the inside.

He then put his hand up to his head to find that he had lost a chunk of grey matter the size of an orange. He recovered, and his pictures are better than ever.

Our brains run on a fairly small amount of electric current, about 20 watts. But when the brain starts to decay this may increase and produce the type of hallucinations that my grandmother sees.

The area is a fascinating one to study, not least because recent research into dreams has indicated that long dreams possibly take only fractions of a second. If not subjected to a barbiturate cosh, the gentleman with his mouth open in the

armchair may be experiencing several lifetimes in his last years.

As more of the generation that embraced lysergic acid start to take the last 'trip', the late Timothy Leary said we should embrace death, study and enjoy. The trouble is most families tend to prefer the *Brideshead Revisited* approach with a priest rather than a psychologist brandishing brain trace monitors and trying to record electrical activity at the moment of death, to attempt to find out what the person is experiencing. 'Wow, granddad, that's amazing.' I wonder what will happen to granny's bomber? Will the nice blond-haired airmen give her a lift, and save her from a life of domesticity in Rotherham? She should certainly be at liberty to explore the possibilities unfettered by the health service. What is really puzzling however is that the aircraft she sees are Heinkels when only Dorniers were used to bomb Sheffield. But then, people should be allowed to have whatever bombers they choose in their brains at 96. Surely this is the kind of freedom generations of English men and women have fought for?

The ambulance crew had to lasso her and strap her into a stretcher

Pin-ups

Keith Waterhouse picks his top six

1 Edgar Wallace
Boyhood hero who inspired me to become a writer/journalist.

2 Alfred Hitchcock
They are not making them like him any more…and I once had the privilege of working with him.

3 Hugh Cudlipp
Friend and mentor – the last newspaper genius.

4 Judge Tumim
Most determined prison reformer since Elizabeth Fry.

5 Thora Hird
One of my favourite actresses and my personal Oldie of the Year.

6 Sarah Lancashire
Adorable Raquel of *Coronation Street* – why did the chumps let her go?

ILLUSTRATION BY JOHN O'CONNOR

Plumpton Racecourse, Sussex

I WENT TO Plumpton Racecourse at eight o'clock the other morning expecting to find it empty. Gaggles of sullen unwashed 11-year-olds, who had not slept for a week, were packing up Pony Club Camp. They moved reluctantly among Rice Trailers under the oak trees while their mothers marched annoyingly and purposefully about, carrying piles of tack and plastic buckets and automatically admonishing them. I parked my car. 'You can't let your dog out here,' a furious woman shouted at me. 'We have to keep the place germ-free you know… We're all absolutely shattered.' Perfect high summer England …

I walked away across the track, which, when John Oaksey first saw in it 1958 as a jockey, made him want to go home again. It's a tough track to ride, with a steep hill, sharp bends and the main railway line to London streaking hard by the third fence. Oaksey feigned a migraine to his mother-in-law, whose horse he was about to ride, but in the end he braved it and won.

It was that race which got him going as an amateur. Riders feel strongly about Plumpton. Dick Francis refused to ride there, so did Fred Winter.

The Prince of Wales chose it as the course on which to make his horseracing debut and the young Clement Freud as an ordinary punter was so keen to attend meetings at Plumpton that he would sit on the elegant railway bridge with its criss-cross ironwork and get a very good view without having to pay the entrance money.

Plumpton racecourse is unwrecked, unbeset with imitation Tesco supermarket stands full of corporate entertainment boxes. Around it stretches well-tended, voluptuous Sussex, with tile-hung, tall, chimneyed cottages basking behind laurel hedges and the high bold Downs as a vertical backdrop to the south end of the course…

Six hundred feet up on the bush-scattered crest lies Plumpton Plain where the Barons formed their ranks to meet Henry III in the Battle of Lewes and where in the 18th century, a shepherd called John Dudney, while tending his sheep, dug a

study and library in the chalk in which to keep his books and papers. He taught himself mathematics and languages – even Hebrew – and ultimately became a school teacher in Lewes.

A track winds down from those heights, leaving behind it hidden combes and Bronze Age settlements. Over the road to Haywards Heath, a lane leads past the once moated, now Lutyens-restored Plumpton Place – home of the great 16th-century horticulturalist Leonard Mascall, who wrote and translated many books on orchards and apple trees.

On down the road, an ancient track crosses from East Chiddington church to Street and skirts the southern end of this forever England racecourse, saved from extinction in the early Sixties by the legendary Isidore Kerman who bought it lock stock and barrel. Plumpton is a far cry form the Palace Hotel in St Moritz, Mr Kerman's favourite watering hole. At the age of 91, he skis regularly and works every day from nine till four in his hugely successful law firm in New Cavendish

123

Street in London. He then plays bridge in the Portland Club every evening. 'It keeps him sharp,' says David Williams who works for the racecourse.

Kerman came into racing by mistake after he defended the famous jockey Tommy Weston in his divorce in the Thirties. 'He was so pleased with my services,' recalls Kerman, 'that he insisted on buying me a yearling at Doncaster sales.' He named it 'Kybo', (short for his mother's great maxim, 'Keep your bowels open') and from then on all his horses and even his famous dairy and pig herds carry the prefix.

Kerman used to be a big punter. In 1936 he landed the Autumn Double gamble with Dan Bulger in the Cambridgeshire and Fet in the Cesarewitch. 'That was money in those days and I bought my first Rolls with it.' He has never looked back. In traditional Jewish fashion he is a magnanimous philanthropist.

Kerman never misses a meeting at Plumpton, and though he has won over the years at most of the great racecourses in Britain, it is still his favourite.

The Wandering Bloom

What was the rare and mysterious peony that **Charles Elliott** *brought across the Atlantic wrapped in his socks?*

The big red peonies are collapsing. They've had their day in the sun, or rather rain. A week of heavy showers has left shattered heaps of petals sticking to the stone wall at the edge of the perennial bed, and only a few of the massive blooms are able to hold their heads up. In a few days we must go round with the clippers and finish the job.

Peonies, as the expression goes, are generous. It may just be that they are over-generous, considering the spectacular and wholly impractical size of their blossoms. They seem to be trying to please us, rather than the bees. Once those chunky buds have broken, a good cloudburst is all it takes to bring on floral disaster.

No peony (no double peony anyway) is immune to this dire scenario, but I am talking about the most common kind of Paeonia officinalis, the sort you find growing everywhere in cottage gardens in England. In America, it is the familiar crimson 'Memorial Day peony', often appearing less luridly as pink. When we arrived at Towerhill Cottage, there was a healthy clump among the weeds; we have since split it up and replanted it in various places, with no apparent diminution in its vigour. In fact, I question whether you can kill the thing – six or eight roots abandoned in a bucket started growing without soil before I put them out of their misery.

There is, of course, a lot more to peonies than these big red ones, pleasant and appropriate as they are. Even as the scarlet monsters are disintegrating, I'm waiting to see what will happen to another more precious specimen I've got growing in our garden. At the moment it has two buds – only one of them of a size likely to bloom – and instead of the lush coarse foliage of officinalis, a rather delicate collection of stalks and very deeply-cut leaves. This is a peony with a history. I planted it last October, in the latest chapter of its extraordinary life.

My acquaintance with this particular peony began 25 years ago, when I bought a house in western Massachusetts from a New York attorney named Frank Adams. Adams (or his wife – I was never sure) was a good gardener, judging from the plantings he turned over to us along with the keys to the house. The peony was growing at the front of a small bed above a drystone retaining wall, in a spot well-drained and enriched with manure.

One autumn day not long after we moved in, Adams came by to take away the peony. He had, I admit, warned me; that was a very special plant. Many years

'Powerful sermon, Reverend'

before, he explained, one of his wife's forebears had brought it over from England and installed it in the family garden near Boston. It flourished there, much admired. When, in the 50s, Adams bought the house in the Berkshires, he made a point of rescuing the peony and bringing it west. Now he was moving again, to Connecticut, and felt that he should take the peony too. It was, after all, a beautiful and rare variety, and wonderfully fragrant.

By this time I had seen the peony in bloom, and fully agreed with Adams's opinion. I was distressed to think of losing it. Being a nice man, Adams agreed to leave a few bits behind. I carefully dug them up and replanted them, at precisely the right depth, at several spots in the now-empty bed. In the spring spindly green shoots emerged, gradually bulked up, and before long the display was as glorious as ever. For the next 15 years the peony went from strength to splendid strength.

In 1985 I moved to England. For various reasons, I had no opportunity to bring the peony. I often thought of it, though, and occasionally contemplated trying to identify it, so as to buy one here. At the Chelsea Flower Show one year, I went so far as to hunt through a display of bloom in search of a variety like it. No luck; it was plainly too rare and unusual. My only hope, I figured, was somehow to get a piece of rootstock from the bed in the Berkshires, and bring it over to England.

Finally, last fall, I got the chance. Visiting our old home for the first time in 10 years, I dug up a good-sized piece of root with four or five eyes on it, shook it in a bag with some powdered sulphur to sterilize it, wrapped it in a couple of layers of plastic, and sank it deep in my suitcase, between the socks and the undershorts.

In principle, smuggling plants is a lousy idea. Eleanor Perenyi, in her delightful book *Green Thoughts*, describes how she smuggled a couple of pounds of French *jaune d'hollande* seed potatoes into the United States by mailing them to herself in a shoebox marked 'shoes', and got away with it. After her account was printed in a magazine, I'm told, the law descended. Ms Perenyi found her vegetable garden under quarantine for two years. The same thing might happen to my peony.

Yet as I pushed my trolley

unchallenged through customs with the peony root stashed among the socks, I felt nothing but satisfaction. My enterprise was restoring an unusual plant to its native place, and moreover adding to its improbable story. Think of it – Britain to Boston to the Berkshires to Britain!

Moreover, once the peony bloomed I'd be able to identify it. Some book or expert would be able to tell me. It would be exciting to know just how rare it was. I could remember a lot about it – its wonderful scent, brilliant coloring, size and abundance of its blossoms. But identification is tricky and even an expert was likely to insist on seeing the real thing.

I was wrong. A few weeks ago, long before the peony bloomed (if indeed it ever does), we spotted a garden in the 'Yellow Book' that sounded well worth going to visit. Green Cottage, in Lydney,

Far from being unusual, 'Festiva Maxima' is one of the most common peony cultivars, and has been bred in France since 1851 – whole fields are grown.

advertised itself as having 'many herbaceous peonies, including the National Reference Collection of pre- and early post-1900 cultivars'. I had decided that peonies were something worth knowing more about. You can only learn so much from books, although I had already learned that if you count the number of buds on your peony and come out with an odd number, someone is going to die…

A somewhat more dependable source advised that the first peony to appear in England came from the Eastern Mediterranean, possibly Crete, about 1548 and was a red single. John Gerard, the 16th century plantsman who was a good gardener but a plagiarist, planted peony seeds surreptitiously so that he could claim (unsuccessfully, I gather) to have discovered a new English wildflower.

Though it had been an early spring, the peonies at Green Cottage (except for a few officinalis) were not yet in bloom the day we arrived. One large bed contained the

National Collection, the plants growing in rows like so many vegetables, with stakes and stretched wires to keep them from falling over. Their names sounded like a guest list from Proust – 'Duchesse de Nemours', 'General Mac-Mahon', 'Felix Crousse', 'Madame Calot', 'Monsieur Martin Cahazac', 'Inspecteur Lavergne'. But there was no way to guess what they would look like when the buds opened. If I was going to find my peony here, I'd have to come back a few weeks later.

As we were leaving we encountered Mrs Baber, who was tending a small collection of plants for sale in her garage. No peonies – but when she noticed us eyeing some potted specimens beneath a wire netting nearby. We assured her that we were simply browsing and got talking about her great love and how she sometimes imports rare specimens from a breeder in Washington State. Which led naturally to my telling her about my precious peony and its adventures.

What did it look like? she asked. I described what I remembered of its huge white blossoms, the flecks of scarlet, the amazing perfume, its obvious rarity. Mrs Baber smiled. Was it a true bright 'ice' white, not cream? Were the flecks of red at random, sometimes deep among the petals? I agreed that they were. ' "Festiva Maxima"!' she said firmly. 'No doubt about it. It can't be anything else.'

So much for rarity. Far from being unusual, Mrs Baber explained, 'Festiva Maxima' is one of the most common peony cultivars, and has been since it was bred in France in 1851. Whole fields of them are grown in the Channel Islands for cutting and export to florists' shops. Dozens of nurseries carry them in this country; checking an American catalogue I see 'Festiva' described as 'The old reliable white… One of the most generally planted peonies in cultivation.'

I'm not too unhappy about this. Even Mrs Baber, whose taste in peonies is about as refined as you can get, admits that 'Festiva Maxima' is a wonderful plant, well worth growing even if the whole neighbourhood is growing the same thing. I trust it will thrive at Towerhill Cottage. In the meantime, I have developed a strong interest in peonies, and intend to try more. They needn't be rare, by the way.

Other People
N Fretwell

MR FRETWELL – I never have found out his Christian name – lives four doors down from us at No 30 ****** Street, London SW15. I first became aware of him as a brooding, gimlet-eyed presence behind a privet hedge, later as a small, belligerent figure (Mr Fretwell might be 5ft 3in but throws out his chest like a guardsman) stomping past our window on his way back from the corner shop with half a dozen newspapers wedged under his arm.

Those newspapers! I used to wonder where he found time to read them all, still more at the catholicity of taste their range implied. The *Guardian* and the *Independent* (borne face outward), the *Daily Mail* (tucked discreetly into the heart of the package), supernumerary *Telegraph*s and *Times*es, *Wandsworth Guardian*s and *South London Gazette*s. What could he want with them all? What purpose did they serve?

Then one day, browsing in the *TLS*, I chanced upon an extremely cross letter rebuking a biographer of Beatrice Webb ('It is surprising that so eminent an authority as Professor X should…'). Immediately the fragments of this scattered jigsaw fell into place. Mr Fretwell, I divined, was a professional writer of letters to papers.

There is, of course, no bore like a newspaper letter-writing bore. Mr Fretwell – 'N Fretwell, London SW15' his professional title – is not quite in the big league, a select pantheon that includes Keith Flett of Hornsey, London N8, Gary Slapper of the Staffordshire Law School and Nicholas Walter of the Rationalist Press Association, but he is certainly one of those six or seven individuals whose opinions, promiscuously advertised in the correspondence columns of national newspapers, are a source of such irritation to their readers. You who read this, I guarantee, will almost certainly have seen one of Mr Fretwell's effusions in the past week – seen it and remembered it, for the Fretwell style, that odd compound of self-righteousness, sarcasm and weary outrage, is quiet inimitable.

To whom does Mr Fretwell write, and what does he write about? The most perfunctory enquiry reveals the breadth of the Fretwell compass. Naturally he turns up a lot in the *Guardian* and the *Independent* (along with Keith, Gary and the others), but the *Spectator* knows him well and the *New Statesman* greets him like an old friend. He has been seen in the educational supplements, and is happy, in a lean week, to unburden himself to readers of *The Lady*, *Good Housekeeping* and the *Literary Review*. Mr Fretwell's communications, which incline to pithiness, are generally of four kinds. Firstly the facetious suggestion: ('On the banks of the Cherwell yesterday I witnessed a minor altercation between two punts-women. Is this the first recorded instance of punt rage?'). More common is the solemn correction. Woe betide the columnist who gives Dickens's birth date as 1811, refers to Anthony Powell's wife as 'Lady Powell' ('Surely, as the daughter of an Earl married to a commoner…') or thinks that Sir Edward Heath MP sits for Bexley and Sidcup. Then there is his unanswerably satirical one-liner ('The Secretary of State for Transport's advocacy of the bicycle would be more impressive if the government of which he is a member…'). Finally there is Mr Fretwell's hobby horse. Each of the newspaper letter-writing bores has his hobby horse. Mr Fretwell's is God, or rather the absence thereof, and his position – that of the fervent atheist who doesn't so much disbelieve in the existence of the Deity, as regard him as a personal enemy. Mr Fretwell is particularly down on the Christian Pro-Life lobby, and last month's abortion rows inspired several savage epistles ('For too long the dead hand of bigotry has lain over…' etc, etc).

Why do editors print this stuff? I don't suppose Mr Fretwell ever had an original thought, and if he did, it was never expressed in anything other than those peculiarly carping and omniscient tones ('It is surprising that…', 'It is hypocritical of…', 'No rational person could…') beloved of the fraternity. And why, more importantly, does he write them? Once, when our acquaintance had improved to the point where we were invited to No 30 for Christmas drinks, I asked him this very question. His reply was lost in the surrounding chatter, but I am pretty sure I caught the words 'democratic intervention' – pretty sure, too, that they were attended by not the faintest glimmer of irony.

Never mind. No one could deny that Mr Fretwell means well, despite his views on censorship, the Civil List and freemasonry (his politics are leftist but with idiosyncratic lurches to the libertarian Right). For myself, I rather relish Mr Fretwell's conversation. Dogged, relentless, quite without humour, he is wholly convinced of his status as a force for the public good. Even his detractors may allow that there are worse ways of making a nuisance of yourself. **DJ TAYLOR**

Robert Geary

The World According to
Enfield Snr

Horsham's favourite son remembered – in a nutshell

THE OLDIE reaches the furthest corners of the civilised world, such as London, Ontario. From there a Canadian journalist who says his name is Inkblot has written to me to say that he thinks Damien Hirst should be pickled in formaldehyde and exhibited at agricultural shows. It seems a good idea and might be called Reverse Art, the exhibiting of pickled artists at cattle shows being the reverse of pickled cows at art shows.

There was a bit of a fuss not long ago when they refused an export licence for a picture by a living artist. I forget which artist, but it seemed to me to be a fault on the wrong side, if you can have such a thing. I would be in favour of exporting a lot of living artists, never mind their art. I suppose the works of Damien Hirst would be caught by the beef ban, but there could be no objection to exporting the artist, even in formaldehyde.

All of which serves as an introduction to the fact that they have put up a memorial to Shelley in Horsham and it looks like a nut. The milk-chocolate-coloured husk is peeling back to reveal an aluminium kernel, and it is of course symbolic. It is also a fountain, but they had to turn it off as it worked too well and sprayed the pavement with water which froze and caused the people of Horsham to fall over. The fountain may symbolise the poet spouting, but possibly not, because on the edge are some lines which begin:

The everlasting universe of things
Flows through the mind...

So if you understand that, you may understand why the nut is a fountain, (though possibly not why the fountain is a nut). As well as the big nut there are four little nuts, which may symbolise Shelley's four children; but then again, they may

not. It is sited outside McDonald's and, being empty of water, serves as a convenient receptacle for polystyrene boxes.

It is all due to Sainsbury's. For the best part of two centuries the people of Horsham went about their business indifferent to the fact that Shelley was born a few miles away, until Sainsbury's were allowed to desecrate the town with a superstore, and in return gave £100,000 for a 'public work of art'. In consequence Shelley was declared to be Horsham's Favourite Son and they put up a chocolate nut fountain in his honour.

It was inaugurated at a ceremony with the fountain spouting water and Paul Foot spouting verses written by Shelley and called *The Mask of Anarchy*, which was inspired by the Peterloo Massacre and written in the style of Cyril Fletcher.

The poet starts by declaring that he has had a dream, which, from what follows, could well have been brought on by raw pork and opium taken in the company of Keats. Fraud appears personified, inexplicably weeping tears which turn to millstones:

And the little children who
Round his feet played to and fro,
Thinking every tear a gem
Had their brains knocked out by them.

Why a child should mistake a falling millstone for a gem is not explained, but otherwise the Cyril Fletcher style has been very well hit off.

Anarchy arrives, also personified, and

He was pale even to the lips
Like death in the Apocalypse

Which would be well enough if 10 verses later we did not find that:

Anarchy, the Skeleton
Bowed and grinned to everyone

So here we have a fully fleshed skeleton complete with lips and pallor. The poet is not more happy with his horses than his skeleton. Anarchy is riding a horse, and:

With a pace stately and fast
Over English land he passed.

Now I defy the most accomplished horseman in the Spanish Riding School to ride at a pace that is both stately and fast. It means, if it means anything at all, that Anarchy hurried past slowly. Another horse, the Horse of Death:

Fled and with his hoofs did grind
To dust the murderers thronged
behind.

Whatever the product of murderers ground by horses may be, it certainly is not dust. There is plenty more like this, and all in all, I think Paul Foot and the committee are to be congratulated on choosing a poem so entirely appropriate to the peculiarities of the monument.

'Forget it, Marcia. I'll put an advert in Exchange and Mart'

Modern Life

What is…
Feng Shui?

I CAN'T FIND that quote about belief anywhere. You know the one I mean: something along the lines that, when a man loses his faith in God, he will believe, not in nothing, but in anything. I think it was G K Chesterton, in one of the Father Brown stories, but how astonishing that it should be in neither the second nor third editions of the *Oxford Dictionary of Quotations*; astonishing, because it must surely be one of the most telling observations about modern life, and if you need convincing, how about Feng Shui?

Feng Shui means 'wind and water', and is described by Lillian Too*, a businesswoman and Feng Shui exponent, as 'a vital and exciting component of a wisdom from ancient China, a science [sic] that goes back at least 4,000 years to the days of emperors and mythical legends,' or, in other words, the days when nobody had the remotest idea how the universe worked, so simply made it all up as they went along. 'Ancient Wisdom' is one of those self-cancelling phrases like 'harmonium music', but for some reason that no longer seems to matter. Feng Shui is In, and must not be gainsaid.

Strip away all the obvious balls, and Feng Shui turns out to be an effective recipe for harmonious architecture and interior design. The trouble is that it's the balls which devotees seem to find most attractive. They carry small compasses with them so that they can sit in their best direction in meetings. They believe that crystals should never be used in the northern sector, being detrimental to the career corner. They consider that Chi flows through watercourses, and the ideal house nestles in the belly of the dragon. The Form School of Feng Shui demands that good locations need the presence of the dragon, and 'where the true green dragon is found there too will be the presence of the white tiger.' If that worries you, you might prefer the Compass School of Feng Shui, which uses the eight trigrams of the I Ching, the eight-sided Pa Kua symbol and the Lo Shu magic square. You might want to determine your most auspicious direction; first calculate your Kua number, which is based on your birth date (curiously enough, the Gregorian calendar seems to do the trick), then make sure that doors leading into your bedroom, study or office face the right way.

Don't forget, either, the Eight Life Aspirations of the Pa Kua; Kan is north and deals with career prospects, while Chien is northwest and affects the presence of Helpful People. To be sure that everything is going to plan, you might want to install a globe and twirl it daily to stir up auspicious Chi, while installing a light in your southern sector to enhance your personal fame. On the other hand, you might find yourself wondering why, given that just about everyone in Hong Kong believes in Feng Shui, the island is about to be handed over to the Chinese; not, you might think, something which can be considered Great Good Fortune, as is demonstrated by the tide of well-to-do business people leaving Hong Kong for good.

But on it goes. I can understand the sweet old woolly crystal-toting, ley-line-aligning, hand-knitted organic New Agers, brains addled from sleeping under pyramids, swallowing Feng Shui whole, beak, bones and flippers. It couldn't be more up their street, coming, as it does, with the multiple warranties of antiquity, exoticism, and a systemised irrationality so profound as to be virtually unfalsifiable. Secure in their relativism, these lovable fools simply get hurt when you try and criticise any of their shibboleths. 'It may not be like, er, your truth,' they say, very quietly and sadly, 'but it's like, er, my truth.' Bless them. But it's not just the woollies. Big businesses believe in it too, and spend fortunes on Feng Shui consultants to arrange their five ghosts, 12 water-flows, heaven-luck, earth-luck, man-luck and dragon's breath, and to protect them from poison arrows and the Six Killings. This, of course, shouldn't surprise us, since the

'What happened to our marriage, Jeffrey?'

hard-nosed, clear-eyed businessman of corporate myth is so often, in reality, a credulous, irrational infant, as nervous as a virgin in a barracks and prone to bolt at the slightest excuse.

What's more worrying is that even normally rational people become defensive when you mention Feng Shui. 'Yes,' they say, 'but there must be something in it.' 'Yes,' they say, 'it's all very well for you to criticise it, but I must say it works for me.' 'Yes,' they say, 'but I just did over my flat according to the principles of Feng Shui and, do you know, my life has turned around. Explain that in your tired old Rationalist Western Philosophy.'

I'm not sure that it would be worth the effort or that I'd be up to the job, but I'm equally sure that that's not the point. The curious thing about our tired old RWP is that, the more rational our received world-picture becomes, the more a sort of innate credulity bubbles thickly to the surface. Perhaps it's indeed the result of some deep flaw in our philosophy, or perhaps Chesterton (if it was Chesterton) was right. But I can't help wondering if the Oriental mind is as credulous and as hungry for belief – any belief – as the moderately-educated, vaguely liberal Westerner. Perhaps the true Wisdom of the Ancients was more a matter of knowing what would sell.

MICHAEL BYWATER

* The Complete Illustrated Guide to Feng Shui, Lillian Too, Element Books, £16.99

'No pudding for him – he didn't eat his greens!'

Albert Schweitzer

MOST PEOPLE will probably remember the name Albert Schweitzer as the founder of a hospital for lepers at Lambaréné in Gabon, West Africa. He was a missionary surgeon and was awarded the Nobel Peace Prize in 1952. He was also an accomplished musician, an authority on JS Bach, and a widely travelled organist.

I was in my second year as organ scholar of Keble College Oxford (1932) when I received a message from John Dykes Bower, fellow and organist of New College, inviting me to assist Dr Schweitzer in his forthcoming recital on the New College Chapel organ. Schweitzer apparently always needed two people to pull out the stops. I was to be in charge of stops on Schweitzer's left-hand side and his wife would manage the stops on his right. The height of the organ loft, plus some curtains, shielded us from public view.

The directions for the stops were printed in the score in two colours – red and blue. The red referred to my side and the blue to Madame Schweitzer's. As we came up to a marking Schweitzer would call out 'Yetst' (German 'Jetzt' meaning 'now') and one of us would act according to the colour.

All seemed to go smoothly for a while until on the call of a 'Yetst' Madame Schweitzer unaccountably pulled out *her*

stop despite the fact the writing was in red (my side).

Dr Schweitzer cut short his playing and in a loud voice thundered abuse at his poor weeping wife and ordered her out of the organ loft.

I remember being in a state of slight shock and stayed in my corner. Then John Dykes Bower, who had been listening down in the Chapel, appeared in the organ loft. Pretending not to notice that anything was amiss, he suggested to Schweitzer that he might like to hear the sound of the organ in the chapel below.

So Schweitzer clambered down the steps and Dykes Bower played. He was a better player than Schweitzer whose playing was efficient rather than inspired and whose tempi were very slow. When Schweitzer returned it was a relief to see that the little diversion had dispelled his black mood. He congratulated Dykes Bower on his playing, Madame Schweitzer was reinstated, and we continued with the rehearsal.

After all these years, I still wonder how Madame Schweitzer made that mistake and why Dr Schweitzer was so terribly angry with her. But I wouldn't have missed the bizarre happenings in New College organ loft for anything. **JOSEPH COOPER**

Still With Us
Sister Lucia

EIGHTY YEARS AGO, on 13th May 1917, three ragged, illiterate children looking after their relations' sheep in the arid Portuguese countryside saw a vision of a 'Lady brighter than the sun'. She returned on the 13th day of each month up to October.

She is now invoked as Our Lady of Fatima. Fatima is the nearest village to the spot where she appeared, the Cova da Iria, 80 miles north of Lisbon. The Pope is very keen on devotion to her because it was on her feast day, 13th May, that he was shot and wounded, in St Peter's Square in 1981. He visited the shrine a year later and donated the would-be assassin's bullet to decorate the crown of the statue in Fatima, to which up to a million pilgrims flock on high days.

Of those three little shepherds Francisco died aged 11 of Spanish influenza on 4th April 1919; his sister Jacinta died aged nine on 10th February 1920 (three weeks after doctors had decided that her pleurisy would benefit from two of her ribs being removed under local anaesthetic). Only their cousin Lucia remains alive; she was 90 on 22nd March, 1997.

Lucia dos Santos is now known as Sister Lucia and lives at the Carmelite convent at Coimbra where she has been cloistered away for 50 years. She is short and a little dumpy. She wears the traditional Carmelite habit and spectacles; her skin has that translucent quality common to people who have never worn make-up and always wash in cold water. She does not give interviews, indeed she does not go out of the convent. One of the very few exceptions was when the present Pope visited Fatima. Pope Paul VI did the same thing in 1967.

She has stuck to her story for 80 years. And any idea that the visions were childish imagination followed by an understandable fear of admitting a falsehood cannot stand up against her decades of contemplation, prayer and self-examination.

Sister Lucia still begins her day early with prayer before the Blessed Sacrament. She then hears Mass and receives Communion. The rest of the day is given to manual work punctuated by singing the Divine Office in choir. There is an hour's recreation. The food is fundamentally what would now be called vegetarian: bread, soup, porridge, that kind of thing. On Fridays and in Lent there is fasting too.

Not that Lucia's fare was very lavish when she was a little girl. Even then, encouraged by the lady who came to see and speak to them every month on the 13th, they would practise self-denial. The idea of these mortifications was to offer them up for the conversion of poor sinners around the world. At the same time the visions filled the children with happiness.

The visions of Fatima are surrounded by the personal theories of a type of Catholic given to the crazier sort of speculation. That Sister Lucia herself is level-headed has nothing to do with this. The Virgin Mary was said to have entrusted the children, Lucia specifically, with three secrets. The first two concerned the World Wars and the spreading throughout the world by Russia of her errors. Why these were called secrets when Lucia willingly publicised them is a good question. Like most private revelations the 'secrets' are conditional. The real message is to pray and do penance. If you do not pray and do penance the wars, errors and suffering will be worse. Pius XII, prompted by Lucia's vision, consecrated the world to the Immaculate Heart of Mary in 1942.

The Third Secret will not be revealed until after Sister Lucia's death. She wrote the Third Secret down in 1957, put it in an envelope and gave it to Pope Pius XII. Excitable enthusiasts say he fainted when he read it. There is no evidence for this tale. In 1960 Pope John decided not to reveal it. A schizophrenic hijacked an Aer Lingus aeroplane at Le Touquet in 1981 and demanded the Third Secret be revealed; it wasn't. Sister Lucia has said the Third Secret is 'Good for some, bad for others'. So there it is.

Another madman (who had been ordained) tried to stab Pope John Paul II when he visited the shrine on 13th May 1982 to give thanks for his deliverance from death a year before. His violent attack hardly demonstrated that he had got the message of Fatima right.

Lucia's cousin Jacinta said: 'If people only knew what awaits them in eternity, they would do everything in their power to change their lives.' The Virgin Mary told Lucia that she and her cousins would go to Heaven. She has had a long wait to join them.

CHRISTOPHER HOWSE

ILLUSTRATION BY JOHN O'CONNOR

The Fourth Floor at Fortnum & Mason

IF THERE WAS a war, this is where I'd go. I don't think anything could go wrong here. You get the feeling that whatever was going on outside, the waitresses would go on serving afternoon tea. Although in Piccadilly, London, it is a corner of quiet, undisturbed England and is deeply comfortable. There is an air of everything being just right, as though royalty is just about to arrive or has just left.

Like the dining room at Sandringham House, the paint work is in that favourite Edwardian colour, eau de nil, and the wall-paper is swathed in Regency swags. The tablecloths and napkins are of pale lemon linen, and when you sit down you get tucked in by smiling waitresses in white aprons. If you are sitting on one of the banquettes against the wall it is almost like being tucked up in bed.

There are olive coloured velour curtains along the windows of Duke Street, where the traffic roars below like a far away river in a gorge. The gilt framed oil paintings around the walls glow with over

restoration and include surprisingly dramatic seascapes by Henry Scott – 'The Glory of the Sea', 'Dashing Wave', and 'The Battle of Trafalgar' by Leslie Wilcox, depicting the rescue of Jeanette who had stowed away on a French ship to be near her husband.

The tables are so spaciously set that you don't have a chance to listen to anyone else's conversations and anyway there is always a hallowed hush in here; you never get any booming voices or guffawing laughter, you get polite chit-chat and gentle glances. At least that is how it appears. I have often thought that very important spies meet here. It is such an unlikely place that it seems blindingly obvious. At lunch-time there are regulars whose privacy and identity is closely guarded by the staff. I tried asking once, 'Who is that distinguished looking gentleman in the corner wearing the Savile Row suit?'

'Oh madam we would never reveal our customers' names'. So I was left surmising that he was the world's greatest

code breaker and he had walked from his discreet sett in Albany across the road, an equally hushed establishment. (A few months later I saw him sitting at his usual table with Jilly Cooper, but I still don't know his name.) At tea-time, when the strains of a string quartet or a piano waft over the brown pile carpet, there are whispering gaggles of Japanese tourists who flutter in and out, and well-groomed American women in camel coloured cashmere bring their sad looking husbands who would probably rather be playing golf at Sunningdale. Quite often there are beautifully mannered couples who have come up from the country; most of the older women wear hats.

You can eat clotted cream and scones, crumpets, teacakes, gentleman's relish on thin toast, cucumber sandwiches, pastries and cakes and any number of the nice waitresses will come up to you and ask: 'Everything all right madam?' They know their business. Miss Cassidy has been working here for 27 years, Frances McNamara, sometimes called The

Headmistress, for 23, Miss Barreiro for 13 and Miss Alvarado for 11. Mr Maatouk, the manager, runs a steady and settled ship.

Perhaps this steady feeling has something to do with the fact that Fortnum & Mason has been around for two decades short of 300 years. Mr Fortnum who came from Oxfordshire originally rented a room off Mr Mason who had a small shop in St James's market. He became a footman in Queen Anne's household. One of his jobs was to refill the candlesticks every night and, as one of his perks, he was allowed to keep the old candle ends. These he re-sold to other members of the household and in his spare time he gradually built up a little grocery business.

As private establishments sprang up around St James's Palace so the grocery business grew. After two generations, Fortnum & Mason had taken the lead in luxury trade. By the 19th century they had become a household name.

Luxury is still as thick as ever – the lemon yellow ladies' powder room on the fourth floor has Crabtree & Evelyn soap. On your way down the red carpeted oak stairs, call in at the perfumery department on the first floor, which is groaning with Lalique. In the plush Guerlain-scented air a glass-topped cactus table forms the centre piece, made by Marc Lalique in 1951. (It is for sale for £41,860).

'I see another Sunday paper has been re-launched'

Gored by the bore

Age cannot withstand him, nor custom stay his infinite moreovers, says **Anthony Sampson**

How on earth do non-stop talkers maintain their momentum, and how can they be stopped? It's a problem that grows with the years. As Ogden Nash put it: 'Oh, to be with people over sixty / Despite their tendency to prolixity!'

There's nothing new about the techniques of the bore. When Samuel Pepys in 1661 encountered Dr Thomas Fuller, the greatest scholar of his age, he was given some invaluable advice. Dr Fuller, he recounted, 'tells me that the best way of beginning a sentence, if a man should forget his last sentence (which he never has) is to begin with an Utcunque' (however).

Dr Fuller had understood a critical device for any serious bore: the means to connect up disconnected thoughts, and to pause for breath without providing any opportunity for a potential interrupter. One useful trick much used by Michael Foot in his speeches is to pause for breath in the middle of the sentence. But an emphatic link-word like 'however' is more effective, for it suggests that the climax is just about to come, and listeners must wait for it.

Any visitor to clubland will recognise the armoury of phrases in the bores' vocabulary nevertheless, moreover, all the same, that being said – which provide the keys to their monopoly. People who live alone, who form the core of clubland, are specially skilled in the kind of monologue which turns into a self-contained internal dialogue.

The accomplished bore must first create his own dialogue, to leave no need for others, and then provide infinite detail, to spin out the time, and prevent the story ever becoming clear. The two secrets were brilliantly combined in the book-title for the world's most boring memoir, once proposed by the publisher Alan Maclean: No, I Tell a Lie, It Was the Tuesday.

Armed with this weaponry, the accomplished bore can remain blissfully unaware that anyone else has tried to get a word in edgeways – let alone that they resented the monologue. Most non-stop talkers, we must remember, began their careers long ago as lively conversationalists, much in demand at dinner-parties: they simply failed to notice that they had crossed the border between the brilliant raconteur and the crashing bore. And after a marathon performance they will leave a lunch party saying 'How nice to have met you,' without realising or caring that they haven't heard a word from you.

There is, it is true, a more sensitive breed of compulsive talkers who are pathetically aware, as they pile up their details, their howevers and that-being-saids, that they are confronted by yawns and half-shut eyes, like dinner-guests in Max Beerbohm's cartoon of Coleridge. They may even give sad glances as they drone on, as if to say 'Let me out of this !'

But they are just as hard to stop. For all thoroughgoing bores deploy an artillery which leaves a wasteland around them. And when a loud, long monologue does come to an end it often leads to an uneasy silence, as the

Lady Thatcher was actually silenced by Garret Fitzgerald who held forth with blarney and brilliance

audience waits for another bombardment.

How can any mere amateur talker break through these defences? Sometimes I've tried protesting: 'Can I just finish the sentence . . . ?' But that merely allows time to prepare ammunition for a new burst of gunfire.

An obvious technique is the diversionary tactic: to start a humorous conversation at the other end of the table. But this can be suppressed by turning up the volume, or using the first-name trick to force you back into his camp – 'as I'm sure Anthony here would agree . . .'

No, the only sure way to defeat compulsive talkers is by outgunning them. Thus at one summit meeting Lady Thatcher, one of the world champions,

was actually silenced by Garret Fitzgerald, then the Irish prime minister, who held forth with both blarney and brilliance for half an hour without stopping. Lord Carrington, who was sitting next to Thatcher, wrote her a note saying: 'You're talking too much!' No doubt he hoped that after this taste of her own medicine she might be more circumspect in future; but it had no visible effect.

In fact Thatcher's own doctrines of individualism provided an obvious boost for bores by rejecting communal attitudes and encouraging competition – in conversation as much as in hospitals or schools. Under the new rules the prize goes to whoever picks up the ball and runs with it longest: the game ceases to be soccer and becomes rugger, in which only a head-on tackle can bring down the player. The trouble is, there are no real rules in British conversation for social tackling, so the bore always gets through.

But the bore still has a problem in this age of individualism, for his captive market is dwindling as everyone feels they have the right to speak – or to stay away.

The club boredepends on the club; and if he can't be stopped, the club may just fade away – like so many London clubs in the evenings. So where do the bores go next? The answer must be all too clear to you, dear readers. As conversation is killed off at dinner-tables, it is artificially reconstructed in the media, in TV quiz games, interviews and late-night discussions.

And the bores find their last refuge in the newspaper columns, safe from any potential interrupter or rival. They can fill in every detail, reminiscence and name-drop without interference. They may lose their thread, run out of argument, or even forget what their point was, if there ever was one. However. . .

Akenfield author **Ronald Blythe** *remembers the life and paintings of his old friend John Nash, whose Essex home he now lives in*

A Fruitful Brush with Nature

IT IS NOT uncommon for us to make some revision of our long established identities in old age. In his eighties John Nash began to stress a side of him which he felt his long career as a landscape painter had obscured and wrote a little book, *The Artist-Plantsman*, to put matters straight. It was as though he had been breaking faith with a boyhood conversion which he now saw as one of those experiences which had been of crucial importance in his development. It was his being shown the difference between his father's conventional garden, all croquet lawn and virtually plantless, and the rich impacted flower-filled plot of five maiden ladies just down the road.

From that moment on, his botanical drawings and vision of the countryside would be correctly 'earthed'. His brother Paul would see nature in poetic and symbolic terms and this would be their chief difference as artists.

They were the sons of a Buckinghamshire lawyer and Paul's first inspiration, like John's, arrived as he sat among the caged trees of his father's bird garden. The boys acknowledged miserable school days, but Paul saw another pupil drawing – Eric Kennington – and John won the botany prize at Wellington, so something good emerged for both. Paul studied at the Slade, which, in the years immediately prior to the First World War, was at its

About a Pig (1913)

zenith as an art school. John thought he would be a journalist but a walking holiday with the young artist Claughton Pellew convinced him otherwise. In 1913 Paul and John held an audacious two-man show in a gallery in Pelham Street which was very near a sell-out.

It was because of this joint exhibition that the uncomfortable description of them as 'the Nash Brothers' took root, something from which they would never

completely escape although they were totally different as artists.

Similarly, John's reputation as a self-taught artist ignored the fact that a number of the greatest painters of his day, including Harold Gilman and Walter Sickert, welcomed this slight youth to their studios and taught him a host of things. But his real instruction came from rural England. Sir Charles Tennyson, the poet's grandson, used to say that nobody who had not

Sunlight and Shadow: Trees in the Chilterns (1920)

glimpsed the last of pre-car Britain could have any notion of its beauty. It was this immediate pre-motorway Home Counties countryside which was to make John Nash the landscapist he was. Beginning at Iver, his father's house, he would, for more than 60 years, uniquely capture a native scenery which stretched from Cornwall to Wales and Skye. There would be nothing wistful about these scenes, no hankering after a vanished world, in fact very much the reverse. An agricultural historian could find in John Nash's pictures an undisguised statement of what has happened on the farm since 1920. He was fascinated by the marks which ploughmen, quarrymen, ditchers, china-clay diggers left on the land. He knew how corn grew and hedges held up. He liked ponds, gravel-workings, fencing and rivers. If one was out driving with him, he would pull-up abruptly with, 'That's a good bit!' and we would contemplate the way in which a small woodland had 'sat' between cultivated fields, maybe for centuries, throwing its timeless shadows. Nash had curious glassy eyes which seemed to focus on such sights more like lens of a camera.

His method was to fill Rowney's sketchbooks with pen, pencil and wash drawings, first covering the paper with a grid. He would then add many neat notes on the weather and the time of day, with its special colours. A pile of sketchbooks guaranteed a long autumn and winter's work in the studio. This was famously poorly-lit, with 40 watt bulbs and with ivy darkening the windows. These overlooked the Stour Valley, a part of East Anglia which he discovered in 1929. Although it was both 'Constable Country' (and Gainsborough Country) Nash never showed the slightest interest.

He was, without being in the accusative sense egotistical, intensely self-absorbed. He lost his natural melancholy when he was painting and when friends arrived, otherwise there could be days of 'the black dog', as he called his sadness.

He married a Slade girl, Christine Kuhlenthal, in 1918. She was the friend of Dora Carrington and a very good artist. Ill health made it impossible for her to paint and during a long marriage she created the right conditions for his art. She seemed to know every lane and cliff in the land.

He was, like all men of his generation, deeply scarred by the two wars, metaphorically speaking. He fought on the Western Front as a sergeant in the Artists' Rifles and as a major in the Royal Marines

The Three Carts (1914)

during 1939/45, and was an Official War Artist, as was his brother Paul, in both conflicts. He used to describe with one of his wry grins how they rented a seed-shed in Chalfont St Peter in 1918 and were paid 30 shillings a day to paint what are now some of the greatest war pictures. Paul used to say that it was such a lot of money

that they must never lay down their brushes until six o'clock. This is why John's celebrated picture *The Cornfield*, now in the Tate, has long shadows. It was his thankyou for having come out of the trenches alive.

An intriguing glimpse of his world can be seen at the New Grafton Gallery, Barnes, later this month. Here a number of his beloved plant drawings and book illustrations are displayed as well as some examples of his wit. Flowers apart, an early influence was Edward Lear. John's Aunt Gussie had been engaged to Lear, hence the display of many of that comic master's pictures in her house.

Whilst Paul Nash found in the view from the house the mysterious Wittenham Clumps, the ancient tumuli which would haunt him for the rest of his days, John met there a strange genius whose funny view of mankind matched to some degree his own. Like Lear, he was a tender person with a ruthless sense of humour. If life could sometimes be calamitous and dark, there remained the radiancy of the countryside and the perfection of plants.

One of my least favourite and, alas, all too frequent real-life scenarios goes like this:
Fellow Party-Guest: What do you do?
Myself: I'm an actor.
FPG: Really – what are you in?
Myself: Nothing at present.
FPG: Ah (*with a sort of amused and knowing triumph*) RESTING!

At which point I edge away – concealing, I hope successfully, pique and, above all, embarrassment. I feel embarrassed for the FPGs. They think that they are using the correct 'in' jargon, whereas in over 30 years as an actor I have never heard a fellow-professional use the term 'resting' to mean out of work.

The expression, if it was ever used, belongs to the era of the old Victorian ham beloved of *Punch* cartoons – lank-haired and red-nosed, in an astrakhan collar and a sombrero, he greets a colleague with 'What news on the Rialto, laddie?' before touching him for a half-sovereign.

To speak of actors 'resting' today is like saying to a modern schoolboy, 'I bet you get up to some spiffing japes in the tuck shop.' It also implies that such idleness is not enforced but a matter of carefree choice. The idea of an unemployed actor appears as much a matter for clichéd hilarity as a stingy Scotsman or a henpecked husband – though no one rocks with mirth at the thought of a redundant bank manager or a briefless barrister. Many, it seems, regard actors – working or not – as intrinsically ridiculous.

This conclusion is reinforced by a new horror: the current expression 'luvvie'. It has the same contemptuous resonance as 'resting', and is almost as absurdly out of date. I *have* heard theatre people calling each other 'lovey', but not many and certainly not recently. As used in *Private Eye* and the tabloids, 'luvvie' suggests a successful, fashionable show-person, but I connect it with the seedier repertory players of my youth – usually in purse-lipped sarcastic mood: "Don't you know your lines – luvvie?' Terms like 'Darling' and

Don't call me luvvie…

… or smirk knowingly and say 'resting' when I'm actually unemployed. **Jonathan Cecil** *on phrases and stereotypes guaranteed to send an actor into a rage*

'Sweetheart' are still fairly common in the theatre – often as handy substitutes for momentarily forgotten names. As a newcomer I found such gushing endearments, however insincere, a liberating change from public-school reserve. It was delightfully incongruous to hear a non-effeminate hulk like Robert Morley call Gielgud 'John darling'.

These days theatricality is decidedly unfashionable, and 'luvvie', with its breathless, stagestruck overtones, seems peculiarly inept when applied to the modern, laid-back generation. Nowadays for one young player to say of another, 'He, or she, is not a typical actor' is invariably complimentary, though I'm increasingly unsure of what a typical actor actually is.

In my early days, there were certain definite stereotypes – sometimes tiresome, always amusing to observe. The Shakespeareans, flamboyantly resonant in pubs ('Another pint if you will, dearest heart!') and dressed with somewhat studied untidiness, were in sharp contrast with the immaculately suited variety types, competitively swapping gags ('Working well tonight!' if the gag got a laugh, 'Went down better first house!' if it didn't).

The late 1950s brought in a new breed of working-class actor – determinedly anti-actorish, but with their own kind of Brando-inspired moodiness. These were counterbalanced by the raffish, self-consciously posh set, epitomised by the recently departed Ronnie Fraser, whose lives revolvedround bars and quitting rehearsals on the dot of one o'clock, ('This is the time of day when I generally repair to the nearest local hostelry…')

Conversation among most pros appeared to be dominated by anecdotes, divisible into the good, the bad and the trad. The good ones depended largely on the teller, and were vivid, original and personal. The bad had seemingly no point at all except that they featured a famous name, enabling the raconteur – usually male – to demonstrate a) his gift for mimicry and b) his intimate acquaintance with the great ('old Johnny G' or 'Darling Dame Peg, bless her').

Trad anecdotes could be good or bad, but had been handed down and embellished by generations of thespians and were shamelessly attributed to all manner of different protagonists, depending on whose voices were most easily imitable: Ralph Richardson, John Gielgud and Edith Evans being particular favourites, even if the stories didn't quite fit them.

It is partly because of such dated thespian stereotypes that actors are still considered ridiculous. But jealousy comes into it as well: it is hard to match actors – vain and childish as they can be – for perennially young enthusiasm, warm camaraderie and sheer high spirits. Perhaps we should be less sensitive and more defiantly bohemian; proud to be outsiders.

About to embark on my stage career I was asked by an appalled upper-class hostess: 'Won't you meet the most frightful people?'

'No more than in other professions' was my youthful reply: a trifle pompous but still, I think, correct. Yet now and again I wish I had answered simply: 'I hope so.'

Faking it

Modern recordings may be technically perfect, but **Robert Tear** *longs for truth in music*

Hi! is that Pro Pecunia records? It's Garry Grab from California!'
'Hello Garry, this is Charles Clutch, how can I help?' 'Now hear this Chuck, Mario Masturbani feels he could have a high B tomorrow. Send someone over to catch it quick.'

Cyril Slurp the ancient retainer took the next plane to America and trapped the said high B with the skill of a lepidopterist. He returned with it palpitating on his tape and filed it for future reference.

At another place, but at a similar time one could have read: 'Here is the violin concerto to top them all!' The critic had zoomed his CD through the rafters. A couple of months before, a short sighted man had sat Scrooge-like piecing one bum note to a similar.

These seemingly irrelevant scenes are part of that industry which has suddenly found Nemesis as its near neighbour. In the early days it was all so different. Recordings were made for the music to be loved, to be learned from.

It began in such an innocent way, each producer seemed to wear a tweed jacket with leather elbow patches, a pucelle, a sad creature just down from Cambridge who had just missed that job at the BBC. Soon, less salubrious characters appeared, the till ringing smart in their ears. They realised with commendable elan that their oysters would have two precious pearls – the composer and artist.

They began in a hesitant way, but, as fate and greed willed, tottered to fortunes untold. Soon the company vultures were directing music and deciding balance,

MATERNITY WARD PUBLIC OPENING

tempos. Those who couldn't tell a B from a bull's foot were the princes of discrimination. Fourth rate middle men decided careers, enthusiasts created or trashed real talents.

Within 15 years all the finest music had been well and truly taped. But the jackals weren't at a loss for long at all. Here the boffins came in inventing new tricks, 78, 33⅓, 45, long play cassette, and, of course, CD.

Through this mendacious period contracted artists were unashamedly favoured, their voices boosted to Herculean size as their colleagues were consigned to the back of a six-acre field. Orchestras now had to join this circus in order to work enough. Festivals were formed almost exclusively for the musical barons.

Then the doctoring of sound and time began. A singer would arrive at a session and say, 'Sorry, don't feel up to it today, may we leave bars 52-93 till later?' A soprano who never had a C would say: 'At this time of the month I only have an A, I'm sure you can fix it.' And fix it they did. Machines were how musicians' grinding, winding low notes moved to high ones, splicing the porkies seemlessly into a seemingly perfect sound, which became more spoof by the hour.

My opening sentences are an illustration of the everyday morals of this industry. Whereas, generally, a photograph freezes one moment, the producers began to box moments taken sometimes from years before in a vain and philosophically misconceived attempt to create perfection.

Having recorded everything for the second time and mastered perfection, the pecuniary taste buds were to be reactivated with the invention of 'authenticity', that spurious academic theory which was to reinvent music's sound and thus re-record everything again. This movement sent performances backwards, not into truthful clarity but into an imaginary world where the ill-understood mores of the 17th and 18th centuries could be turned into financial certainties.

The consequences of 25 years of hubristic lies and double dealing have been almost wholly malevolent. It can be argued that recordings have been seminal in selling classical music to a wide

'Miss Honeyball, I smell money. Check it out, will you?'

audience, but the BBC had done the hard work and moreover had done so without notable self-interest.

Performers have been twisted. Eager young pianists practise 25 hours a day until they play with bleeding knuckles in a hopeless attempt to achieve the perfection

great performers and performances from the more truthful past. These thunderous artists are now being released to recapture the world. Modern conductors, singers, all sorts of musicians are having their contracts terminated. Projects fall like autumn leaves.

'Now hear this Chuck, Mario Masturbani feels he could have a high B tomorrow. Send someone over to catch it quick'

which the record companies have planted in their ears.

Young tenors endeavour to ape the sound of the 'star' (his sound often enhanced by steroids, taken to satisfy corporate cupidity). Concert halls have emptied because a natural sound no longer satisfies the ears of those used to the cans.

Well, it's all over. The companies – fidgeting in their dungeons – have all the

May we hope that the outcome will be a revival of truer, more honest performances, where small imperfections will be regarded as a part of life and when audiences and performers alike realise that imperfection is the order for things.

And that when perfection does perch on a shoulder it does so when it will – and not at the behest of greed or obsessional graft.

The Little Doctor

O F Snelling *remembers one of the originals of London's antiquarian book trade*

He was a small, frail elderly man of benign countenance and disposition. Once he was known to almost every new and second-hand bookseller in the country, if only by correspondence. But that was half a century ago, and more. He lived in retirement with his maiden sister, in a pleasant row of mansion flats in Prince of Wales Drive, facing Battersea Park. After I had got to know him well I visited him several times. There wasn't a book to be seen in the place, although I was aware that he was an indefatigable collector. Indeed, it was through books that I had got to know him. But he appeared to be dominated by his prim sister and an autocratic manservant, both of whom bullied him unmercifully. I don't think they allowed such dust-gathering things as books in their spacious flat.

Cleverly, he had overcome this problem. He must have got on well with his next-door neighbour, whose own flat was too large for his needs. The little doctor had had a hole knocked in the far wall of his bedroom and a door put in, to which only he held the key. With private access to a fairly large room in his neighbour's flat, he was able to house one of the most remarkable collections of books, prints and ephemera I have ever seen.

I first met him in about 1950, when he used to drift into the old Hodgson's Book Auction Rooms in Chancery Lane, where I was working in the saleroom. Many years previously, I gathered he had been responsible for successful research into respiratory diseases contracted by chimney-sweeps and other similar unfortunates, which brought him a great deal of money in the form of a grant or an award. I never knew the details, for he was reticent about his medical achievements. Although I came to love the little man, I don't think I would have trusted him to bandage a cut finger or prescribe an aspirin. His talents lay in a quite different direction.

He had begun his book-collecting career with Charles Dickens's novels in the original parts – pristine condition only, naturally – but after his medical success he started to accumulate everything he could lay his hands on which referred in any way to chimney-sweeps. Dome-pated, bowlerhatted and mittened, Dr Sidney Henry perennially cruised the West End bookshops for items on sweeps. I doubt if there was a single book, story, article or newspaper snippet about sweeps which he did not possess. If he didn't have an item, he certainly knew about it, and was tireless in its pursuit. His collection was racked all round the room on dark green metal shelves. The solitary window hadn't been opened for years, and its panes were never cleaned; it was airless, musty and gloomy.

Early on I guessed that he might be homosexual, but it was a long time before I knew him well enough to broach that subject. It finally came about after he had told me of this stern and stolidly Victorian upbringing, of how one day in the 1890s he had happened to mention the name of Oscar Wilde. His father had clamped down immediately, forbidding any mention of this most depraved of beings. The little doctor confessed that he had felt a certain affinity with that pariah of the '90s, but he had lived in silence with his predilections.

Over the years, as I got to know him better, he tended to confide in me more and more. His pursuit of the chimney-sweep in literature and art remained unabated, embracing even the 70-odd-volume set of Voltaire's collected writings, which contains one short reference to the subject.

Our social acquaintance ripened, mostly in local Lyons' teashops or ABCs. A lonely soul, he seemed delighted to have found a sympathetic listener, with whom he could joke about his solitary plight. Throughout this poor old chap's life, to be 'queer' was virtually a crime. He didn't live to see the day when relationships 'between consenting adults' would no longer be frowned upon by the law. And I never felt able to mention my suspicion that his absorbing interest in sweeps had such a basis. The rather obvious Freudian symbolism of their going up dirty chimneys was entirely lost upon him.

One day, a colleague of mine was sorting through an enormous private library for a sale. On one side of the room was a shelf or two of the 'chuck-outs', with no saleable value. For a laugh, my colleague threw me a slim volume from this shelf. It was a privately-printed book of verses, mostly flowery and sentimental doggerel. The most interesting things in the book were some pasted-in sepia photographs of prepubertal boys in the nude, with beautifully slim limbs and well-rounded buttocks, all in idyllic leafy surroundings, with sunlight filtering through the trees.

It was duly sent to the little doctor, and eventually absorbed into his enormous collection. Where it resides today I do not know, though his accumulation of books and ephemera on chimney sweeps came to rest in the library of a northern university.

Many years later, long after my old friend had died, I read an essay by Donald Weeks called 'A Corvo Collection', including in Cecil Woolf's and Brocard Sewell's 'New Quests for Corvo'. It refers to a book of verses, by one John Gambril Nicholson, entitled *A Garland of Ladslove* and issued in 1911: Nicholson and Rolfe had been at school together in the 1880s. I recognised the title immediately. This was the slight book that had been thrown aside, and passed on for a laugh to the butt of our amusement.

A Garland of Ladslove is not easy to come by, but it is an essential item in any serious Corvo collection. And who took those sepia pictures I wonder? After all, Frederick Rolfe Baron Corvo – artist, translator, poet, biographer, and novelist – was no mean photographer, either.

'Soup of the day's crap, by the way'

Service from the old school

Jermyn Street's shabbily elegant Cavendish Hotel was a draw for London's beautiful people, thanks to its owner Rosa Lewis, who was an eccentric and admirable law unto herself, recalls **Alastair Aberdeen**

By the time I came to know Rosa Lewis in early 1940 the Cavendish hotel had acquired a shabby elegance and had suffered twice from German bombs. You went through the front door into a square hall in which was a large table stacked with letters from exotic countries, addressed to habitués, men who (during the war) might not show up for a year or two, if ever.

Rosa would be sitting in her armchair, beadily eyeing any stranger that came in. I have no idea how many bedrooms there were, but if anyone came in whose face didn't fit, Edith Jeffrey, her constant companion, standing nearby, would tell the stranger: 'Sorry, we're full up.' One person, more persistent than the rest, argued his way into getting a room. Rosa then woke up (she slept a lot in her old age) and said, 'Do we have to oblige it?' ('It' was a master stroke of contempt.)

Habitués, on the other hand, were accepted as part of the place on any terms. Terms, indeed! Rosa would dictate bills out of her head. Impecunious favourites paid little or nothing. Richer ones who weren't favourites paid the difference according to her whim.

This Robin Hood attitude was well known, and for some people could have disastrous consequences. There is the story of the man who, in the 1930s, took his mistress to the Cavendish for a weekend – a silly thing to do, since Rosa was fond of *his* wife and *her* husband. When the man came for his bill on Monday morning it was £120, a vast sum in those days. 'Really Rosa,' he said, 'I'm not going to pay *that* amount.' Rosa fixed him with her laser-blue eyes and said meaningfully, 'Oh yes you will.' (The perfect blackmail.) Rosa was all for people having plenty of illicit sex, but in her book this was cheating and had to be paid for. Dalliance had to be discreet – Edwardian style.

She stood in awe of no one, not even Edward VII, and she called the young, red-haired Winston Churchill 'Coppertop' to his face. It is well known that she disliked writers, especially after Evelyn Waugh had lampooned her as Lottie Crump in *Vile Bodies*. Thus it was when a stumpy little American arrived with several pigskin suitcases. 'Can I have these taken to my room?'

he asked. 'Just leave them there, dear,' said Edith (everyone was 'dear') 'and Charles will take them up when he comes on.' 'Then can I have lunch?' 'No, the dining room isn't ready, but there is a nice place down the road called the Aperitif if you want lunch now.' Off went the man, thoroughly chastened.

'Really, Edith,' said a friend of mine who had witnessed this scene, 'the way you treat your guests!' 'Well you see, dear,' said Edith mildly, 'Mrs Lewis and I don't like him much. He wrote a rather nasty play – *A Streetcar Named Desire*.' So much for Tennessee Williams.

I have said that the exterior had a shabby look, and so too – for my generation – did the interior. But, before we were born, the Cavendish, in Edwardian days, was the fashionable meeting place for the beau monde. They were enchanted by the beautiful chatelaine who could swear like a trooper and drink as much champagne as any of them.

It is almost certainly nonsense that Edward VII gave the Cavendish to Rosa for services rendered. She acquired it, and neighbouring houses in Jermyn Street, out of the profits made from cooking for the great and the rich. When the Kaiser or a grand duke took a house for the season, she moved out the resident kitchen staff and installed her own team of 12: she took on the running of parties in great London houses. If Escoffier was the finest chef in London, Rosa was his female counterpart. Each admired the other.

This is why the new generation of gourmets, headed by the King, flocked to Jermyn Street and the delights of the Cavendish, both culinary and sexual.

If Rosa saw a sad-looking young bachelor she would say: 'We'll have to find him a nice clean tart' (to cheer him up, so she thought).

In early 1944, when I and others were back in London after two years in the Middle East and Italy, we gave a party at the Cavendish so that our friends would know we were home. Rosa reserved six double bedrooms for the guests, none of which was used, and she was heard to mutter: 'Can't think what the young generation is coming to.'

Later, she presented us with a bill of £140 for the party: gin, whisky, champagne, wine, tonic and, most bizarre of all, £33 for kümmel. It took all of Frank Waldron's charm – and he really was one of her favourites – for her to knock £100 off the bill without any fuss.

Rosa was more wayward in her illogicality than anyone I have known. She condemned a famous madame of wartime London as 'that wicked woman: she'll come to a sticky end, and well-

It was well known that she disliked writers, especially after Evelyn Waugh had lampooned her as Lottie Crump in Vile Bodies

deserved'. Her eccentric moral judgements kept everyone on the hop, which was intentional, for Rosa was clever at keeping people in line by making unexpected jumps of mood and pronouncements.

One evening, the big circular table in the dining room was alive with a group of Polish officers knocking back glasses of neat vodka and becoming very merry. I was sitting next to Rosa, who was, to cheers, matching glass to glass with the Poles. 'Don't worry, dearie,' she confided to me, 'it's only water.'

All at once there was a commotion. The Colonel, a large, affable man, was being screamed at by his Polish girlfriend. As she turned to flounce out, the Colonel grabbed one buttock and gave it a hard squeeze, provoking a different kind of scream.

'What was all that about?' we asked.

'Oh,' said the Colonel insouciantly, 'she wishes to go to bed with me again tonight, but I have decided *No*, and she is enraged!'

Rosa chortled delightedly. She loved high-handed men.

In the latter days, it was a mystery how this rackety place was run. The answer is that it ran itself. Edith was in charge, and there was Charles, a stocky factotum, who padded about on splayed feet and seldom showed any expression other than 'nothing ever surprises me'. He must have known of many clandestine goings-on but rarely gave a sign of recognition.

Bennet, who served in the dining room, was partially deaf, wore horn-rimmed glasses, and could have been a solicitor's clerk or a mortuary attendant. He was in the habit of telling bawdy stories – very confidentially – to any mixed gathering. Once, when he was doing this, and my guest and I were longing for a drink, I became exasperated and shouted, 'Hurry up, Bennet, we're thirsty'. 'Shut up,' he shouted back, 'and wait your turn.'

Cissy was the waitress. Nothing was too much trouble for people she liked, but for people she didn't like, service was very slow, or just no service at all.

Charles, Bennet and Cissy made their own rules and you had to lump it. There were, presumably, other employees in the background, but they hardly showed. One itinerant 'employee' was my six foot eight cousin, Peter Royds, who occasionally manned the creaking old telephone switchboard. (In fact, anybody who made a call usually did it themselves.) Peter's voice would be heard, behind a kind of trellis, thus: 'Who's that? Mrs Buxton-Waters? Oh, you want to speak to your son? He's in his room with a hangover. I'll put you through, but he may not answer.'

A sad reminder of the comings and goings during the Second World War were the stacked tin trunks belonging to regular soldiers who deposited them at the hotel when they went overseas. Many of them were never to be reclaimed. As the war came to an end the place was running down. It had suffered bomb damage, and its coterie of habitués had thinned out. I happened to be in London on leave from Germany on VJ night, so I called in at the Cavendish on my way to a night on the town. It was as quiet as a morgue.

But the hotel could burst into life, unexpectedly and spontaneously, much to the delight of the ageing Rosa. I gave a party there the night before I left for Kenya in 1948, where I was to be best man to my friend Frank Waldron. Late that night I was called to Rosa's bedroom. In her negligée, her long silvery hair unpinned and flowing, she sat on the fabulous sable bedspread given to her by the Grand Duke Michael of Russia, who had stayed at the Cavendish on his honeymoon in 1904. She wanted me to take a pair of silver candlesticks to Frank as a wedding present. I had to make excuses – my main baggage had gone ahead to the docks in Liverpool and I had no way of carrying such a precious cargo.

'But Rosa,' I said comfortingly, 'Frank will be here in a few weeks on honeymoon; you can give them to him in person.' Thankfully my excuses were accepted.

In 1949 I came back from Kenya, having become engaged (by post). I took my future wife to see Rosa, who clapped her hands and sent for a bottle of the best champagne. When this had been drunk she told us to go upstairs and choose a piece of furniture as a wedding present. Edith took us to the rooms (by now never used) where the Grand Duke had stayed. The most modest piece we could see was a Sheraton card table, so, diffidently, we chose that. A Sheraton-*type* card table was delivered to our flat. Edith was having no nonsense about us having the *best* of anything. She was protecting her future.

For our first years of married life we seldom went to the Cavendish: Rosa seemed to spend more and more time asleep until, finally, she died in 1952. St James's, Piccadilly, was overflowing for her funeral. Old friends had many happy reunions. Happy? Well, not really, but nor was it a time for mourning. The old order had gone and with it the Cavendish life had gone – *forever*.

Never again can there be a place like it. In fact there never *was* a place like it. A unique woman was the catalyst, and when she died the whole ambience died. Edith tried valiantly to run it for the next 10 years, but the lease ran out, the demolition men moved in and up went a hotel just like all the other hotels.

Rosa's Cavendish attracted people who appreciated eccentricity and who were not interested in efficiency. Modern society proscribes the free spirit. The Cavendish would never have passed health inspectors, fire precautions, traffic wardens, tax inspectors or auditors; nor would it have escaped from litigious customers.

A sad postscript. When the old Cavendish had been pulled down and the new one was being built, a friend of the old days, staying at a quiet hotel in the neighbourhood, saw the slight elderly figure of Edith asking pathetically if they had a room. 'Sorry, madam we are full up.' she was told. And they *were* full up.

> Guests were enchanted by the beautiful chatelaine who could swear like a trooper and drink as much champagne as anyone

'Mother! we were just talking about you'

OCTOBER 1995. The last time I saw Kinglsey Amis he was in a private room in UCH a fortnight before he died. Even though he was very poorly indeed he reminded me of the first time I'd ever seen him walking into our lecture room in Swansea University in 1949. I suppose this was because he had lost stones in weight and was too ill to summon up the intolerant, crosspatch, impatient expressions that had scarcely left his face for more years than was good for him. What do I mean, good for him? I have to remember that even at his most disagreeable he went on producing a novel a year, one of which won the Booker Prize. More years than was good for his friends, shall I say. Excluding those cronies at the Garrick Club who adored him at his most Blimpish…

October 1949. 'Don't look now, but here comes dream-boy,' said my girl friend in the back row of the lecture hall where we could knit unseen in the boring lectures. A blond, very good-looking chap took up his position at the rostrum to give his first lecture. I was cold and he was wearing an officer's great coat dyed a rare maroon. We gave him an easy eight out of 10 straight off for looks but by the end of his lecture this new Mr Amis had scored 10 and the rest. When had we ever been kept interested through a whole hour of literary criticism? And laughed so loud and for so long?

It wasn't too long before he, and stunning-looking Hilly, his wife, became the pub companions of our gang. And we were baby-sitting for their incredibly blond-haired children Philip and Martin, and later Sally. And gaping at their house with its Swedish furniture and porridge-coloured curtains and pastel rugs.

We thought they were glam beyond belief – the Scott and Zelda Fitzgerald of our days. And bohemian. Well, sort of – not in the way Kingsley looked. His clothes were immensely square: check shirts and ties and sports jackets and suits – his maroon army coat was soon replaced by a camel belted number that set more hearts a-flutter. He was undoubtedly attractive at this time because he was clever in a scornful way which included you on his side. He made us laugh with his imitations of motorbike engines and Lord

Two Kings

Mavis Nicholson *remembers her old friend Kingsley Amis*

David Cecil. He was generous and very good company.

This was a time of parties, parties, parties at their house – at one of which a horse, tethered in the pocket front garden, stared unblinkingly at our goings on for all the world like a Methodist aunty not wanting to miss a thing. Hilly had bought it on the spur of the moment and hadn't yet found, that night anyway, a field for him.

She'd inherited money, which is why they could live in such style, and the horse was succeeded by an Afghan hound which she hadn't told Kings about. He'd come back from college, gone into the dining room, sat down and started to read before he was aware of a pair of eyes right up against his face and teeth which were bared any time he tried to move. There was a word that 'Barbie' would obey, but he didn't know it. So he had to stay rigid

without food or drink for several hours until Hilly and the children came home. Some of us thought this was a hoot, a piece of natural justice since he was too often footloose and fancy-free. A pity, we thought, that Hilly had ever told him the word.

These Swansea days were his golden days, he'd later say. He got on with the South Wales Welsh. We suited him. He thought us warm-hearted and we made him laugh too; he was tickled by his children's Welsh accents – their Marm and Dard. On the Gower beaches nearby, like most Welshmen he kept his town clothes on. He did quite enjoy a game of cricket on the wet sands, but you could never have called him an unbuttoned sort of chap, and perhaps that should have warned us.

I blame the mother. His had been,

according to him, a difficult birth – such a big head – that she vowed she was never going through such pain again. (Pardon me for breathing, Mum.) She had wrapped her only child in cotton wool, so much so that she had stopped him, at the very last moment, going with all the other boys to school camp, just because he had a small spot on his face. She'd grabbed at this obviously feeble excuse just to keep him at home with her. He was devastatingly disappointed.

Geoff (my husband) and I remained friends of the Amises after we moved to work in London. They often stayed with us in our flat in The Cut near Waterloo, for this was the start of his success. *Dixon and Christine,* the novel he'd been working on in Swansea and from which he used to read out excerpts, emerged as *Lucky Jim.* Great, gleeful sharers of their new-found wealth, they took us out to restaurants we could never have afforded at the time. If we protested, Kingsley would ask: 'If you'd come into money, would you be treating us?' And then he'd answer, before we could, and with exaggerated emphasis: 'Yes, you would!'

He bought jazz records and left them with us so that when he came up, he wouldn't be without them – and to educate our taste, I suspect. He did.

At one point I got a message at my office in St Martin's Lane that a Mr Amis was in casualty at Charing Cross Hospital. Could I go and pick him up? We'd been expecting him to stay the night with us, but he'd been knocked over by a car after lunch at the *Spectator.* He was sitting on a

bench when I got there, all woozy with anaesthetic and bandaged up to his eyeballs – literally, for one eye was injured. I was dumbfounded they were letting him go in this state. He had no idea where he was or what had happened.

I rang Geoff, who was already home, and asked him to call our doctor while somehow I got a leaden Kingsley into a taxi. We put him to bed in vest and pants and waited. It was a warm summer evening, and a neighbour whom we had never spoken to stopped at our kitchen window to introduce himself. We offered him a drink and chatted. He was doing an MA in English literature and Amis's novels were mentioned. At which moment K walked dopily into the kitchen in bandages and underwear and we introduced him to his fan. His name was Paul Du Feu, who would go on to become the first male frontal nude in *Cosmopolitan,* the husband, briefly, of Germaine Greer, and more durably of Maya Angelou.

None of us could ever get over how Kinglsey never had hangovers. While the rest of us were feeling like Lucky Jim, resolving never to use our eyeballs again, you'd hear K Amis whistling jazz tunes loudly and expertly in the bathroom, hurrying to join the rest of us, not to be on his own.

Why did he change so? It was the booze, you see. There he was, a man who liked being liked, who liked liking people, and who ended up making it impossible for anyone to show him that they liked him still. Now that he has died he can't do that any more.

The Oldie
45-46 Poland St.
London W1V 3DF

Readers Write

Better on a Camel?

Sir: Airline acronyms used to be very popular – as indeed did airlines. With all but a handful of the world's airlines going or already gone out of business we oldies could perform a most useful service for future generations by recording, before it is too late, a colourful footnote to a more colourful time of travel.

Laying aside my magazine and leaning back against the bedhead (the irony of my now reaching for my *Oldie* when we go to bed is not lost upon Mrs McKeag) I found to my dismay that I could remember but two.

Quantas, the Australian government always led us to believe, stood for Queensland and Northern Territories Air Services. Those of us who have ever enjoyed the hospitable attentions of its solicitous but occasionally somewhat outré cabin staff know of course that it stands for Queens and Nymphos Trained as Stewards. Then there was (is) Alitalia: All Landed in Turin All Luggage in Athens. Apart from BA, which ever stands merely for the obvious, I discover that I can recall no more of the so very many I have heard.
Malcolm McKeag
Lymington, Hants

Brutish Airways

Sir: On the subject of airline acronyms, I recall:

Aeroflot – Air-o-Flop

Pakistan International Airlines – Please Inform Allah

PanAm – Punctuality and Navigation Absolutely Minimal

TWA – Try Walking Across

Alitalia – Always Late in Take Off, Always Late in Arrival (an alternative)

SAS – Stays Airborne Sometimes

I seem to remember that TAP was Try a Pee. El Al's was a screamer but lost to my memory as are those for Lufthansa, Swissair and Sabena who all benefited (!) from acronyms. Perhaps others will oblige.

Dennis Bates
Bromley, Kent

Sir: My favourite airline acronym is Such a Bloody Experience Never Again, although – truth to tell – I have had a perfectly decent flight with Sabena.

Revd Peter Kettle,
London, SW19

Fear of Flying

Sir: Ref – Airline Acronyms
Here are a few more:
BOAC – Better On A Camel
TAP – Take Another Plane

George and Alison Sassoon
Lochbuie, Isle of Mull

Sir: BWIA (British West Indian Airways) can also stand for 'Britain's Worst Investment Abroad' and 'Best Walk If Able'.

John Sampson
Highfield, Southampton

Sir: I like Gulf Air – Get Used to Late Flights And Irregular Reservations.

Jean Latham
Chedington, Dorset

Brief details

Sir: Victoria Wood is evidently too young to be an oldie, if she doesn't realise that Celia Johnson – Laura Jesson in *Brief Encounter* – would never have gone to a public library. She would have gone, certainly by train in those pre-Beeching days, to the main branch of Boots in her country town. There she would have handed her booklist (filled in while reading the book reviews in the Sunday paper) to the girl behind the counter who would take one or two from her selection and thread the little Boots shield bookmark through the eyelet on the spine.

Having got this far, I watched the film and found it was all exactly as I had written, Boots and all, with the Kardomah for added nostalgia.

I also found that the setting is not the Home Counties, because there are coal mines, and definitely non-Home Counties countryside where Laura and Alec go in the borrowed car. In fact Laura takes only one train from what is evidently a small village halt to Milford Junction, which is within walking distance from the centre of the town.

Anyone well up on railways (I think it is the LMS) would know exactly which station was used for the film. There are direction boards for Skipton, Keighley, Leeds and Bradford, Grange, Ulverston and Barrow, as well as Lancaster and Morecambe. And of course the boat train passes through non-stop.

Incidentally, what does Fred Jesson do for a living? He always seems to be hanging around at home being solid and dependable, but something must pay for the nice but not terribly modern house with at least one maid (and possibly a cook).

Come to think of it, in those days jobs really were nine to five, and evenings were free for listening to a concert on the wireless while the wife got on with the mending. Darning socks became obsolete with the advent of television.

Penny Aldred
London SE13

Briefer Encounter – Letter No 94

Sir: Re *Brief Encounter*. Some of the background shots where the two meet in the street, are of Beaconsfield, Bucks. There is a mock-Tudor gable-end which is on a site now occupied by a supermarket, and in another shot there is a bay-windowed cafe called Five Ways. I used to eat there in the Forties. However, the shots outside the hospital are not of Beaconsfield.

Fred Jesson must have been in an office of some kind, possibly bank or insurance.

The Kardomah always reminds me of the Cadena. There was one in Reading and

one in Oxford. They smelled deliciously of coffee beans and had basket chairs.

I do still darn occasionally – with one eye on the television. At the time I first saw the film, I was unpicking a cotton jumper to re-knit it in another style as knitting cotton was not on coupons.

Esther J House
Tiverton, Devon

Even Briefer Encounter – Letter No 95

Sir: Yes, Penny Aldred – the station in *Brief Encounter* was LMS. It was Carnforth. From there you could catch a train to Morecombe or Keighley, Skipton or Leeds via the old Midland Railway line.

You could get to Ulverston and Barrow via the Old Furness Railway Line. And you could get to Lancaster on the old London and North Western. The only boat train which would pass through would be the Stranraer to Euston, which had connected with the boat from Larne, conveying the good people of Ulster who had business in London.

Martin Barnes
London EC1

Further briefing

Sir: In *Brief Encounter*, the local station was unmistakably Carnforth, of course, but the atmospheric night shots of speeding trains, which still have the power to stir the senses, were actually taken at Watford Junction.

The cinema where the star-crossed lovers purport to see the cod Hollywood epic *Flames of Passion* – an indulgence of Coward's, I've always suspected (he invariably knocked Hollywood whenever possible, but never hesitated to unload his work there) – and where they spot the organist as the cellist from the Kardomah/Cadena cafe orchestral trio, is still recognisable as the one-time Metropole in London's Victoria.

I know because, pre-war, you could see a second-run West End film and supporting feature, any day of the week (except Saturday) for the princely sum of one shilling before midday – a pleasure I often enjoyed. Halcyon days!

Harry Wilson
Exeter, Devon

Pin-ups

Sir Les Patterson picks his top six

1 Michelle Roberts
To me brains are more important than looks and this talented lass fits the bill. I always read one of her raunchy poems at bedtime. A turn on.

2 Princess Anne
Just about my favourite royal, next to old Chazza. She likes a laugh and enjoys her freedom (like me).

3 Tamara Beckwith
A well connected little hornbag who can connect with me any time she likes.

4 Charlotte Rampling
Now she's ditched that Frog she needs a real man, and I'm ready, willing and able.

5 Lavender Patten
Fellow RC, and real spunky little goer. My horny Honkers helpmate.

6 Mary, Lady Archer
Fragrant? I wouldn't say no to a closer sniff.

I once met...

The whole Royal Family

QUEEN ELIZABETH II came to the throne in 1952 and after 25 years it was decided that the event should be remembered with suitable celebrations. This meant that the poor lady had to go round the suburbs of London, meeting various local dignitaries and receiving their loyal best wishes.

The day was scheduled to close with a display of fireworks on the Thames. The great and the good had been invited to watch these from the top four floors of the Millbank Tower and a splendid champagne supper had been laid on for them there – presumably at tax-payers' expense.

The lower two floors were for very important people; the floor above was for really important people; and the top floor was strictly reserved for royals and prime ministers only.

Someone had decided that the music to accompany the fireworks should be chosen by that fine artist, John Piper. Piper was as vague as he was talented, and the job of

giving him technical assistance, as well as a few practical suggestions, went to my wife Faith.

She and Piper made up a short tape comprised of little bits of British music – Handel, Britten, Vaughan Williams, etc – to which the pyrotechnic display would somehow be matched. When the evening arrived, the whole royal family, with the exception of Princess Alexandra – who had been sent to Alexandra Palace, and would have become Queen if a bomb had destroyed the tower – assembled for the party on the top floor.

Faith and I were on this floor too, because it had been decided that we were the only ones who could start the music tape, and thus the firework display, on cue.

The evening did not start well. It was pouring with rain and the clouds were very low. The Queen arrived a little bit later than the others and was whisked straight into the lift. As soon as she arrived at the top, she made a bee-line for the Queen

Mother, who happened to be standing beside me (and who must have been wondering who on earth I was).

'Where are my dry shoes?' demanded Her Majesty junior.

'I left them in the lobby for you,' replied her mum. 'They are in a Harrods plastic bag.'

HM junior turned to her lady-in-waiting. 'Fetch them at once. My feet are soaking wet.'

After a few moments the lady-in-waiting returned with a very nervous-looking detective. 'I am afraid, Ma'am, that we can't get your shoes,' he said.

'WHAT?' A look of thunder crossed the royal brow.

'The lifts have all been sealed as a security measure.' (Yes, thought I, so that all the detectives can have an hour off and enjoy the party 'below stairs'.)

From then on HM not exactly in a party mood.

Various dignitaries were presented. I

149

chatted lightly, very lightly, with Princesses Margaret and Anne until the time for the fireworks drew near.

Then everyone – everyone except the Queen, that is – moved to the windows to watch. Faith went into a special control room and I stood in a doorway from where I could give her the signal as soon as the Queen got to her vantage point.

Ah, but majesty doesn't work like that, especially if it happens to be in a bad mood, with wet feet.

No courtier murmured in the royal ear. No field marshal waved a gracious, gloved hand in the direction of a red carpet or a gold chair. Was the Queen going to stroll over to an empty window on her own and peer out? She was not. She did not budge an inch.

The Prime Minister, Mr Callaghan, to whom she was talking, risked his neck with an interruption. After all, the whole nation was waiting, via the BBC.

'There are fireworks starting now, I believe Ma'am.'

Her Majesty took no notice whatsoever. Frantic commentators on radio and television made renewed efforts at small talk as the cameras showed only the barges – silently waiting in the teeming rain.

The heck with it, I thought, and gave the signal. Whoosh! whoosh! The music blared and the rockets shot into the clouds. 'Why don't they blow up the barges?' cried the Duke of Edinburgh, leaping from window to window.

But the Queen never moved a muscle, even though the fireworks were for her.

I expect that she has mellowed a bit, now that she is a gran. **COLIN CLARK**

Sidelines

David Ransom

'Death must go on, I suppose,' I joked. 'One can but hope,' he said, with the slyest of grins

Not-so-grim reaper

IT'S AN ILL WIND and all that. As I write snow is piled against the front door and a bitter frost bites at my toes. The sky is grey as only East Anglian skies can be, but at least some people are happy. A parson came into the wine shop where I work the other day, and having written a cheque for his purchases, suddenly decided he wanted a bottle of our best malt whisky. 'Alter the cheque,' I suggested. 'I'd rather not,' he mumbled. 'My wife is apt to glance at the cheque stubs and I don't want to have to explain.' He reached for his wallet, and with a contented smile said: 'I'll use some funeral money!' Peeling off two £20 notes he said. 'Do you know? The Archdeacon rang me last night and said 27 people died in Ipswich hospital yesterday. Twenty-seven in one day! I hardly dare leave the house in case an undertaker requires my services!' 'Death must go on, I suppose,' I said, handing him his change. 'One can but hope,' he replied, with the slyest of grins.

It's difficult to put your finger on why death and all its attendant paraphernalia is so interesting, even amusing, but it is. Maybe it's the sheer nervousness with which we anticipate our own demise that makes us giggle about death, but giggle we do. We try to cope with death by formalising it in ceremony, but it doesn't work. We perform the rituals of committal and burial to bring order to shattered lives, but it's only when we can see the funny side of it all that perspective returns, and grief is somehow relieved. My uncle died suddenly. He went off for his morning swim, and dived into the pool never to breath fresh air again. His funeral was a dramatic and tragic affair. Everyone was overcome. At the end of the service his widow was to be escorted down the aisle of the church by another of my uncles, Jack. As they left their pew, a button on Jack's coat suddenly flew off and bounced towards the altar. The widow stopped the procession, turned, and retrieved the button. Tears streaming down her face, she held it out for all to see and could be heard saying, 'You can never match 'em, can you? You can get new buttons, but they never seem to match.' People murmured agreement, heads nodding with approval and understanding.

It didn't end there. We repaired to the Dewsbury crematorium, high on a hill outside the town, which on a bleak February day is as cold, windy, and inhospitable as anywhere in Christendom. I took two aged aunts in my car and when I opened the car door to help them out, one said: 'Shut that door David! Else we'll all be dead!' I remember thinking of Al Read, Norman Evans and all those other northern comedians. I understood where they got their material from. Just listening to folk around them.

Some deaths, such as that of a child, can never be assuaged, but the fact remains that the professionals like my parson friend have to be able to view their work as a job like any other. I couldn't help being tickled by the thought of him concealing a bottle in his cassock, and taking a surreptitious slug of Highland Park Orkney Malt as he stamped his feet in the freezing cold outside Ipswich Crematorium and then rushing home to see if the Co-op had rung while he'd been out.

Father Georges

IN AN INNER London parish, the third floor of the Roman Catholic presbytery, as the late afternoon rush hour begins, with tramps and down-and-outs queueing downstairs for tea and sandwiches, Father Georges sits in his armchair. It has been a hard day. Up early this morning to celebrate Mass, he has had to endure the shock of an unannounced visit from a member of his order, and the loss of his best suit, which he suspects Father Doug of having stolen. It is hours until dinner. The rain beats down… Before he has even started to think about a quick nap, Father Georges has fallen asleep.

Next week he will be 83. It is 36 years since he came to this parish, when it was run by his own obscure Belgian order, for reasons no-one can now remember. He was sent as a temporary replacement until a new padre was appointed. 'You'll be back in six months,' his bishop assured him. A year later Georges was still waiting. 'Just another six months,' his bishop wrote. In a way he was right; six months to the day the bishop died in the middle of an ordination. The recall never came.

Georges served as parish priest for 15 years, until someone in authority noticed that the parish was being administered by Belgians and arranged for control to be transferred to the London diocese. He once again awaited the order to return. Now he was ambivalent about returning home. What with one thing and another, he hadn't visited Belgium in a decade, and had barely thought about it for years. It would be different now. Much as he detested his parish, he at least felt he understood it.

To the large, settled Irish and Italian population, the church fulfilled an important role. It also ministered to an ever growing influx of unfortunates, as the area's long nurtured sense of community was eroded by drug abuse, prostitution and dubious batik stalls selling second-rate hippy accessories to hordes of gullible tourists. There was still work to do here. Fortunately the new parish priest, Father Tony, was a practical and sensitive man, who was happy for Father Georges to stay for a long as he wanted.

As the years passed, Father Georges came to realise that he did want to stay, permanently. He had met Sheila, a kindly widow obsessed with the church and her budgie, in that order. Georges would saunter to her flat at lunchtime, eat a feast, hear Sheila's latest news (which revolved around supplies of Trill) and doze on her sofa. On Sundays he would drive his ancient car to the local old people's home to celebrate Mass. Now in his late seventies, healthy if not hearty, Georges was beginning to feel safe. Then, one day, a letter arrived. A Father Norbert would be visiting London the following week, and wished to pay Georges a courtesy call. Georges was mortified. This would be it: the summons. He would be deposited in some home for decrepit priests and left to rot. The day Father Norbert arrived, Georges contrived to be out. Father Tony said that Georges had been getting a little forgetful, and offered Norbert a cup of tea as consolation.

Six weeks later, Father Georges came downstairs to breakfast to be greeted with an unfamiliar face which hailed him in fluent French. 'Good morning Georges,' said Father Tony at the head of the table. 'I don't think you have met Father Norbert. He has come to stay for a few days.' Tony, with his customary generosity, had given Father Norbert an open invitation to stay any time he was in London, and Father Norbert had been delighted to accept. Father Georges could scarcely utter a coherent sentence. He withdrew to his room. Later Father Norbert sought him out. 'There is no-one here!' came a muffled voice from behind the locked door of Father Georges' room. 'Go away!' When the coast was clear he fled to Sheila's house, and didn't return to the presbytery until midnight.

Since then Georges' health has declined noticeably. Thanks to the initial welcome afforded by Father Tony, Belgian priests come to stay at the presbytery with increasing regularity. Each time Georges pretends not to be in or claims to be someone else. Father Tony has tried to persuade him that his suspicions are unfounded. Father Georges does not believe him. Now young Father Doug has arrived to assist Father Tony, and Georges worries that he won't protect him as Father Tony has done. Today his best suit disappeared. He has told Father Doug he suspects him, and will take him to the highest court in the land before he lets him get away with it. Later he will remember that he took the suit to the dry-cleaners on Monday.

The truth is that the Belgians have no desire to take back Father Georges. The irony is that Georges' mounting paranoia, secrecy and shouting fits are placing a strain on the shoulders of Father Tony. As Father Georges snores in his armchair, Father Tony drafts a letter to the Belgian order, requesting that alternative a arrangements are made. Father Georges' fears are going to come true, and the last person he'll think of blaming is himself.

MARCUS BERKMANN

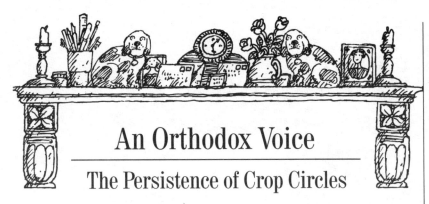

An Orthodox Voice

The Persistence of Crop Circles

Love Thy Enemas

The FT's African editor, **Michael Holman**, *explores uncharted territory*

THE RESPONSIBILITIES I have incurred in taking on this column seem to me to be two-fold; first, to expose the errors in modern thought and conduct through the touchstone of constant truth and philosophy; and secondly, to keep you informed about things like crop circles.

Unreported in the press, this summer's display of designs imprinted on farmers' fields was magnificent. The formations were larger, finer and more widespread than ever before. A consistent feature of this phenomenon is that it discredits every theory which purports to explain it. I had wondered how it was going to deal with the prevalent theory, that the whole thing is the work of unknown hoaxers, and I was deeply impressed by its response. Early in the season, formations in oil-seed rape gave warning of exciting things to come, and my neighbour John Neal, owner of a scruffy canal boat, proposed a visit down to Wiltshire to inspect the latest local developments.

It took about a fortnight, navigating from Regent's Park, up the Thames and into the cranky old Kennet and Avon canal at Reading. On the way we called at the riverside mansion of Uri Geller, recently vilified in *The Oldie*. We found there a handsome, charming Israeli gent, as honestly confused as the rest of us, who willingly demonstrated those 'gifts of the Spirit' with which, through no fault or virtue of his own, he has been endowed.

After many days on the canal we finally moored up at the Barge Inn near Alton Barnes, in the heart of crop circle country. That, it turned out, was the pub chosen by the 'croppies' for their evening gatherings and blatherings. The leading experts, American, German and British, showed their faces there; news and rumours were at their hottest; ufologists, sceptics, philosophers and cunning rustics mingled together, and the conversation was the best in Wiltshire. Midsummer evenings outside the Barge Inn, with good fare and good company, and with the four elements – earth, air, fire, water – were exactly as you can remember them in the Golden Age.

The crop formations we saw were fantastic. Approaching Devizes, on the main road from the north, you were confronted by a field-long scorpion and, if you stopped, you could read scrawled notices by the maddened farmer, denouncing it as mindless vandalism. As perceived, it was a work of art, and so were many of the other designs and wheatfields around Avebury and the old Wessex sanctuaries. Circles often appeared in the same fields as in previous years, infuriating landowners who suspected they were being mocked by their peasantry. From Devon and Sussex to Yorkshire and the North, crop circles this year were spotted all over England.

The designs are intelligent, so (unless you want to think the unthinkable) they must surely be man-made. One thing I learnt from my week at the Barge Inn is that certain people have become obsessed and are inspired by dreams or inner compulsions to imitate the original patterns or to surpass them in artistry. The phenomenon has taken to using human agents to further its work. That work has to do with the changing of minds. I do not say this lightly, but because I have observed the effects of crop circles on the minds of those who have fallen under their spell. In some cases the result has been personal shipwreck – which was no doubt deserved and needed – but others have been awakened to an interest in life generally. These are times of revelation, and crop circles are a powerful catalyst in this process. This is not a theory or opinion, just a straightforward perception. **JOHN MICHELL**

FORGIVE ME for discussing the state of my colon, but my tale has a happy ending. So please read on. Don't be embarrassed. Here follows a story that could, just possibly, save your life.

Bottoms and the noises they emit have always provoked mirth; but any malfunctioning of or within that part of our anatomy is usually a taboo subject, even between patient and doctor. It certainly was with me.

Until, that is, the day I got this frightful pain in my abdomen, and before I spoke to Mr John Northern, a bowel concern specialist who advises the Imperial Fund for Cancer Research.

The pain had been intense, located somewhere under my ribcage. Various ailments, including wind, had been eliminated as causes. But the pain continued, and further investigation of a particularly nasty possibility – cancer of the colon – was needed.

'I am sending you in for a barium enema,' said Dr Joseph Teeger, the *FT*'s doctor in Johannesburg. And so it was that two days later, I was stretched out on an examination table in the city's Brenthurst Clinic.

I suppose it was the response from sympathetic friends that made me especially apprehensive, almost as much about the process as as about the possible outcome.

The words 'barium enema' prompted sharp intakes of breath, expressions of profound sympathy over the phone, and winces if I were talking to them face to face. I braced myself for what was to follow.

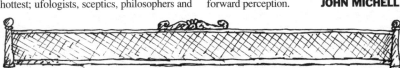

Like a cat having its temperature taken by the vet, I looked rigidly into the middle distance while an ignominious intrusion on my privacy got under way.

'Just relax,' said the lady who was about to apply the KY jelly.

It is not easy to start a conversation with someone whom you cannot see, and who is busying herself where the sun doesn't shine, and whose name you do not know.

But introductions affected – 'Pleased to meet you, Mrs Finch' – I did my best.

'You must have seen more bottoms, Mrs Finch, than I have had hot dinners'.

Her reply was most comforting. 'I could write a thesis on the subject. Now just relax and I'll slip it in. You may find it a bit uncomfortable.'

For 48 hours I had been dreading this moment, as much for the embarrassment as the anticipated discomfort. But I had carefully prepared myself for the occasion.

I had followed instructions, and subsisted on tea, crackers and clear soup, and drained the contents of a bottle with a most interesting label. 'Patients should be advised,' said the instructions, 'to expect a strong, thorough bowel action

approximately six to eight hours after taking the liquid.' I cannot improve on that admirably phrased warning, other than to say it was an understatement.

'What is going to happen?' I asked, as I lay on the table, wrapped in a skimpy blue cotton dressing-gown, designed to be put on back to front.

Mrs Finch was admirably matter-of-fact. 'We squirt in some barium, pump some air, rather like a balloon.' I wanted to turn tail, but it was too late. With a deft movement, the tube was inserted.

Uncomfortable, but not painful. Then in went the barium, followed by what Mrs Finch called 'a few puffs of air'. I am bound to say that this was a misleading description which in no way prepared me for the sensation that followed, for it was as if a Force Eight gale had

disappeared up my bottom.

For the first time, I had an inkling of what it must be like to give birth. My entire sense of being was concentrated within my nether regions, coupled with an overwhelming sense of a presence that nature urged me to expel.

Were I not gripping the table so firmly, I believe that I may have drifted up to the ceiling, like a World War II barrage balloon. A dreadful thought now

Bottoms and the noises they emit have always provoked mirth, but any malfunctioning of or within that part of our anatomy is usually a taboo subject, even between patient and doctor

preoccupied me. What if my sphincter let me down?

I had visions of Mrs Finch bowled over by a blast of barium from my buttocks, but thankfully the seal held. But a further test of my muscle tone was to come: the perilous journey to the loo, buttocks tightly clenched.

I have been flatulent in my time, but what followed was truly something special. Had nature blessed me with a musical ear, I swear I could have played 'The Trumpet Solitaire'. As it was, I suspect that horses bolted, the neighbourhood dogs started barking, and young children clutched their mothers' skirts.

So get to the point, I hear you say.

It is this: bowel cancer is the second largest killer of adult males, and the third most common cancer in Britain, with over 30,000 new cases every year. Yet 90 per cent of the cases are curable, provided they are diagnosed at an early stage. But most people wait for as long as six to nine months from the onset of symptoms – constipation, blood in the stool, pain in the abdomen – before seeing their GP. By then, half have a cancer that is very hard to treat.

So why do they wait? I asked Mr Northern. For the same reason, he replied, that this column might be regarded as a delicate subject. And the moral? As Mr Northern puts it: don't die of embarrassment. My test, by the way, was clear. I told you: my tale has a happy ending.

'We got us a nice quiet little town here, mister, and I aim to keep it that way!'

Still With Us

Jonathan Routh

IN THE SIXTIES, Jonathan Routh was often referred to in the press as 'Britain's Number One Practical Joker', as a consequence of the pranks played on an unwitting, but generally cooperative, public in the ABC television series, *Candid Camera*. I am continually surprised by how many people of a certain age still recognize my surname, and ask: 'Any relation to Jonathan?'

When I tell them that I am his son, they ask: 'What's he up to now then?' And I answer: 'Well actually, he's a painter living in Jamaica.' As is generally the case where my father is concerned, nobody quite knows if they are having their leg pulled, or not.

Somehow, *Candid Camera* crept into the national consciousness, and is still fondly remembered for infamous pranks like the car with no engine, and the plumber who is summoned to deal with a girl in the bath with her big toe – allegedly – stuck in the tap. Some found the stunts cruel, saying they humiliated people, but permissions always had to be given for a sketch to be shown, with the disappointing result that the best material of all, where

people made complete prats of themselves was never allowed to be shown.

As more and more people began to recognize Jonathan though, it became increasingly difficult to keep up the programme's standard, and he wisely decided to quit before it lost its edge too much. It wasn't just that, though; he felt that by the Seventies, people had lost their sense of innocence and gullibility, and were becoming too knowing and cynical to let themselves be the object of gentle ridicule. I possess an old video of Jonathan attempting to fly on Wimbledon Common, with the help of a bicycle, some old feathered wings, and a child's twirly windmill attached to his headgear. There was no problem then in enlisting the help of the general public, and sweet old ladies in particular, to pull his string like a kite, while he flapped and cycled furiously, anxiously claiming that he'd been blown off course, and had an urgent appointment in Basingstoke. Today, I suppose, he would either be arrested or mugged for such behaviour.

Making a clean break from the medium, Jonathan embarked on a series of relationships with rich female companions who were able to indulge his whimsical craving for exotic travel and impractical homes. Foremost amongst these was the eccentric oil heiress, Olga Detterding, who allowed him to cram her large Piccadilly penthouse with stuffed sheep (with raisins scattered behind them), and a ludicrous fountain in the entrance which sprayed you as you came in. *Hello* magazine would have loved it if only it had existed then.

Eventually, Jonathan tired of this excessive and unreal lifestyle, and married Shelagh, a good woman who was able, more or less, to put up with him, and still does. Apart from a series of not particularly helpful travel articles, such as 'A weekend at the Ritz', Jonathan had been dabbling with painting and illustrating since he walked out of television. This had led to a series of books about the adventures of a group of nuns, with titles like *The Nuns Go East* and *The Nuns Go West*. Whether these were meant for adults, children, or the clergy, was never clear, but nonetheless he persisted, and one day, with the addition of a few bold brushstrokes, the nuns had turned into Queen Victoria. This led to his most enduring book, *The Secret Life of Queen Victoria*, a chronicle of an adventurous holiday she is supposed to have taken, without Prince Albert, in Jamaica, in which she is seen tightrope walking, water-skiing, etc.

Since its publication in 1979, Jonathan has been working full-time as a painter, rising at dawn as he always did to make the best use of the day's light, wherever he may be. Most of the year, he and Shelagh are to be found (after a long search) at Fort Victoria, the spacious house they have built for theselves in a remote corner of Jamaica.

A smidgin of electricity is supplied by a windmill, made from a kit he bought in Wales, and there is no running water, apart from lots of small Jamaican boys tearing round with full buckets on their heads. They seem to live happily enough though, surrounded by a large group of local youngsters whom 'Miss Shelagh' looks after, and enjoying the frequent visits of globe-trotting guests, including rock superstars and American millionaires, who always look relieved in the photos to have escaped from the machine-gun patrolled perimeter fences of the high-security official holiday residences.

During the spring, Jonathan and Shelagh often go to Haiti, if it's safe, and America, to reciprocate hospitality, before spending the summer months in Tuscany, in a vast and beautiful house they have mysteriously managed to purloin. On their annual return to Jamaica, in September, they tend to stop off in London for a few days, where they hold court at San Lorenzo's fashionable Knightsbridge restaurant, where there are still some of Jonathan's splendid murals downstairs, which he occasionally has to renovate after severe pasta damage.

A lifetime of hedonism has meant that Jonathan has had to give up his beloved cigarettes and alcohol in the last year, but he is nonetheless able to continue his exotic, or maybe it's quixotic, lifestyle, which is part Gauguin and part British eccentric. I've never really understood how he sustains this, but it works, and he has fun, so long may he continue to do so.

CHRISTIAN ROUTH

A doleful experience

On a back-to-work scheme, **Amanda Gee-Smyth** *finds the benefits highly debatable*

AT 10 O'CLOCK on a dull Monday morning I enter a dilapidated Victorian house, open a door marked 'Restart Scheme', and find myself facing a room crammed with old plastic tables and chairs, a corner of which is strewn with mugs, teabags, coffee and sugar sachets. Twenty faces stare as I take the last seat on a bench. I am on the dole, or income support, and obliged to take a course to get me back to work. The instructor, an ex-army sergeant, stands beside a blackboard on which is written 'Why I Want to Work'.

I look around at my fellow captors. They range in age from 17 to 58, and are down-at-heel, desperate and hostile. There are only two other women – a secretary and the 'assistant tutor', who turns out to be a former auxilary nurse. My eyes are drawn to the back of the head immediately in front of me: shaven and covered in blue and black tattoos, twining over the ears, skull and down the neck. 'Made in England' has been neatly printed at the base of the skull in largish letters. Its owner stands up, revealing jeans and bovver boots, lights a rolled fag, winks at his buddies and says 'f- this'. As a fortysomething journalist who has spent years abroad, out of regular employment for the past year, what am I doing here?

I get £48 a week from which to pay heat, light, water, food, clothes and travel. Our 'benefits' consist of exemption from community tax, free health services, dental and eye check-ups. We are not allowed to earn more than £5 a week: anything in excess of this is deducted from our weekly money. (Some lucky ones can claim housing allowance.)

We are on a week's course, which is obligatory, to help us find a job. If we fail to attend lectures we lose the benefit completely and have to re-register. If we find a job, we are no longer entitled to anything. To keep abreast one would need to earn £170. Most jobs on offer in this neck of the woods are around £2.50 an hour, and mainly part-time and seasonal.

Lectures, or 'education', consist of filling in forms about what we have done in the case of the previously employed, or would like to do if never having been so. Our tutor tells us how good we will feel even if our employment consists of 'voluntary community work', where you receive about £10 a week, which almost covers fares and a sandwich. It will look good on our CVs, we're told.

The assortment of plumbers, builders, electricians, and hotel staff – all of whom have been hit by the recession and/or age – barely contain their frustration as the 'HOW TO USE A

TELEPHONE, HOW TO BE POLITE AND WELL DRESSED, HOW TO WRITE A LETTER ENCLOSING A CURRICULUM VITAE' is written up on the blackboard. 'What's that?' mutters Made in England, setting off a murmur of 'Don't want a mortgage, why am I here anyway?', etc. Most of the men slip out for a smoke every 10 minutes or so.

We are handed slips of paper from the Job Centre to select anything suitable in the job line. There are about 30 unsuitable jobs. The tutor says nothing, but his assistant twitters on about going for interviews and how daunting it can be. The older men reply, 'I've been a plumber, mate, for 30 year, I'm too old, they won't take me on.' At this point Made in England – who also has a Union Jack tattooed on his forehead – announced that he has done time in Broadmoor. Under the facade lies a rather lost teenager. He is intrigued by my accent, and has to have my reply interpreted. He decides I am not a Tory spy and I become an ally.

Then, to his revulsion, a large tray of sandwiches appears. They are free, and clearly an insult. What filth could be inside? Egg, tomato, cheese, chicken, salad, chicken tikka. The Bovvers stumble round to the pub on the corner for a couple of pints and some chips. The rest of us gratefully choose our lunch.

On the second day we write up our CVs onto a computer. As there are only four of them and 20 of us, and hardly anyone knows how to use one, the result is lots of smoking and sitting about looking in the local paper for the jobs we already know about. On day three the CV saga continues, and some lucky ones are loaded into a minibus and taken to be lectured for two hours on how nice it would be to work for nothing if nothing turned up. The tutors, aware of the apathy and sheer stupidity of the whole course, admit to some of us that the job is hell. Pride, it seems – and about £12,000 a year – dragged them into it. Most resign within a year.

On day four we press computer buttons which ask us questions to which we answer yes or no. The programme is designed to offer a choice of job areas which might suit us. Some print-outs only offer three suggestions – our sole graduate is put down

'He misses the Cones Hotline more than he'll admit'

as a potential carpet layer. The simple girl looking for a chambermaid's job – which she gets – might like to be a fork-lift truck driver, and I am put down as a shop steward or receptionist. There are shouts of laughter as lists are exchanged. The thought of Made in England being a chemists' assistant has sinister undertones.

On the last morning we all attend, threatened by loss of benefit if we don't. We're told that nothing more can be done today as the tutor is ill, but that if we do not 'voluntarily' join the Job Club, or take up unpaid community work, we will be forced back onto a similar course in six weeks time, which lasts for three weeks, with attendance obligatory every afternoon. I opt for a six-month membership of the Job Club, with voluntary attendance for three weeks.

Two people out of the 20 who attended the first course got jobs, and about three from the Job Club. This all took place some time ago, and although Job Centres continue, the system of interviews with your 'signer-on' seems to have taken over, with little improvement. But it takes you, temporarily, off the unemployed list.

Video
Larry Adler

Samson and Delilah 1949

'Be careful, Samson, the Sodomites are out tonight.'

This is the third film I've seen recently where I recall seeing or hearing something that didn't turn up on the video I watched. And I have to admit, this does seem an unlikely line to be uttered in a DeMille film. I'm also partial to one of the credits: 'Based upon the history of Samson and Delilah in the Holy Bible, Judges 13.16.'

Victor Mature is the perfect Samson and Hedy Lamarr is the perfect anything. And guess who Delilah's sister is, assuming you knew she had one... Angela Lansbury, that's who.

As you would expect in a Cecil B DeMille epic, the scenes are spectacular. And the last minute or so where, after having been blinded, he pulls down the temple... well, they don't make 'em like that any more.

That particular scene gave birth to one of the best of all Hollywood stories. Obviously it could only be shot once; if a retake were needed you'd have to rebuild a whole new temple. After the great

climax, with huge idols toppling to the ground, crushing people beneath them and with the temple in ruins, DeMille called to his crew: 'Camera One, did you get that OK?'

'Boss, I don't know what happened, but when the first idol fell it raised such a cloud of dust that it blotted out everything.'

'OK, what about Camera Two?'

'Boss, the crowd panicked and when the idols were falling, some of the people ran into the camera and knocked it over.'

'Oh, fine. That means I've only got my long-shot camera three left. OK, Camera Three, what about you?'

'Ready when you are, Boss!'

Pin-ups

John Mortimer picks his top six

1 Veronica Lake
The small, tough girl with the heart of gold and the memorable hair-do. The star of the best movies of my youth. I believe she's still around somewhere and I would love to find her.

2 Lord Byron
A sensible romantic, a Calvinist Casanova and conservative revolutionary. *Don Juan* is an epic of good sense in a dotty world. I wish he could have written me a letter.

3 Paula Yates
In spite of recent history, funny entertaining and very pretty. Full of wonderful stories about her dad from *Stars on Sunday*.

4 Muriel Spark
Our best contemporary novelist. Her prose leaves me breathless with envy. When she started, Graham Greene gave her a small allowance on the condition that she didn't pray for him.

5 Oscar Wilde
Not only the author of one of the finest comedies in our language but, in spite of all the affectations, a sweet-natured man who managed to make his friends feel as entertaining as he was. I could apologise to him for the Old Bailey.

6 Henri Matisse
He said that the purpose of art was to give tired, hard-working people pleasure, and he provided it as generously as anyone.

Where have all the **real** toys gone?

Real toys vanished from High Streets long ago. The '70s saw the beginning of the "there's-no-demand-for-that-sort-of-thing-nowadays" approach to retailing; then in the next decade came a torrent of 'Safety' and 'Consumer Protection' legislation with which almost everything else of interest failed to comply.

One astonishing source of real toys and knick-knacks remains. Anyone who buys anything for children (or even indeed adults) should have the HAWKIN catalogue. Unfortunately, though, you have to ask for it: it doesn't drop out of other things, and it isn't mailed to those who haven't requested it.

Here are just a few of its five hundred offerings which might ring bells:

- ❏ Jacks
- ❏ A Soap Cat which grows hair
- ❏ A Ginger Beer plant
- ❏ Jumping Beans
- ❏ Loaded Dice
- ❏ Water Flowers
- ❏ A Kazzoo
- ❏ Gunge in a tube to make 'balloons' out of
- ❏ "The Tower of Hanoi"
- ❏ An Egg-Laying Chicken *(It lays "when depressed" or so its instructions used to say)*
- ❏ A Submarine with a tube to blow down
- ❏ Magnetic Fishing Game
- ❏ Card Dress-me Dolls
- ❏ Clockwork Tin Robots
- ❏ A candle-powered 'Pop-Pop' Boat
- ❏ Cricket Dice

- ❏ Jacob's Ladder
- ❏ Rubber-band-powered Flying Birds
- ❏ Swanee Whistle
- ❏ A Water Diviner
- ❏ Vanishing Ink
- ❏ 'King Tut' who stays in his coffin only if you know the secret
- ❏ Wooden Dolls' Houses
- ❏ Crystal Growing Kits
- ❏ Wood-framed Slates
- ❏ Cardboard Theatres (including one not unlike The Globe)
- ❏ Snowstorms
- ❏ A "Milkman's Wallet"
- ❏ Wooden double-decker Pencil Boxes
- ❏ A Jack in the Box
- ❏ Magnetic Marbles

- ❏ Terracotta Bricks (1" long, with real mortar)
- ❏ Finger Puppets
- ❏ Paper 'Scraps'
- ❏ Modelling Balloons
- ❏ Steam Engines
- ❏ A wooden Noah's Ark
- ❏ Gyroscope
- ❏ Flick Books
- ❏ The Dynamo Torch
- ❏ Crystal Sets
- ❏ Tinplate printed Seaside Buckets
- ❏ Kinetic Wheel
- ❏ A Clockwork Tractor with four gears
- ❏ Rainbow Pencils
- ❏ Spillikins
- ❏ Tin 'Penny Whistles'
- ❏ 'Magic Boxes' which make things vanish

The catalogue is free, entertaining and fully illustrated with colour photographs. Goods from it are despatched promptly on a 'money-back-if-not-satisfied' basis. There's nothing quite like it. Ask for a copy now!

HAWKIN & Co.

St Margaret - Harleston - Norfolk IP20 0PJ
Telephone 01986 782536   Fax 01986 782468

CLASSIFIED

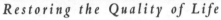